hell bent for leather

hell bent for leather

Confessions of a Heavy Metal Addict

seb hunter

Fourth Estate
An Imprint of HarperCollins*Publishers*

HarperCollins books may be purchased for educational, business, or sales promotional use. For information, please write: Special Markets Department, HarperCollins Publishers Inc., 10 East 53rd Street, New York, NY 10022.

Book design by Charles Kreloff

FIRST EDITION

Printed on acid-free paper

Library of Congress Cataloging-in-Publication Data is available upon request.

0-06-072292-4

For Fa

I was in the pub with my friend Andrew and the conversation turned to "What specialist subject would you choose if you were to appear on *Mastermind*?" He came up with the very good point that in order to proceed to the later stages of the competition, you would need a store of different specialist subjects for each new round. But as the heats progressed, the standard of fellow competitor would rise, so not only did you have to prepare—we guessed—four rounds' worth of different specialist subjects, but you probably needed to gamble your weakest in the early rounds and save your best one 'til last. We imagined the dreadfulness of early-round elimination on some hastily cribbed topic, with our fountains of knowledge waiting primed and unused. So assuming there actually are four rounds, including the final (and yes, we're taking huge liberties with our levels of general knowledge here), Andrew chose:

1st round: Bob Dylan

2nd round: Samuel Beckett

3rd round: Tennyson (yes, he's a fop and a show-off)

Final: The Beatles

He really likes the Beatles.

In response I installed my beloved Beach Boys at the top of the pile and started to ponder my remaining three stages.

"Can I have Brian Wilson as a separate round?"

"Definitely not, or I'd have John Lennon."

"Oh, I see."

It was then that a horrible truth began to dawn. It grew in my brain until I couldn't hold it in anymore. Although I am very good on the Beach Boys and, indeed, my hero Brian Wilson, there was a subject that, if I was honest with myself, I knew more about than any other. And it wasn't big, or clever, or cool, or relevant to anything at all useful in my or anyone else's life (unlike Brian, of course). I covered my mouth with my hand.

"Heavy metal," I said quietly.

"What?" Andrew appeared confused.

"My number one isn't the Beach Boys. It's heavy metal."

"Really? Heavy metal? As random as that? No focus or specification? Just the whole thing?"

"Yes." My head hung in shame. "The whole goddamn thing."

"You never told me about this before."

"It's kind of a secret," I muttered.

"So if you got to the final of *Mastermind*, you'd sit there in the black chair and when asked for your chosen specialist subject, you'd calmly reply 'heavy metal'?"

"I'm afraid so."

"That's fantastic!"

It was true. And this book is all about what I have learned, and my charmless stabs at emulation.

And hey, before you say anything—I'm not proud.

Chapter One

let's get it up

I'm ten.

*I*t's 1981, a late summer evening in an underground common room at a boarding school in deepest Wiltshire. Someone is playing "Can-Can" by Bad Manners on a cheap yellow record player and we're all running around in a sweat, playing off the musical momentum, though hardly paying it much attention. And then comes my big moment, the only real eureka, blinding–light moment I've ever had. Some wise child peels off from the fray and clunks down AC/DC's "Let's Get it Up," and that's it for me. That was the light switch—the world suddenly became three dimensional and my ears popped open.

It was so raw, so suggestive, that I had no idea how to react. This was a whole new set of rules for my body; a sudden and unexpected DNA tattoo. I stood motionless on the flagstone floor, beads of sweat hanging off my fringe, waiting for this skull-splitting rheum to end so I could calm down and return to how things had been before, but I never quite managed to get there.

"Hey! Hey! *What was that?*" I stood open-mouthed over the record player.

By the end of the week, having heard "Let's Get it Up" a further sixteen times, including the B-side, "Back in Black" (live), all other thoughts in my head had evaporated. I taught myself how to do this, fast:

Back at home that Christmas I knew exactly what I wanted. For the last few years my parents had been feeding my thirsty *Star Wars* obsession, however this year I'd requested just one solitary item: a cassette by AC/DC. My mother asked me where she was supposed to purchase such a thing and I was forced to admit I had no idea. So I spent an anxious Christmas morning worrying that I'd be getting yet more *Star Wars* figures and not the one thing I craved so badly. But halfway through the communal giving I was handed a tape-shaped package. Slowly I peeled at the wrapping until I could clearly see a gold cover and a picture of a giant cannon, and on the back cover—oh my god—the album contained "Let's Get it Up"! I felt sick and slightly dizzy and my hands started to shake.

My mother, sensing my existential distress, plucked the plastic box away.

"'Let's get it up,'" I whimpered.

My mother frowned. "What do you think that means?"

"It means . . ." I paused. "Let's all get it sort of 'up' and have fun."

"Well you're wrong, it doesn't mean that at all, it means something entirely different."

"Like what?"

"I'm not telling you. Just be careful, that's all, don't go around saying that sort of thing in public. And 'Put the Finger on You'? What do you think that one means?"

"It just means putting the finger on you. I don't know." *She doesn't understand*, I thought to myself. *She just doesn't get it!*

She ran her finger through the rest of the songs, muttering under her breath, and handed it back. "'Let's Get it Up' means something rude. In fact quite a lot of these songs sound rather rude."

You're mad, I thought, embarrassed for her obvious misunderstanding.

As soon as the Queen's speech was over and the family had thanked each other for their biscuits and condiments, I interrupted proceedings by loudly demanding we play my new tape.

"Everyone will like it!"

"But Granny . . ."

"Granny will like it too!"

My father raised an eyebrow. I had up until this moment been a thoroughly charming and dutiful child, so after a moment's consideration, the cassette player was reluctantly dragged in from the kitchen.

With my back to my extended family, I slid the new cassette into the machine and covertly inched up the volume in preparation for AC/DC's grand opus *For Those About to Rock . . . (We Salute You)* in all its corrosive pomp. As the guitars snaked out I turned, grinning and blushing heavily, and grabbed onto the aerial to steady myself. Then the bass began to throb and I noticed some awkward shuffling on the sofa. Next came the drums—crikey they were loud! I glanced at my scary Uncle Geoff and he'd started turning purple, but still I sensed a thrill of expectancy in the room. Then came the singing—or rather some wordless yelps like a rusty iron lung—and with it a sharp, horrified wince

from the entire family. It was slowly dawning on me that perhaps not everyone would love AC/DC quite as much as I'd hoped. Finally, just as the chorus came blazing through (*For those about to rock! We salute you!*) and I was at the very peak of excitement, my father shouted "Enough!" and my mother leapt at the eject button, and I was hastily sent upstairs by Granny.

My mother and father married in 1968. My mother was an artist and a teacher, and my father ran his own property development businesses. Three years later I came along.

And then two years after that, my sister, Melissa.

For the first six years of my life we lived in an old farmhouse in the Hampshire village of Meonstoke surrounded by farms and fields, until my father grew bored with the country and discovered a gigantic run-down Victorian house in Winchester. It looked like it would need years of work but was irresistibly cheap, so he decided to buy it. We all slept on brown corduroy cushions in the drawing room for the first few months, while the electrics were recast, water was coaxed back through the miles of disused

I'm Rupert the Bear, Mel's a mouse.

black pipes, and the child-sized gaps in the floorboards were hastily covered with lino. This was an amazing house: it had thirty rooms, a cool vaulted cellar, and a giant warren of an attic. My sister and I liked to change bedrooms whenever we felt like it because there were just so many to choose from, while my mother painted huge colorful murals on their walls for our entertainment. My father meanwhile took this sprawling house to task, attacking it with sledgehammers and drills, knocking up arches through walls in a comedy hard hat. The garden was a giant overgrown jungle in which I constructed dens out of old beehives, played laser wars with imaginary friends, smashed a football against the green garage door, and goaded our cats.

At eight years old I was sent to a small boarding school miles away in the countryside near Salisbury. For the first few terms I was poleaxed by homesickness, but after a while I lightened up, and then suddenly—for the only time in my life—school became a complete delight. We wore cool navy blue boiler suits when we went outside to play, and there was an old quarry in the vast school grounds, and hardly any girls to be scared of. I was extremely lucky to be there; my parents had had to borrow money to send me in the first place, and slowly I began to repay some of their investment. I developed a random obsession with Austria and, aged nine, began a James Bond–style novel, casting myself as the heroic Austrian protagonist. I supported Austria passionately at soccer and in the skiing on television on Sundays, and had an Austrian flag on my bedroom wall. No one knew what had triggered this Austrian obsession, not even me; I'd never even visited the place.

During my school holidays back in Winchester I made friends with my next-door neighbor. Alexander was a spoiled only child, which meant he could get hold of almost anything. We liked playing toy soldiers, sci-fi laser war, and Lego—he had so much Lego he had to keep it in buckets and giant Tupperware boxes, and his armies were so huge that wherever you walked in his house your feet would get spiked by the piles of discarded military enmeshed in the carpet. We also liked ABBA and spent many evenings dancing chaotically in Alex's front room. We even made ABBA compilation tapes, for no better reason than Alex's posh stereo had twin tape decks. And, for a while, that was all we knew about music.

AC/DC changed all that. First chance I got, I rushed over to Alex's to tell him about my discovery. He went straight downstairs to request an AC/DC album from his parents, and a day later he was the proud owner of their 1979 masterpiece *Highway to Hell*. I was so jealous I refused to listen to it, but I couldn't keep this up for long. As we cued up the record for the fiftieth time, I realized that this wasn't just a passing phase—this was the real deal, the *meaning of life*. There were rampant phalanxes of guitars, drumming so hefty it felt like dinosaurs were stomping round the room, and a voice so astringent it could strip paint off the walls. Alex said he was going to change his name to Alexander AC/DC and that his parents had said it was OK, and I, temporarily, believed him.

Together Alex and I learned that AC/DC had had two different singers: Bon Scott, who sang like a snake and was dead (he choked on his own vomit in 1980), and his replacement, Brian Johnson, who wore a flat cap and a vest and sounded like a parrot with laryngitis (maybe that's what had pissed Granny off so much). Alex and I liked Bon the best—too much Brian all in one go was distressing, and Bon sounded sexy, though we didn't know what "sexy" was exactly. We just knew Bon was cooler, and funnier, and being dead we knew he couldn't turn around and decide to write a ballad.

Bon was great, but our favorite thing about AC/DC was their iconic lead guitarist, Angus Young. Angus was a short Australian man with straggly hair who always wore a school uniform: velvet shorts, velvet jacket, velvet cap, shirt and tie. It wasn't the fact that he dressed like us that impressed us particularly—although we respected the gimmick—it was the sheer feral sound he made with his guitar. Every note that Angus played seemed to possess a kind of taut, evil shiver; it got us right in the diaphragm. His perpetually blazing Gibson transfixed us and we devoutly mewed every note in exhausting bouts of keep-up air guitar in Alex's bedroom. While the rest of the DC stood rooted to the spot in their tight mucky T-shirts under their curtains of hair, Angus duck-walked his way around the stage like a depraved goblin Chuck Berry, dripping rivers of sweat behind him as he methodically, ritually disrobed. We duck-walked with our air guitars around Alex's room, careful not to skip the needle.

A month later, Alex's parents took us to Le Havre for a weekend. They were both doctors and were traveling over there for a medical conference. Alex and I spent hours locked in the hotel room, squinting out over the docks, watching seagulls attacking cars. When we were eventually let loose in a giant department store called Les Printemps, Alex was allowed two new AC/DC albums and I was allowed one. It took us hours to choose. In the end I went for *Powerage* while Alex demanded *Dirty Deeds Done Dirt Cheap* and *If You Want Blood, You Got It* (I still feel estranged from both to this day). *Dirty Deeds Done Dirt Cheap* featured songs called "Big Balls," "Love at First Feel," and "Squealer." It was getting harder to avoid the sexual connotations.

We were banned from listening to the tapes back at the hotel or during the journey home, which was probably a good thing anyway with all that talk of big balls. So instead we bickered over whose tape was better before we'd even heard them, and learned the track listings and the times of the songs and every detail from the covers. My tape had a picture of Angus with a crazed, electrocuted expression on his face and wires coming out of his sleeves instead of hands, which I soon discovered was exactly how he sounded inside. But

Me as Angus at my sister's fancy dress birthday party. L–R: dog, sister, me

Alex and I were worried: had Angus *really* impaled himself upon his Gibson SG on the front of *If You Want Blood, You Got It*? It looked extremely convincing. How had he survived that?

Back in Winchester we bought up the DC back catalogue using Alex's parents' money and waited impatiently for their first new album since we'd discovered them. It was called *Flick of the Switch* and had an exciting though mini-

Angus— dead?

malist cover, with Angus and his guitar hanging off a giant switch. My favorite song was "Bedlam in Belgium." I imagined the devastation the DC could cause in Belgium—Angus duck-walking down a blazing street that looked a bit like Le Havre, but bigger and engulfed in flames. Unfortunately for us, *Flick of the Switch* was their worst album to date, but we hadn't discovered the music press yet, so it took a few years to realize.

My family's appetite for AC/DC hadn't progressed at quite the speed I'd initially expected. I was particularly let down by my father's response, who, as a brilliant pianist, bass player, and all-round musical Svengali to our family (when he felt like it), should have been the most appreciative. He became agitated when I played the DC on his fragile and expensive record player at objectionable volume while the family sat watching *The Two Ronnies*. He wasn't completely anti-pop—he owned "Strawberry Fields"/ "Penny Lane," a T-Rex album, and a Chris Squire (out of Yes) solo album that someone had once given him by mistake. But whenever he heard the DC he would wrinkle up his face comically and hold his ears as Brian Johnson screeched out "What Do You Do for Money, Honey?" and "Let Me Put My Love Into

You" and "Givin' the Dog a Bone." I convinced myself that if he listened long and hard enough he'd eventually get it, just as I had. I said, "OK, maybe that one wasn't so good, perhaps not the best, I agree, but hold on, listen to *this* one." And he'd light another Silk Cut and turn up the darts on the television and I would translate an annoyed movement of his mouth into acquiescence.

One Sunday he was lighting a fire with wet kindling and newspaper, a cigarette in his mouth, and I was playing him *Highway to Hell*, explaining each track as they came and went. His face was a picture of resigned indifference, but I was determined he'd like it this time. After all, it was my current favorite album, and Bon's voice was easier than Brian's, and my father didn't have his fingers in his ears for once, which was a start. After "Shot Down in Flames" he slowly took the cigarette from his lips and muttered, "I quite liked that one."

Wow! I played it again straight away, fluffing the rewind button in my excitement, but next time when it finished he said, "But that one was bloody dreadful."

"It was the same one!"

"Aha." Pleased with himself, he turned on the television.

"Well did you like it or not?" I was hopping around, preparing to rewind it again but he'd turned the TV up so loud he couldn't hear me.

What Is Heavy Metal?

Heavy metal is defined by the *Cambridge Dictionary* as: "A style of rock music with a strong beat, played very loudly using electrical instruments." I reckon they've nailed it. The *Collins* calls it: "A type of rock music characterized by high volume, a driving beat, and extended guitar solos, often with violent, nihilistic, and misogynistic lyrics." It's hard to disagree. And by heavy metal, I mean the real thing—the original full-fat knuckle-duster motherfuckers. I'm talking about metal's Golden Age, which took place between 1969 (the first Led Zeppelin album), and 1991 (Nirvana's second album, *Nevermind*). This book only takes into account events that took place between those two landmark dates, so if you're here looking for some Slipknots, or the Limp Biscuits, you should search elsewhere.

Heavy metal comes from two places: the blues, and a strange kind of bombastic neo-classical. Two famous metal bands illustrate this well: Motorhead and Van Halen. Motorhead's seminal (the metal world adores the word seminal) *No Sleep 'til Hammersmith*, an album recorded at the genre's High Temple, Hammersmith Odeon, is a metal classic. Essentially it's just a fast and mucky blues album howled out by a handlebar-moustached and wart-ridden speed freak. In the other camp you've got Eddie Van Halen, guitarist in his eponymous group, who created a new style of Wagnerian arpeggio by playing his guitar's neck two-handed, almost like a piano, using classical scales and phrasing, which went on to influence swathes of bouffant pomposity and Paganini plagiarism. There was no soul in that half—most metal came straight out of the blues and those hoary old three chords, just played at ear-splitting levels and in very tight trousers.

Why is the concept of high volume so important to the genre? It's because otherwise it would be extremely boring. If you think about it, there are no subtle structural dynamics to listen out for— no artistry in construction to be intellectually appreciated and politely applauded—you're not going to miss anything. The only question to ask during a metal song is: when is the guitar solo? That's all you really have to think about, so you're free to jump up and down and make devil shapes with your hands, headbang if you feel like it, and brazenly punch the air to the battering flood of watts coming at you from all those Marshall amplifiers.

It's primal, all the way through—stick-of-rock primal. Sound, volume, pummeling. It even *hurts* the next day. Brilliant!

The loudest musical performance ever recorded (so far), hitting a marauding 129.5 decibels (louder than a jet plane take-off), was achieved by an American band called Manowar during a concert in Germany. Manowar was one of those bands that gave metal a bad name. They epitomized the clichés we were all so ashamed of. Manowar wore animal hides and fur, had huge biceps and Viking-style handlebar moustaches. They cut themselves with a ceremonial dagger and then signed their record contract in their own blood. They had names like Scott Columbus, Ross the Boss, Death Dealer, and Rhino. They believed in True Metal (their own music), and dedicated their entire career to the vanquishment of their nemesis, False Metal (music other than their own).

Manowar set out to wither the competition with decibels and gesticulation. They succeeded up to a point, inspiring their huge and loyal fanbase to write letters into *Kerrang!* magazine accusing bands like Poison and Mötley Crüe of peddling False Metal, in terrible spelling. Every album Manowar released was even more epic than its predecessor, more grandiose in its warrior vision.

Manowar

They're still going today, still topless and wearing loincloths, their moustaches just slightly craggier. False Metal is still out there winding them up, and they remain committed to destroying it. Joey, Manowar's muscled bass player, sums up their ethos well: "The whole purpose of playing live is to blow people's heads off. That's what we do; that's the energy of this band. We're out there to kick ass. We're out there to turn our gear on and blast. We're out there to kill. That's what metal is. Anyone saying otherwise is not playing heavy metal. We will melt your face!"

Metal's love of volume is ubiquitous. Here are some song titles celebrating, and, in some cases, frantically urging you to turn the volume up to aid your listening experience:

"I Love it Loud"—Kiss. A simple paean to loud music. Gene Simmons, the bat/demon character in the group, wants you to feel it *right between the eyes.*

"Blow up your Speakers"—Manowar. Speaks for itself. They also criticize MTV in this song, for not playing their music, a statement that to this day remains unrequited.

"All Men Play on 10"—Manowar again. Ten refers to the volume dial.

"Blow up your Video"—AC/DC. Because it's not loud enough, and the speakers have already been blown up, elsewhere. This is another protest at lack of television airplay. It also makes the point that videos are commercial and unnecessary and somehow False Metal.

Loudness: The self-explanatory name of a Japanese metal band of the eighties, humorously nicknamed Roudness by the metal press. They wrote songs called "Rock Shock (More and More)," "Burnin' Eye Balls," "Bloody Doom," "Dogshit," and my favorite, what-does-it-mean? "Hell Bites (from the Edge of Insanity)."

"For the Sake of Heaviness"—Armoured Saint. Almost poetically honest.

"Too Loud (For the Crowd)"—Venom. (Metal loves brackets too).

"Louder than Hell"—Mötley Crüe. Strangely, this song comes from the height of their poodle period, when you'd have thought being louder than hell was the last thing on their minds. This song isn't loud at all.

(Manowar had a song called "Louder than Hell" too.)

Although lyrics about how loud you play are evergreen, there are several basic lyrical themes which are even more beloved. These are: anything involving or referring to sex or the sexual act;

traveling really fast; blowing things up (rebellious violence in the name of rock); and (preferably Norse) mythology. Any combination of these subjects is also completely fine, indeed combinations are essential if you're going to have enough to write about over the course of a long career.

If a metal band decides to stray from these well-trodden paths, they will usually end up producing a concept album. The concept album is heavy metal's ultimate High Art statement, its holy grail of spiritual and intellectual achievement. Most metal musicians will, at some point in their career, be inspired by a film they have seen, an obscure mythological tale they have read, or a social injustice they have stumbled across, and decide to retell that story via one continuous piece of music which often stretches over an entire double album. The result is usually a paper-thin narrative crudely welded onto a set of lyrically clumsy songs that are all still about sex and rebellion and mythology, but with spooky incidental music breaking up the individual tracks. These concept albums often come in expensive and showy packaging, fold-outs with poems and encrypted messages for their fans to unravel. Then, on the subsequent tour, at some point in the show they'll play through the whole thing from start to finish, using tapes to fill in the linking bits they can't play themselves, boring everybody in the audience who came to hear the songs which celebrate how loud the band is. Almost every metal group makes a concept album at some point during their career, even Motorhead; it was about the First World War and it was called *1916*.

Metal fans occasionally like to argue over what was the first ever heavy metal song. Often the answer is "You Really Got Me" by the Kinks. It's got a rhythmic fuzzy guitar line and is clunky and unsupple; it piledrives. But the Kinks obviously weren't heavy metal, so what bands can you call metal? And are there different types? There are loads of different types, so here are a few handy pointers:

The Scorpions—classic heavy metal from Germany

Def Leppard—new wave of British heavy metal (NWOBHM)

Meat Loaf—panto heavy metal, but no one likes him, he's too fat, and uses too many keyboards

Slayer—thrash metal (slightly frightening)

Bon Jovi—kind of heavy metal (especially if you are a girl)

Europe—(as above)

Marillion—prog rock (we tolerate them because we think they bring us intellectual credibility)

Genesis—(as above, for those slightly older)

Poison—glam metal (completely different than '70s glam)

Michael Bolton—heavy metal (when he first started, believe it or not)

Led Zeppelin—heavy metal (though it pains me to say it)

Thin Lizzy—*Trad. Arr.* Irish heavy metal

Iron Butterfly—heavy metal with an organ

If you think I'm being free and easy with my heavy metal tagging, I don't care. It's how artists were perceived by metal fans that's important here, not what their music actually sounded like. If metal fans tended to like something, then whatever it was, it was allowed into the fold. Pretty much anybody could record a piece of pop fluff, but so long as it had a cranked-up guitar in there somewhere, no matter how low in the mix, or one of those solos (you know, a whiny one), then metal fans would give it the collective thumbs up and allow themselves to buy it, or at least watch it endlessly on shitty pop TV, often it was the only way metal could get anywhere near the charts.

At the absolute far end of metal's acceptability were Roxette, the Swedish Eurythmics of the late 1980s. Their music was primary color Euro synth-pop with shouty choruses, however because their portly guitar player had vaguely rock hair, wore his big rock guitar low, pulled the right shapes, made Os with his mouth, and wore a tasseled leather jacket, some of us kidded ourselves into thinking we could actually hear a guitar in there, so in some quarters Roxette were tacked sheepishly onto the very edge of the metal landscape. *Kerrang!* magazine would review their singles. They mocked them of course, but acknowledged their existence nevertheless. They weren't so bad.

When Samantha Fox burst from Page Three onto our stereos, she too had the good sense to apply some "raunchy" guitar to her miserable repertoire, with the same effect—grudging acceptance from the metal community. At least she was "keeping it real," with "proper instruments." She also wore lots of denim, which helped slightly. There was even a time when Kate Bush was considered borderline metal, but I'm still not sure why. I think it might have been a simple sex object thing. Maybe it was just because she had really long hair. Or because she crimped it.

Heavy metal is essentially a club, a gang with an allegiance to a musical and social set of values. It might be frowned upon by society at large, but that's something that binds metal even more tightly. Metal has always retained a dubious conservative mindset—black or gay metallers are rare indeed. I'm not claiming the whole metal community are a bunch of *Daily Mail* readers—heaven forbid, only most of them—but as a movement, and right through its thirty-odd-year history, those not of a WASP predilection have tended to align themselves somewhere else. They take one look at this bunch of clowns and for the rest of their lives say to themselves, "Well, at least I'm not one of *those* . . ." Metal fans know that people say this about them and they resent it; this partly fuels the "nihilism" mentioned in the *Collins* dictionary definition. This conservatism probably stems from metal's lack of outside stimuli from other musical or social trends; its bonding conformity has tended to squeeze out any progress society might have made since metal's inception, so ever since it has revolved around the old-fashioned ideals it's always felt comfortable with.

The closest metal has ever come to genuine interracial embrace (ignoring revered icons such as Jimi Hendrix, Carlos Santana, Phil Lynott, etc., who were unique individuals and succeeded despite rather than because of the prevalent racial perception) was in the late 1980s, with the sudden appearance of funk metal and the all-black band Living Colour. These four chops-laden dudes from New York knocked down doors the genre had assumed would remain closed forever, were tentatively embraced by an ethnically parched community, and fundamentally altered the rock landscape for the better. They set the pace for a glut of nonwhite rockers, who now had the freedom to express themselves within a format they had always loved but had nevertheless felt excluded from all these years. A few months down the line from Living Colour's hit single "Cult of Personality," every metal band in the world had shoehorned a turgid funk track or two into their set, and were claiming Sly Stone and Funkadelic as deeply influential to their music. Funk was metal's "next step" for a while—another blast of life-maintaining oxygen like the New Wave of British heavy metal (an exciting young vanguard of leather and perms in the late '70s that included Iron Maiden and Tygers of Pan Tang), the arrival of Guns N' Roses in 1986, and the revolution of thrash metal, popularized by the likes of Metallica in the mid-'80s. These arrivals kicked heavy metal's perpetually fat and lazy ass and forced it into different directions—or at least kept us busy objecting to them. Metal would have died long before without their cumulative influences.

Homophobia is an accusation that one can direct much more easily. Heavy metal has always been almost comically heterosexual, professing a collective horror at the antics of the homosexual pop fraternity and the gay community in general, which is ironic when you think about the basic trappings of the genre: long hair, tight leather trousers, phallic symbolism, makeup, bondage gear—the look is steeped in sexual ambiguity. The magnificent irony of this came in 1998, when the lead singer of arguably the ultimate heavy metal band, Judas Priest, left the group and outed himself live on MTV. Throughout his career Rob Halford had dressed in leather peaked caps, shaved his head, and showered himself in blindingly camp iconography. Yet the sound of the metal community's jaw hitting the floor on his confession was loud indeed, and delightfully naive. As with Freddie Mercury, it was suddenly all so obvious. Halford had even alluded to it in his anthem "Hell Bent For Leather." But how were we supposed to tell from *that*?

The most obvious visual sign of allegiance to the heavy metal cabal has always been in the long hair. In many ways it's all you ever really need to demonstrate your purity, your unarguable virility. Short-haired metallers always protest about this, but that's only because they've been told they can't have long hair by their parents or their bosses. Long-haired metallers know this only too well and will always feel superior about it. Occasionally you get long-haired metal musicians who cut their hair to be clever. They always grow it back again, though, unless they've done it because of baldness, in which case they wear a big hat, or a bandanna, or both at once with some sunglasses.

Wigs are more common than the world of heavy metal would like to admit. It's vital to maintain the pretense that your hair will *never* fall out. Famous wig-wearers include all of Kiss, David Lee Roth, and Ritchie Blackmore; W. Axl Rose is just a rumor. Spinal Tap caused controversy just by wearing wigs in their film. It was as if the metal community was saying, *If they're going to make a film about metal, at least use people with real long hair.*

Rob standing outside his mom's house in Birmingham

The heavy metal community has never been one hundred percent comfortable with the film *Spinal Tap*, despite its earnest claims to the contrary. The film's frightening accuracy horrified metal bands and fans alike when it was released in 1984, and the metal community, as one, complained that it just wasn't funny. But director Rob Reiner's fondness for the subject and his attention to detail eventually won us over, until eventually it became bad form to protest. That is until the bastards decided to come back in the late '80s, this time as a "real band," with a new album and gigs and everything. *Oh no, not again*, said metal, and all the rock mags handed *Break Like the Wind* terrible thank-you-very-much-now-go-away reviews. The "band" thought metal fans would love it, as they'd been claiming to love the movie, but they didn't, they hated it, and the whole project died a messy death.

Ha ha ha, who's laughing now? we gloated.

Keep it True. Death to the False.

Silver

It always troubled me that Alex got everything before me, if indeed I ever got it at all. It didn't really matter because I was round at his place all the time anyway, but it still rankled, so I came up with a foolproof idea: I would invent my own AC/DC album, design a cover and a track listing for it, and try to convince Alex that it was the real thing—a "lost" DC album, never mentioned anywhere, found exclusively by me. It was a brilliant idea, except for one key element: I had no music to go with it. I would have to say that, unfortunately, I had mislaid the actual cassette along the way. Frustrating, yes, but these things happen. But it was brilliant, trust me. In fact *Silver*, the superb and legendary missing AC/DC album, was, in my humble opinion, the Greatest Record They Ever Made.

I constructed the cover out of black cardboard and wrote my much-practiced AC/DC logo in silver pen in the middle. Underneath that I wrote *Silver*, all classylike, hardly smudging at all. Then I carefully listed ten made-up songs which I thought sounded like DC titles: "Stick It Further In" and "Give It to Me Heavy & Hot" and "Let's Rock Hard (All Night)" and "AC/DC Forever." I wrote those in silver pen on the inside, and the credits too—all tracks by Young, Young and Johnson, without a single mention of Hunter anywhere.

One afternoon as we walked downhill from home toward the water meadows, I showed Alex my cassette box with great pride and no hint of shame. I explained the extraordinary story behind the album, and the tragic tale of the lost cassette. Alex listened politely and toyed with the case. I described the songs, even sang him a few, then it went back in my pocket and we never mentioned it again.

It was around this time that I started my weekly charts in a green exercise book that I'd stolen from school. It was 1982 and I was sick of the charts on the TV and radio because there was no AC/DC in them. (There was that year actually—"Nervous Shakedown" sneaked in at the low thirties for one solitary week. I bought it, of course, and then pretended not to be disappointed when I realized it was exactly the same as it was on the album.) So to redress this imbalance I came up with the idea of compiling my own charts, based on my current favorite songs. Each week I solemnly transcribed my list of favorite songs by AC/DC into my exercise book. I would apply myself to this task with professorial fastidiousness, and pore over the slight drop of "High Voltage," or the exciting new entry of "Let There Be Rock." When I'd finally written out the placings, I'd spend half an hour reading down the chart in hysterical detail in the style of a Radio One DJ, comparing this week's chart against last week's. The track that spent the longest time at number one was the stunningly average "Up to My Neck in You," which stayed up there for thirteen weeks. It shrugged off all comers, even "Bedlam in Belgium," until, on a winter's morning in 1983, two new songs from one new band gatecrashed the party.

The songs: "Flight of Icarus" and "Run to the Hills."

The band: Iron Maiden.

Alexander AC/DC is on the right—his rifle is real.

Chapter Two

ready and willing

As my boarding school was what felt like a hundred miles away from Winchester, and my parents couldn't afford the fees any more, I sat exams to try and get into Winchester College for free, but failed them with flying colors. So at eleven years old I took another exam and got into a school in Southampton for free instead, just ten miles down the road, which meant I could catch the train there every day. Money was suddenly so tight that we were forced to move into a much smaller terraced house, and it suddenly felt as if we were all living on top of each other.

By this time I had worked my way methodically through the Maiden oeuvre, pausing only briefly to return my cassette of *Killers* because Bruce Dickinson, the singer, sounded nothing like he had on *Number of the Beast*. That was a tricky conversation in the record shop, believe me. I went back a few weeks later, in disguise, and bought it again after I found out they'd changed singers between albums.

It seemed to me that Iron Maiden were slightly more serious than AC/DC—no gimmicks, no dirty words, no flat caps; just a lot of long hair, leather and spandex, and songs with epic themes. AC/DC functioned on three chords and thinly veiled sexual metaphors, but Iron Maiden were all puffed chests, complex guitar solos, and songs about the wind and flags. They were operatic and overblown and I was extremely excited by their blustering cutlass sound. Alex and I did the Maiden—we raced through it, constantly trying to outdo one another with Maiden facts and figures which we often just made up.

But our friendship wasn't to last. Our schools were miles apart and my plunge into metal's rich belly was starting to pick up pace. One day outside the school gates some incredibly cool kid played me some Judas Priest on his Walkman. The snippet I heard was enough; it was awesome. To me, the Priest sounded like the future, so the following week I burst into Winchester's metal-friendly Venus Records and bought *Defenders of the Faith*. Aside from the impressive hulking robot monster on the sleeve, the album's aural innards gleamed with razor-sharp sounds. The guitars were so heavy and fast! The singing was like molten shards of glass! The lyrics were about how great heavy metal was, and how we were right and everyone else was wrong! And in the picture of the group on the back, not only were they wearing just leather, they were also completely covered in studs and rivets. This was easily the greatest record ever made, and, despite the fact that one of the group had short hair and one even had a beard, these were the coolest bunch of guys I'd ever seen.

I bought up a few of their records from the 1970s, but became slightly disillusioned as parts of them weren't heavy enough, especially *Sad Wings of Destiny*, with its great big flouncing angel on the front. Still I knew that allegiance was particularly important in metal, so despite their ballads I felt sure I was the Priest's number one fan in Hampshire. I pored over their checkered history, filling the space reserved in my head for traditional academic subjects with facts about beardy Ian Hill's bass technique (there wasn't one), the making of the seminal *British Steel* album (it didn't take long), and the controversy around the *Stained Class* album and an American teenager's suicide. I was genuinely shocked to find no Judas Priest entry in my father's complete set of *Encyclopaedia Britannica*; I even went so far as to compose my own, which I posted to the compilers for use in the following year's edition, but my father refused to buy the whole set again so I don't know whether they put it in or not.

Nobody seemed to appreciate my precocious charm at this huge new school in Southampton. It was swallowed up by the screaming playgrounds and the echoing wooden halls, and my complete lack of street wisdom played into all kinds of hands. I made friends with a few other Winchester first-year students, but as a group we were easily capsized, and I clung harder to the heavy metal dinghy in my head. I wasn't bullied, just trampled underfoot, so I spent more and more time carving out the logos of my favorite bands on my exercise books, which, I was sternly informed, was naughty, and to stop it.

Heavy metal was taking me over. In fact, I couldn't get enough of it out in the real world so I decided to invent my own imaginary band. I named them, cryptically, "ER," and gave them the most convoluted, soap-operatic career curve in the history of metal. Singers quit, axe gods were mysteriously fired, and a trail of humiliated part-time synth players littered their checkered career. ER's canon of around twenty-five albums was the very peak of my early-teen imagination; even today their memory still holds the residual weight of a genuine musical entity. My long daily walk to the station, and then from the station up to school and back again, consisted of me surreptitiously muttering out the life and times of ER under my breath, twitching at invisible instruments as I slouched. I'm not exaggerating when I say that for each of those imaginary masterpieces I had designed artwork, song titles, lyrics, pyrotechnic guitar solos, song times, tours, set lists, and gatefold double live albums.

Their logo was shit, though.

My social life improved in my second year when I discovered a pupil a year younger who was also from Winchester and also liked heavy metal. He was disreputable, and his name was spelled disreputably: Marc.

Marc was radical in his musical tastes. He liked Whitesnake and Ozzy Osbourne, both of whom were crossed off my list of potential bands to get into because they used keyboards. He liked some Iron Maiden too, on the side, because at that time you just did. Our age difference wasn't a problem since he was twice as streetwise as I was; he introduced me to a glut of bad habits including masturbation, lying about ejaculation, and spitting. I was already a proud smoker and had worked my way up to Marlboro within a matter of weeks, having started on packets of ten menthols and the occasional stolen Silk Cut from my father. Marc and I clouded the smoking compartments on the train to school each day and practiced smoking poses in trees behind Winchester Station before we went home.

One weekend, sensing ourselves as grown-ups, we decided to take the train to Southampton to buy ourselves our first heavy metal T-shirts. This would be the first time I was to wear anything not selected and purchased by my mother, so I'm not keen to elaborate on the clothes I was wearing at the start of this journey, except to say that I had a pretty cool Batman shirt that I liked to wear a lot, which had big, pointy, bat-like collars.

We marched down the Southampton main street with open minds over which particular T-shirt we were going to choose in HMV. It was 1984, the summer of Frankie Goes To Hollywood, and it was difficult to find a T-shirt that didn't resemble a billowing white sheet proclaiming "Frankie Say . . ." something we didn't understand. We eventually uncovered a few piles of black shrink-wrapped treasure, laid them out over the racks, and filtered out all the smalls we could find. After much dithering, I chose a Judas Priest one and Marc got two Maiden ones. We rushed over to the park opposite and pulled on our new T-shirts and suddenly we were cool, suddenly I was a sexual animal, suddenly I cared about my hair. We strutted very slowly back to the station, eyeing up older girls along the way, one more thing that Marc had shown me how to do.

A week later I acquired a denim-style jacket (actually my mother did—thrift store, black corduroy, baggy armpits), which meant that Marc and I were now officially metal. It was becoming hard to tell the difference between ourselves and any passing member of, say, the Maiden, and we didn't change our clothes for almost two months. Passing similarly attired young fellows in the street, we'd blush and push back the edges of our jackets to properly display the T-shirt design.

The winged flying steel robot beast on the front of my T-shirt was called the Hellion. He featured on a sequence of Priest records in a variety of guises. In this illustration the Hellion is *Screaming for Vengeance*, the image on the cover of the Priest's best album, I think.

How to Dress Metal

People think the standard metal uniform of band T-shirt and jeans is easy. And in a way they're right. But passions run high—high enough for the choice of T-shirt not to be taken lightly. Not only must you worry about what band you're going to choose, which is a perilous decision in the first place, but you also need to think about its rarity value, its kudos, the effect it would have on a fellow, say, Molly Hatchet fan, were you to bump into one on the main street. If that Molly Hatchet fan saw you in a bog-standard latest-album design with its colors still vivid on the print, you'd feel obliged to explain that you are a real fan, and haven't just got into them recently despite the pristine appearance of the T-shirt. What you want to be wearing is that limited edition tour T-shirt, the faded one and, most importantly, the one with the tour dates on the back. Having the tour dates on the back (preferably for a gigantic, world-straddling tour with tons of dates in Germany and places you've never heard of in America) makes you a proper fan. And if the tour you're advertising on your back took place over five years ago, you're pretty much there. Every metal fan has at some point in his or her life walked down the street in the depths of winter with their denim or leather jacket slung over their arm, just to show off the tour dates on the back of their T-shirt.

The T-shirts have to be black. In the '70s they were occasionally red, but red fades to pink which is unacceptable. Black fades really nicely into "old," "old" becomes "favorite," and "favorite" often turns into "second skin." When it comes to the design itself, the most important feature is the band's logo. This is a straightforward branding exercise. The logo should be elaborate and embellished with one of a few standard lettering effects—gothic, or spiky, or three-dimensional, or even all three—but not so complicated as to be impossible to replicate in felt tip on the back of a denim jacket or in an exercise book. Uriah Heep really messed up—their labyrinthine design was much too difficult to draw without artistic training, so people tended not to bother trying and wrote UFO instead. Here are a few generic-looking logos of bands you may not have heard of, to demonstrate the general effect.

The logo is particularly important when it comes to the heavy metal T-shirt, because the rest of the illustration will often be interchangeable with any other band's. It might be a dragon, an apocalyptic urban scene featuring explosions, a crude image of five or so longhairs (the band themselves), a big motorbike, a large-breasted woman (often with the band's name tattooed prominently on her upper arm), and if the band is American, a top-hatted, half-zombie Uncle Sam figure, cackling and pointing a spindly finger at you. Most of these images have been used at one time or another by everybody. The only metal band whose art is particularly recognizable are the Maiden, with their lifelong mascot, the famous zombie "Eddie the Head." Eddie features on all of the band's album covers and most of their merchandise.

Destruction are German.

Overkill—I don't know why they chose to separate the word in their logo like that.

Dio

Venom

Witchfinder General

Witchfinder General

Jeans are easier. Any jeans are fine, so long as they're not fashionable. If you take too much time over choosing the jeans you'll be labeled a ponce. Bleached tight jeans will see you through without any problems. So too will filthy ones, and good old-fashioned grease

Eddie the Head

This guy knows he's got it exactly right.

never goes amiss either; it signifies a manual job, possibly with hot rods or motorbikes, which is a good impression to give.

If you have spindly legs, you might want to go a step further down the jeans highway and invest in a pair of tight, clinging ones. These come in a variety of different types. The most metal are the legendary stripy spandex, as sported by behemoths all over the world since the early '80s. Spandex is the definitive metal legwear; it's skin-tight and comes in a huge variety of rainbow hues and faux animal prints. Tiger-striped, sequined, leopardskin, black and white, leather effect, pinstriped, spangled, satin, polka-dotted—pretty much anything and everything goes, and amazingly no one (well, no metaller) will raise an eyebrow to question your sexual orientation. For best effect the spandex is finished off with a gleaming pair of bright white ankle-hugging sneakers.

When it comes to coats, you can choose between two: denim or leather. The leather jacket—stolen wholesale from the Brando/Dean model of the 1950s—has, from the '70s onward, been the purists' staple. The only problem with the leather jacket is that you can't really sew patches onto it, but it overcomes this design flaw by looking plain mean. What you could attach to your leather jacket were studs; in the late '80s they sometimes came with studs already on them, if you were a twat.

The denim model, though plainly cheaper and a little more versatile, was always considered the slightly younger brother of the leather. There were all sorts of things you could do to your denim jacket (things that would've ruined your leather one), such as add band patches, strategic rips, hem-scuffing, and writing on them with felt-tip. The denim was an all-round friendlier type of beast—easier to celebrate your favorite bands with, but lacking the sweat and fusty creak of the bad-boy leather. Motorhead, arguably the only genuinely "cool" metal band ever, only wore leather jackets—crusty old biker numbers with wide lapels that flapped in the wind. They probably even wore them in bed (if they ever went to bed, that is).

Leather trousers are completely different. They've always been a big mistake, especially if you spend hundreds of pounds on a gleaming off-the-rack pair, which just give you tree-trunk thighs and a huge baggy ass. The only person ever to have looked cool in a pair of leather trousers (and even then only for about five minutes) was Jim Morrison. In the late '80s, though, during the new glam rock, leather trousers came back with a vengeance. In a way they replaced spandex, which had slipped slowly out of fashion due to bands like Saxon never being out of the stuff. These new leather trousers began to develop accessories such as tassels, sequins, and laces up the sides. This all looked quite nice for a while, but in the end they were just another easy target for Kurt Cobain and his subversive cardigans.

I've mentioned big white trainers, but after Guns N' Roses came along, you had to wear cowboy boots, wherever you happened to belong on the metal tundra. If you were sold on the whole Guns aesthetic like most people (their look would rule the metal school right up until the end), you wore your jeans inside your cowboy boots, showing them off in all their fake chintz glory. But if you were still refusing to bow to the whole sleaze thing, or were on the whole thrash metal trip, you brought your blue jeans out and over like actual cowboys did.

Assuming you didn't do that, assuming you had a shred of cool, you wore them with tight black jeans, much like a goth might.

But—and think about this—have you ever seen a metaller walking around with just a basic pair of cowboy boots? No! For God's sake man, where are your spurs? In my era, between 1986 and 1992, all you could buy on Carnaby Street (the only place to go if ever you want to dress metal) were accessories for your cowboy boots and skull-motif bandannas. But it wasn't just spurs you could improve your naked boots with; all kinds of metallic under-strapped appendages were permissible—studs, stars, flower shapes, bells, rivets, skulls, indeed anything and everything went, just so long as it flattered your ankles, jingled loudly, or hurt.

Have I mentioned sweaters? Good. They're not allowed. Granny's knitted you a woolly pullover with "Warrant" stenciled on it?

Fuck Granny.

Larger than Life

Once Marc and I had the basic gear down pat, it was time to customize the rest of our clothes. The most metal way of doing this was by pleading with my mother to sew on band patches. I got a small AC/DC one on my black corduroy jacket in the area between the shoulders, and I wrote the Iron Maiden logo along the bottom with a toxic silver marker pen. You couldn't really buy patches around Winchester or Southampton—often you had to rely on getting one as a free gift in a special 12-inch single—so building up a backful was something that took time, years even. The problem with this was that you ended up with patches on your jacket of bands you'd liked at the time of sewing, but had gone right off a few months later. Heavily patched denim jackets had the constant potential to become walking walls of shame—lucky for me I never got into the Quo.

My school uniform started to get in the way of this new self-expression. I didn't dare sew a Judas Priest patch onto the back of my blazer, though I was desperate to. The only way to rebel from within the uniform was by stealthily growing my hair down beyond my collar. This sounds vaguely rebellious until you glance at any school photograph from that era, where, apart from the hip kids with their sides-shaved mullets, we all have exactly the same shaggy, bigfoot haircut.

By the end of my second year at this increasingly unpleasant and bewildering secondary school, I was known among my peers as a sad and boring heavy metal obsessive. I'd acquired this reputation on the back of just three bands—the DC, the Maiden, and the Priest. But as I endlessly thumbed the Priest section in Venus Records, I could see a band poking through the racks to the right that made me feel uneasy; they were covered in blood, fire, and terrifying black and white makeup. Despite being frightened, my eyes couldn't help but occasionally stray over in horrified fascination, though I didn't dare pick out one of their records. Little did I know of the clandestine excitement just around the corner—little did I know I was about to embark upon an affair.

I'd heard of Kiss before—who hadn't? But they had such a stupid and uncool name (why not just call yourselves Hug, or Cuddle, or Namby Pamby?), I'd always been loath to investigate. I was also intimidated by the way they looked—I didn't really understand why they wanted to scare everyone quite so much. But then one day, under pressure from Marc, I bought their first double live album, *Kiss Alive!*—and suddenly they were my new favorite band.

Kiss weren't a regular band as such. Instead they were a Demon, a Spaceman, a Starchild, and a Cat, who just happened to play instruments and hang out together in their own rocking fantasy world. The establishment couldn't see this and so therefore considered them dangerous. They claimed that Kiss was an evil acronym that probably stood for Knights In Satan's Service, but this was all wrong because they were really just four young guys from Queens, New York, who became so swept up in their theater that nobody saw them without their face paint on for ten whole years.

Kiss's music wasn't as technically great as Judas Priest's or Iron Maiden's—they played nice easy chords with big choruses in a kindergarten blues style—but their overwhelming visual impact more than made up for the pleasingly rudimentary chops. You couldn't just buy, play, and listen to Kiss records like you did with other groups— you had to buy into the whole rock 'n' roll pantomime. They became the biggest band in the world, a living, breathing pop cartoon franchise. You either swallowed it down or thought the whole thing completely ridiculous, which of course, it totally wasn't.

Unfortunately for me, I got into them just as their album sales hit rock bottom and the band consequently decided that the face paint had outlived its magic. They decided to shake their dwindling audience back into action with an earth-shattering gesture— their true faces revealed for the very first time on the front of 1983's *Lick It Up.*

The album was pretty good, all things considered (it even featured some rapping), but my timing couldn't have been worse— they exploded their myth just as I excitedly approached, and the two coolest members had left the band, too. I was stuck with their anonymous new clump-metal direction and nobody left in the group that I liked.

They eventually came to their senses in 1996 and put the makeup back on—something that ego catastrophe Gene Simmons said they'd never do—having forced their slighted muse through the shame of going grunge in the early '90s. Kiss fans all over the world forgave them everything as the original lineup gathered again, donned their capes, stack heels, and shoulder pads, and set out to conquer the world, via marketing, once more. They'd unwittingly become the world's ultimate tribute band.

Kiss Koffin

Back at school I heard on the grapevine that there was some-one else in my year who liked Kiss. I knew him by sight because he had ginger hair and caught the train from Winchester every morning. His name was Dominic and I didn't like him, or rather he didn't like me, but I was desperate to talk about Kiss with someone, so I regularly tried to approach him in school.

One day he was standing outside a classroom with a group of kids I didn't know.

"Dominic!"

He was ignoring me, trying to edge out of my way.

"Dominic!"

"What."

"You like Kiss!"

"So fucking what."

"Do you like *Creatures of the Night*?"

"Just fuck off Hunter. For once, just fuck off."

"Have you got *Alive 2*?"

He attempted to walk away.

"*Love Gun*?"

He turned and spat—yes, there on the vinyl tiles!

Why didn't he want to talk about Kiss? I couldn't find anyone in this godforsaken place who liked them!

Then I had a lucky break. There was a swarthy kid in my class who told me in passing that he had an older brother who went to another school in another town but who liked Kiss.

"How much does he like them?" I felt nervous.

"He really likes them."

"How much is that?"

"A lot."

"Has he got *Creatures of the Night*?"

"How am I supposed to know?"

"Has he got *Alive 2*?"

"I *don't know*. Why don't you ask him yourself?"

So I wrote him a letter.

calling dr. love

Paul Bavister and I exchanged letters like lovers. Every morning I would enter the classroom and approach his grumpy younger brother who, after toying with me for a while, would reach into his blazer pocket and pull out Paul's daily message. In return I would hand mine over. We exchanged long letter after long letter, packed with Kiss devotionals, but would always end with shy and suggestive allusions to other bands to make us sound more adventurous and slightly less weird.

I was desperate for Paul to like me, but he was almost three years older, so I felt I had some catching up to do in the credibility stakes. I achieved this by lying. I told him I was a member of the Kiss Army, the world-famous Kiss fan club, and it worked. He would ask me what I had gained from the experience, materially and emotionally, but I had no idea, so I just made stuff up that sounded feasible: an Ace Frehley keyring, a Gene Simmons mask, some gold discs on my bedroom walls. He became jealous pretty quickly, so I knew I was on track to a healthy and lasting friendship.

After a few months of this, we began to moot the idea of a phone call. The very thought made me nervous, and I prepared for it by sitting on my bed, looking out of my little window, and repeating to myself: he likes Kiss, I like Kiss, how can this be anything other than beautiful?

When the phone rang at last, our respective parents did the preliminaries. My father picked up at our end, which was a potential disaster; wherever I was concerned he felt it his duty to load everything he said with heavy sarcasm. He could be ruthlessly offensive to anyone who crossed his path: he was usually inspired and hilarious, but back then I thought it was indefensible and humiliating.

My father was extremely thin—pipe-cleaner thin—and sartorially wedded to the 1970s. He wore flares and turtlenecks and had floppy hair and was in love with music and driving fancy cars. He was the exclusive and expensive first to own the digital watch, the calculator, the turbo car, the microwave, the home walkie-talkie system, and the voice recognition radio that, years later, he actually thanked me for breaking (I broke all these things in the end, except the car). He was handsome, irreverent, witty, and financially untrustworthy; a master of shuffling debt. Even within the bosom of our family he maintained a deep independent spirit and everybody simultaneously admired and felt intimidated by his raffish charm. He was, however, fueled mostly by alcohol; not the kind of destructive appetite that wrecks lives and reputations, but more of an insidious ethanol trail, which he disguised with aplomb. He was never drunk, for a start, at least not that I was aware of, but he always carried that subtle scent. He stopped in for quickies whichever the way, and drove up to the Golden Lion every night after we'd had tea. When I went round to friends' houses I'd always be amazed that their fathers were there, and not down the pub. He went on occasional two-day cooking benders, during which the family were strictly banned from the kitchen as he conjured up vast gastric assault courses. Afterward the kitchen was a bomb site; in fact he enjoyed show-ing us the mess he'd made, proudly dis-playing the force of expression that had gone into preparing that one solitary meal. Unsurprisingly he never hung around to clean it all up; this was one of the prices my mother was paying for his companionship. But we all pretty much hung on his every word.

And he struck gold so far as I was con-cerned when he threw another couple of hundred pounds at one of the first domes-tic cordless telephones, which I lugged two-handed up the stairs for my first spo-ken words with Paul Bavister. I was mor-tified when my piping treble pitch was returned with a deep, husky voice. Thinking on my feet I started to reel off a few names of Kiss songs, and he followed with his man's voice, but before long we had reached an important agree-ment over the deep significance of Kiss's "And on the Eighth Day (God Created Rock 'n' Roll)." That it was true and we were on some kind of mission.

Our letters dried up and the phone calls lengthened. Soon we were communicating on a nightly basis—marathon Kiss conferences that were starting to piss off both sets of parents. However, as well as the phone calls, I had secretly decided that I too should become a metal god. For months now as I earnestly listened to Kiss's "Christine Sixteen" and "Plaster Caster," I had gazed at a pair of electric guitars—one six-string, one bass—leaning up against the grand piano in our small living room. My father had knocked these up during his brief hippie phase. He'd bought the cheapest guitar and bass he could find (at Woolies) and taken them apart. He'd stripped off the vinyl finishing, pulled out the wiring, replaced the scratchplates, done something strange to the pickups, and generally transformed these lowly instruments into a pair of hot-wired minimalist axes, onto which he'd then stenciled his cool initials: A.StJ.B.H.

I knew the bass was easier, so one day when he was out I plugged it into his giant Farfisa organ amplifier, hit a bottom E, and made the dog's lower jaw shudder. After a couple of days of furtively standing in front of the mirror, I was still unable to play "Detroit Rock City." My fingertips had turned scarlet and the bass kept sliding off my shoulder because the headstock was too heavy. To counter this I played sitting on a chair, which was an important sign of my dedication to musicianship over style, but it was OK because I leant the mirror against the fireplace so I could still see myself quite clearly.

Then, one evening, Paul said solemnly, "We have to start a band."

We'd both known deep down that this had been coming, but had been too shy to bring it up; I hadn't told anybody about my bass explorations, not even Paul.

"We should, yes."

"It would be a brilliant band," he said in a deep voice.

I was getting excited. "An amazing band," I said. "The best band ever."

"I play the bass," said Paul.

What? Since when? I was silent for a moment.

"I play the bass also," I replied. Oh man, this was a disaster. More silence.

"I've been playing the bass for ages," he said. "I've also got a strap and four plectrums."

"What do you mean, ages? I've been playing for ages too." The dog looked at me.

"Why can't you play something else instead?" he said unreasonably.

"No I play the bass. I'm a bass player. I'm actually really very good at it."

"I thought you said your dad had an electric guitar? Why can't you play that?"

My father's six-string sat malevolently in the corner. There was absolutely no way I was going to be able to play it; for a start it had almost twice as many strings again as the bass—approximately twenty. But then Paul did have the strap and the plectrums.

"I'll think about it," I said.

"You could be an axe *god.*"

"Oh yeah, oh sure."

I hung up, and reluctantly turned my mind to every heavy metal fan's ultimate weapon of choice—our sonic call-to-arms, our horizontal phallic light sabre—the electric guitar.

The Shapes of the Guitars

Think punk, think punk guitars. Could you tell a punk guitar from a nonpunk guitar? Think reggae, think about the guitars reggae groups use. Could you tell these guitars apart from, for example, New Romantic guitars? Think Britpop. Think '60s pop. Think

Stax. Think ska. Think krautrock, think anything. There's only one kind of music where you can tell what you're going to get just by looking at the instruments.

Here is an electric guitar.

It's the most popular and famous guitar in the world, the Fender Stratocaster, a design classic, popularized by Hank Marvin. Pop into any pub that has live music and chances are there'll be somebody onstage with one of these.

Here are some heavy metal guitars.

Aren't they much better?

Metal is the only genre that has thought, hang on, why don't we make the guitars look like us? So that's what they did.

It was probably Jimi Hendrix who first came up with the idea of turning the guitar from a straightforward instrument into something more ambitious. He was left-handed before the invention of left-handed guitars, so he spun the thing around and strung it upside down. Then he played it with his teeth and after that, he set it on fire. He knelt onstage with the guitar lying between his knees, squirting lighter fluid into the flames, coaxing them higher, sometimes up to six inches in the air. The Who smashed their guitars up. Blue Cheer blew theirs up. Kiss made theirs fly! But I'm getting excited. Let's calm down and have a look at some more guitars.

This is a B.C. Rich Warlock guitar, an early metal prototype. It's not as modern as it looks; these guitars date from the early '70s. I've always been deeply fond of this model, it's not as ostentatious and zany as others we've seen, I think it retains elements of classicism. Joe Perry from Aerosmith used to play a red one, which definitely counts in its favor, but then I was always damn keen on Joe Perry as well.

Here we have a Gibson Explorer. It was popularized in the early eighties during the new wave of British heavy metal, and subsequently embraced by groups such as Metallica, whose tough-guy mainman James Hetfield sometimes plays a black one while wearing black clothes. They have a mixture of nice clean lines and a slightly old-fashioned look, but still manage to look very metal. If you're playing one of these in this day and age you're either doing it ironically, or you're rather beautifully unreconstructed.

Bow down to this sturdy mutha. You know this one for sure—this is the definitive metal guitar—this is the Gibson Flying "V." You would be forgiven for thinking this meaty specimen dated from the '80s. In fact it was first seen in the '60s, when Jimi Hendrix no less, occasionally strapped one on. But it was metal that suited it best. Randy Rhoads, Michael Schenker, all the NWOBHM bands, every longhair worth their salt had to own one of these (and it was a good idea to customize it, maybe with an airbrush). One of the great things about Flying Vs is that they are impossible to play sitting down. Look at them—of course it's bloody impossible!—so you had to strap them on, thereby becoming an instant metal guitar god. I don't know how anyone ever got around to taking theirs off.

This is another design classic, the Fender Telecaster. Jimmy Page used to play one of these before he switched to the Les Paul. It's most famous devotee is The Boss himself, Bruce Springsteen. It symbolizes everything he stands for: a complete lack of preten-

sion, no frills, simple plain shape, hardy, manly, it makes a noise
that sounds like chicken wire, and positively thrives on sweaty
forearms. You don't come across them very often in heavy metal.
I once bought a secondhand Telecaster off a guy in a junkie flat
in Muswell Hill. I was selling my Les Paul, going in the opposite
direction from Jimmy Page (not for the first time) and we got into
a discussion over the pros and cons of both guitars.

"The great thing about Telecasters," he said, "is that you can
chuck 'em through a wardrobe door and they come out fine the
other side. You can do anything to 'em, whatever you like, and
they can always effing take it."

"Right," I replied, and paid him in cash.

Here we are, the second most popular electric guitar behind the
Fender Strat, the Gibson Les Paul. This guitar was invented by Les
Paul, way back in 1954. They're not only satisfy-
ingly heavy (weight, not metal heavy, though
they're that too), but they also sustain a note for
hours (when plugged in). They have a very distinctive fluid sound, all belly and full-tone.
Famous devotees of this model include Jimmy
Page, Slash, and Ace Frehley. Mick Mars out of
Mötley Crüe liked these axes so much he
named his first born after them. Les Paul Mars.

Here's Angus Young again, my first-ever guitar hero, with his trademark model, the Gibson
SG, and of course his usual school uniform. SG
players seem to be fanatically loyal to their
instrument; I don't know why, I think they look

crap. They sound good though—raw and fiery—and are probably the sturdiest guitar that Gibson ever made.

A guitar war broke out in the mid '80s. It was triggered by the headstock—the end bit of the electric guitar, where the tuning pegs are. First of all, guitars had normal headstocks. They looked like this:

Normal

Stylish, classic, nobody had any problems. They were just the end bits of the guitars. Then somebody at Jackson Guitars designed the world's first pointy headstock, and the guitar world went completely mad for them. They looked like this:

Pointy

This new development shook the metal world to its stack-heeled foundations. Much like the spandex explosion after years of denim and leather, pointy headstocks smashed the floodgates open. All of a sudden even the most traditional and old-fashioned guitars came with these new pointy headstocks welded on the end. They looked absurd—it was like putting spoilers and racing stripes on a Ford Taurus—but the momentum was unstoppable, and it soon became obligatory for every axe to sport one. These headstock daggers signified poise, sleekness, modernity, fashion . . . and fashionable things were rare in heavy metal, so here was a chance to really get one over on your less streetwise metallist.

Even basses weren't immune. The first pointy bass-stocks followed soon enough, and the usually ultra-cautious steady-Eddie legs-akimbo bass players of the metal world bought them too. These headstocks and the new body shapes that followed had invented a whole new way of expressing ourselves. Guitar bodies started to look like this:

The metal world began to dribble. We'd been the ugly duckling of the music world and at last felt that we were becoming sexy. And we were.

But hang on, what happened to the war? Check this out:

Reverse pointy

Yes, it's the other way around!
Again:

Normal pointy   *Reverse pointy*

This new development threw us all into turmoil, and a nasty squabble ensued as the forward pointys faced off against the Robespierrean reverse pointys. The kingdom was split. This fierce, uncompromising discussion raged for years, until the huge success of Guns N' Roses turned the wheel slowly back in favor of the Gibsons and the Fenders and the plump, rounded, *normal* headstocks.

Even today, if you're real metal, your guitar has a pointy headstock. And if you want a quiet life, it looks like this:

Points both ways

The next picture is the metal equivalent of the bullet that killed JFK or the arrow that hit King Harold in the eye at the Battle of Hastings. It's important to boo when you set eyes on this next specimen. It is an evil Excalibur of a musical instrument; it's the guitar Kurt Cobain used to kill metal.

The Fender Jaguar is actually a damn fine, if expensive, piece of sonic machinery. It resembles a knackered old Thames barge, and can be made to sound quite similar. This is one of those guitars that I want to lick.

At the opposite end from the Fender Jaguar's ramshackle elegance, is Cheap Trick's "madcap" guitarist, Rick Nielsen. Cheap Trick were pop rock, but slid into our territory by virtue of their long hair. They had a moderately successful career throughout the '70s, and happened to write two of the all-time great pop-metal songs; the heart-string-tugging-but-punch-the-air-at-the-same-time "I Want You to Want Me" and the even better "Surrender." Nielsen's problem was that he was short-haired and strange-looking while the lead singer and bassist were drop-dead gorgeous. Cheap Trick album covers always featured the handsome two on the front, and Nielsen and rotund drummer Bun E. Carlos on the back, so Nielsen needed a hook to grab himself a piece of the attention. He came up with these:

Crikey.

This is an accurate representation of Nielsen himself.

This is actually an electric guitar.

Christ.

Point of Entry

May 5, 1985: my fourteenth birthday. Downstairs in the front room, my mother and sister groggily watched me open my presents. As usual, my father was still asleep upstairs, and as usual, he hadn't got me a present himself. But suddenly I had an idea. I padded up the stairs to my parents' room and knelt at my father's bedside.

"*Wake up*," I whispered. "*Wake up*." Nudging didn't work either, so I had to roll him over onto his back. One eye reluctantly flickered open and he grunted and rolled back again.

"You know it's my birthday today?" I whispered into his ear.

He grunted again.

"Well I've thought of something you could give me as a present!"

No grunt this time, he just pulled up the sheet.

"Why don't you give me your electric guitar? It won't cost you anything and you don't have to wrap it and it's not going to leave the house, is it?"

There was a very long pause.

"Well?" I whispered, and held my breath.

"Oh alright. Now, please, fuck off," he mumbled from under the sheet.

It's a fictional chord.

I ran downstairs, strapped it on, and stood in front of the mirror and gazed at myself for a very long time. It was lighter than the bass, and much more complicated. But it was suddenly the sexiest fucking thing in the world and it was mine, which meant that *I was sexy too*. I had my photograph taken with it in the garden that afternoon.

Chapter Four

go!

When my father agreed to teach me how to play the guitar, I had assumed it would take him more than six minutes to do so. He showed me E, he showed me A, and he showed me B7.

"Right then," he said.

"Right what?" My fingers were gracelessly locked into B7.

"I'm off to the pub."

"But what's the next chord?"

"That's all you need," he said, looking for his lighter and car keys.

"I only need three chords? There are more chords than that aren't there? What about . . . what about C?"

"Bollocks."

"Really?"

"Just learn how to play those three and you'll be fine. You can work out the rest yourself."

"Can't you please just teach me a few more?"

"I'll see you later."

"*D?*"

He left, I gazed at my trembling B7, played it, and dropped my plectrum.

What galls me today about this is that apart from being right, he was also being extraordinarily lazy. Had he delayed his visit to the pub by a couple of hours, I would've got through the painful preliminaries considerably faster than the months it actually took. But then again, his laziness gave me the opportunity to be a self-taught guitar player, which is definitely the best way. Your style is your own. Your clumsiness is unique. You can't blame your guitar teacher for your complete lack of technique. You can be utterly rubbish for years all by yourself. And your defense is perfect: *Well how the fuck am I supposed to know?*

I don't know why, but my father owned Russ Conway's old bass player's amplifier—not the speaker or anything, just the top bit, the amp. He talked about it in hushed tones like it was our own Elgin Marble, so I did too. Russ Conway. Who was he?

Later that week he wired the amp up to an old hi-fi speaker and we plugged in the guitar. The sound that came out was fuzzed-up and rancid (he'd overloaded the speaker) and all you could hear was distortion. My father apologized and moved to dismantle the contraption, but I elbowed him away and lugged it up to my room, quaking with excitement. My guitar was already heavy metal!

My sister still owns cassettes that I recorded of my early practice sessions. She likes to remind me of them every now and then as if they're some sort of lost treasure waiting for reappraisal. There's hours of the stuff: no singing, just monster riffs out of time and barking root chords that go on forever. These tapes feature my first attempts at writing a song. It was called "Go!" It's enthusiastic.

Paul and I were now an official band, despite the fact that we'd never actually met, let alone played our instruments together. The tone of our conversations shifted to accommodate this new professionalism as we arranged our first physical meeting. This summit was a logistical headache as we lived miles apart; the journey would involve generosity from one of my parents, and since my mother had stopped driving altogether after a dicey moment in high winds on the highway, it was all about trying to bribe my father.

I was obviously the star of our group—having no singer certainly helped my cause—and as my father drove me down to Paul's house for the weekend, I gazed out of the car window, a supremely confident master of the art of axemanship, off to the country for a few days of rehearsals of original material that I'd written out in my new *Complete Guitar Player Music Writing Book.* I was also feeling quite cocky since my father had recently told me how bar chords worked. It turned out they were agony and took ages.

"Are my fingers supposed to hurt as much as this?" I asked him.

"The pain is good for you."

The Bavisters lived in a big house near the coast and Paul was waiting for me in the drive as we arrived. He was tall and ungainly and covered in spots. We were very awkward with one another and filled the gaps in our conversation by reciting the names of Kiss songs back and forth just as we had in our first telephone call. When my father left, we headed up to Paul's bedroom, which smelled disgusting, and began the serious business of deciding what kind of band we were going to be. He showed me his bass; in fact he strapped it on and played a complete load of rubbish.

"That was 'Ladies Room,'" he said.

"I don't play Kiss songs, I play original compositions only."

Then he told me that he'd invited another friend over for the weekend, somebody called Luke, who also played the guitar.

"But why did you invite him? I thought the band was just us."

"Luke plays *lead* guitar, you see? He'll play lead guitar while you play rhythm guitar. And I play bass."

I was crestfallen. "Yes, but is he actually any good?"

"Yeah, he says he's amazing."

Before I'd had a chance to digest this properly we heard Luke's parents' car pull up in the drive. Luke looked like a spotty cross between Jimi Hendrix and Phil Lynott and had a flashy Fender Stratocaster copy with its own plush case lined with purple Afghan velvet. He wore a leather jacket and a bullet belt and had a high-pitched nasal voice.

"Hello," he said through his nose.

"Have you got an amplifier?" I asked.

"No, I was hoping to use your one."

"Russ Conway's amplifier only has two input sockets, I'm afraid. One for me, one for him," I pointed at Paul.

"I don't mind," he said. "I'm here to play solos."

"But if you're not plugged in then how—"

"Just solos," he snapped.

We set up our gear—the three guitars and the amplifier with the speaker on a wire—in Paul's straw-matted conservatory. Paul and I immediately got on with some pointless sonic jousting, playing random noisy chords while eyeing Luke as he sat on the floor fiddling with his tuning pegs. After an hour, bored with our racket, we sat down and constructed a proper song. Paul already had some epic warlike lyrics, and we attached them to some music I'd written. We practiced it a little and then *bang bang bang*, off we went, noisy as hell, riffs clattering, dreadful, eager, high on it, whooping.

"Right. Shall we record it then?"

"Definitely." So we stuck Paul's cheap tape recorder with its little condenser mic next to Russ Conway's amp and hovered a finger over the record button. We were to yell out the vocals in tandem while we played, which meant we had to play our instruments kneeling down by the machine so it would catch our voices. The song was called "Armageddon's Ring," and its chorus went: "*So can't you hear the distant thunder / growling in the East / the war of good and evil / the righteous and the Beast.*"

It was good.

We recorded pretty much everything we played; with hindsight I don't really know why. Maybe it was in case we came up with some spontaneous masterpiece, our own accidental "Stairway to Heaven." As we played through "Armageddon's Ring," Luke sat on the floor hunched over his Strat. It was still unplugged, and he moved his fingers speedily up and down the fretboard. I watched nervously as we crashed along, knowing that sooner or later it was going to be his turn to be plugged in, and that what he was doing silently with his fingers was scaring the shit out of me.

When Paul and I were satisfied with our performance (take #2), Luke looked up from under his hair and said that he had a guitar solo worked out for the song. We were impressed—we didn't even know how he'd managed to hear himself for the last ten minutes. But how were we going to record him?

"Overdub me," said Luke.

Paul and I looked at one another and gestured toward the tiny cassette machine. "How? It's just a tape player!"

"Overdub."

"How?"

In the end we stopped the tape after the second chorus, plugged Luke in, let him do his solo unaccompanied, and then, when he nodded he had finished, pressed pause.

The solo was truly extraordinary. Paul and I sat open-mouthed while Luke attacked his axe like a man possessed—he even grunted loudly as he played it. The problem was that he couldn't actually play the guitar at all. Not in the slightest. He just ran his fingers blindly up and down the fret board, producing the sound of pigs being slaughtered. He couldn't even tell how bad he was—that's how bad he was. Maybe he'd just watched a lot of video footage of his heroes and believed that some vague speedy finger-aping would see him through. Perhaps I should've suspected something at the beginning of the session when he'd appeared to be having problems tuning. But I'd just thought, *maverick axeman—respect.* Halfway through the pertinent "Armageddon's Ring" ("reminds me of Van Halen"—my sister in the car on the way back to Winchester) comes a loud click and a pause, and then thirty seconds of Lou Reed's "Metal Machine Music," a Situationist guitar solo. We had to leave it in because it appeared that Luke was in the band now. Well, three was better than two I supposed, hating him and his stupid solos already.

We took a break and sat on the swings at the end of the garden and talked about gigging while I smoked and spat, my voice the only yet to break. We agreed that our song "Armageddon's Ring" was sufficiently definitive to name the band after. Our logo was to the point: a ring that you'd wear on your finger, but with a nuclear explosion as the "jewel."

The weekend recording with Luke had brought us to an edgy impasse. To recap:

Seb Hunter: Guitar & vocals. Can play bar chords. Can sing high harmonies. Speaks like a child. Short hair, but almost over eyes. Excitable. Prone to almost wetting pants if things are getting too overwrought.

Paul Bavister: Bass guitar & vocals. No sense of timing. Tone deaf. Tall. Bad skin. Deep monotone voice. Big house.

Luke Foster: Lead guitar. Voice like Kermit. Technique like Kermit. Also tone deaf. Everything deaf. Bad skin as well. (I had bad skin too, I just decline to mention it.)

Back in Winchester my reputation fractionally increased after I told the other kids at school that I was now in a band, and a fucking good band at that. Dominic, who was still extremely aloof even though he secretly liked Kiss too, asked me who our influences were.

"Heavy metal," I said. "Heavy metal generally, and Kiss."

"Well you sound completely shit and it's a shit name as well."

None of this mattered. I was already cultivating a haughty rock star attitude that included a cigarette wedged behind each ear and a pair of my father's aviator sunglasses. Dominic said I should listen to some decent fucking music for a change, like UFO or Aerosmith. He played me some UFO on his Walkman, but two minutes into the track I wrenched off the fuzzy headphones.

"It's got keyboards!"

"Yeah? What's your problem? Don't be such a prick."

"But you can't have keyboards in heavy metal."

"You *are* a fucking prick."

Actually, I thought to myself, *you* are the fucking prick, because UFO were absolutely rubbish—the syrupy washes of keyboards made the whole thing sound like the bloody *Magic Roundabout*.

"Are Aerosmith as shit as this?" I asked.

"It's pointless saying any fucking thing to you."

"Just tell me. Are they?"

A few days later he lent me Aerosmith's fourth album, *Rocks*. What happened next can be anticipated.

Aerosmith

Aerosmith came out of Boston in 1972, fronted by two men known as the Toxic Twins because of their vast appetite for drugs: Steven Tyler on vocals, and Joe Perry on guitar. They played a slightly more aspirational Rolling Stones brand of rock music, but with their twisting guitars turned up much louder. Their songs were low-slung authentic blues-sounding, but were anthemic enough to appeal to us kiddies in need of such sweeteners. The success of their third album, *Toys in the Attic*, meant that they could buy as many drugs as they wanted, which they did, and they managed to look extraordinarily cool while on them (in fact the more zonked-out they became, the more they began to look like pirates). At the height of this giant plane of excess the band entered a studio called the Wherehouse outside Boston and recorded their fourth album, the one Dominic had lent me, which they somewhat ironically titled *Rocks*.

Rocks is the greatest rock album of all time, by anyone, ever. I don't know how Aerosmith managed this considering the state they were in while they were making it. When asked about the record these days, even Tyler says that all he can hear are the drugs. It sounds like something from another dimension; entirely other-worldly, a hazy sonic entity unto itself. It swirls and swaggers but feels arid and fragile at the same time, and although they've had their odd decent moments since, this is the only Aerosmith album you honestly need to buy—it's a rawhide goddamn masterpiece. Its final song, the faux doo-wop coda "Home Tonight," features my all-time favorite guitar solo; it's a weird and unique thing—a guitar solo that makes me cry.

As *Rocks* slowly released its charms, Kiss slipped off the end of my radar, and thus began a holy tumble into an abyss of dark stuff—the music made by outlaws in eyeliner, high on drugs. Aerosmith had opened another big door for me—the gateway to the defining metal giants of the 1970s. In America this era belonged mostly to Kiss and Aerosmith, but in the UK it belonged to the really big boys, the guys who were so big that they became known as dinosaurs. This was the decade where heavy metal started on solids, learned to walk, and grew into the monster that conquered the world, East and West. The '70s were where metal found itself, where the sacred texts were hewn from the death of innocence in the '60s, lines were carved thick in the sand, amps were cranked up to their limits, and the rules of the game were conceived, practiced, and stuck at for over twenty-five years. Let's take a deep breath and enter the Houses of the Holy.

The 1970s:
The Zep, the Sabs, the Purps

Led Zeppelin were the daddies of us all. They were the biggest, the loudest, had the longest songs, went on the longest tours, had the longest instrumental solo spots, had the highest-pitched singer, had the best and thinnest guitar player, took the most drugs, shagged the most groupies, were the first to have their own private jet, had the most songs about knights and goblins and stuff, and, most importantly of all, sold far and away more records than anyone else of the period.

They came out of the ashes of the late '60s and ripped off old blues standards shamelessly but with virtuosic brio. The only weak link was singer Robert Plant, who looked the part with his puffed-open chest and leonine mane, but who sang too high and too squawkily, and wrote silly lyrics, worse than Noddy Holder. But they conquered the world with their first ever tour—as simple as that—the crowds had never heard anything like it before. The Zep were the first to achieve rock's definitive critical mass, to discover its liberational equation: Blues + Power = Destination.

Led Zeppelin were so big and famous that when they got to their fourth album they didn't even bother to give it a name, or even put their name on the outside record sleeve. It says a lot about the doggedness of the metal community that people still fight about what to call this fourth album. Seeing as the Zep called their first record *1*, their second *2*, and third *3*, the argument for calling it *4* would appear overwhelming. But calling it *4* in front of a Zeppelin diehard provokes howls of protest. They know it as *The Four Symbols*. Others call it *Zoso*. Some say it has no name. All you need to know is that it's the one with "Stairway to Heaven" on it, the one you've probably got. It's almost *beyond* seminal. It starts off with "Black Dog," which is really hard to play on the guitar and is about sex. It's followed by "Rock and Roll," which is hard to follow at the beginning if you're a guitarist and you're trying to count yourself in, and is about sex too, and is really hard to sing if you're playing it in the right key. Then it's the medieval epic "Battle of Evermore" which is full of wailing and mandolins and is profound and hard to play on the guitar (and the mandolin). Then it's time to settle back for the main attraction.

"Stairway to Heaven" is perhaps the most famous rock song of all time. It goes on for about fifteen minutes and has many different parts; it's like "Bohemian Rhapsody" but slightly less embarrassing. "Stairway" is a song about nothing really. Plant (known affectionately in metal circles as Percy) wrote some of the words with a hangover a few minutes before he was due to record them. For a song so famous, few other artists have had the nerve to record their own interpretation. Those who have (Dread Zeppelin, Rolf Harris, Dolly Parton) have produced a mixed set of results. Even Percy hasn't got much to say about the song anymore. "I was a kid when I wrote that," he says these days, dismissively.

After this, the Zep got even bigger, and they started to give their albums names—a sign of insecurity if ever there was one. Punk arrived, and everybody assumed the Zep would be one of the first to fall, but instead they ran away to America and played three-hour sets with models of Stonehenge onstage. In the end neither punk nor their own bloated weight killed them: they were killed by Death. The best drummer *ever*, John Bonham (known

affectionately in metal circles as Bonzo), died the archetypal metal
Death, going the same way as Bon Scott from the DC and several
others: he choked on his own vomit while sleeping. He died in
1980, and the rest of the Zep did the right thing and broke up the
band. To their credit they still haven't sullied their legacy by re-
forming, although they've come mighty close over the years, and
probably will some day, but that's OK because that's what people
do. People should be less precious about shit like that.

Black Sabbath were punk before punk was invented, but without
sounding much like it. OK, they had long greasy hair and moustaches, and dressed in black, were obsessed with crucifixes, wrote
songs about witches and stuff, and were probably Satanists, but the
principle behind the noise they made, and their attitude while
making it, was punk all the way. All four of the Sabs were from
Birmingham, and all were really dodgy, especially their delinquent
young vocalist (in metal, always use "vocalist" rather than
"singer"), the deadly Ozzy Osbourne. The noise they made was
instantly terrifying. If you can imagine getting on the *Titanic*
(before it sank), stripping out all its decks and cabins and everything until you've just got the gigantic iron shell, and then in the
middle of the night scraping something rusty and fetid along the
bottom, for hours, then you've got the raw effect of the sound of
Black Sabbath. They did a few ballads too, though these weren't
ballads so much as funereal dirges, which provoked suicidal urges
among those unconditioned to their sound. They scared people,
and people love to be scared, so the Sabs became enormous.

The Sabs were bolder than the Zep when it came to naming
their fourth record—they bit the bullet and decided to give it a
name: *Volume 4*. Like the Zep, it was their best and most famous
album. It came out in 1972 and included a song called
"Supernaut," which has, to my ears, the greatest riff of all time.
And it's these riffs that turned the Sabs from a modest blues band

into bona fide Princes of Darkness. Tony Iommi, guitarist and songwriter (once described by the editor of *Melody Maker* as looking like "a gypsy violinist in an Earls Court pizza joint, or more accurately, like the Italian contestant in next year's Eurovision Song Contest"; Iommi later punched him), is the all-time Master of the Riff. Those thick slabs of chords, jagged grinding motifs, clanging statements of evil intent, were Iommi's alone. So Tony laid down one of those, Bill and Geezer (drums and bass) doomed it out behind him, and at the front, bellowing the runic catechisms, was Ozzy himself. He wasn't a great singer, still isn't, but listening to their early albums there's only one man for the job—though if foghorns were able to elucidate they could've used one of those instead.

The Sabs were always dogged by allegations of Satanism. It was an image they did little to dispel—why would they want to mess with their mystique? Iommi rebuffed the accusations by stating boldly: "We don't do any sacrifices onstage." This kept people off their backs for a while, but not for long. When Ozzy left the group in 1977, worn out from drunkenness and a recent death in his family, the Sabs ploughed on with another singer. Then another, and another. Altogether, if we come right up to date, they've had nine different singers, not to mention several bass players and drummers. Only Tony has remained at the helm throughout, keeping the Sabbath fires burning. And for that, surely, we have to salute him.

The third band in this Holy Trinity, Deep Purple, have had so many members that I can't be bothered, and that's before we get to all the offshoot bands like Rainbow, Whitesnake, and Dio. The Purps were a middle-class group, there were six of them, and one of those played the organ. I never liked them—they had an organ. The Purps didn't set out to be heavy metal (they originally consisted of just the old drummer from the Searchers, and then he found a keyboard player to give him a hand), but after a while they couldn't help themselves. The man in charge of Deep Purple was the legendary "Man in Black," Ritchie Blackmore (not Johnny Cash). He was a great guitar player but a guy with *issues*, and a legendarily short fuse.

The Purps named their fourth album *Concerto for Group and Orchestra*. It was singer Ian Gillan's first with the band, and hardly an auspicious start. It was recorded with the London Philharmonic Orchestra, and it came with Movements. Odd as it sounds, it was only after this ambitious call-to-arms that they really got into gear and produced the body of work that gets connoisseurs into such a froth.

In Rock, Machine Head, Fireball, Made in Japan: don't those names raise the hairs on the back of your neck? These are true foundation blocks of the catacombs of rock. Every secondhand record shop and record fair is virtually obliged to have a set of these albums somewhere within its midst, each for sale at a rock-bottom price. Their sleeve designs should be etched onto your retinas. Which is the one that replaces the American presidents' faces of Mount Rushmore with the Purps themselves? I raise an eyebrow at you if you don't know this one. *(In Rock.)*

The Purps' sound was actually very traditional. Ian Gillan was a true blue, straight-down-the-line classic metal singer, and he had a decent set of pipes on him, but there was none of the spark, none of the pace-setting characterized by the blazing Zep or the grinding Sabs. The Purps were good guys; they could be depended on to churn out the tunes, crank up the juice, dust down their chops, crank up their chops, and dust down the juice, but they never had a dimension all of their own. On a good night, Blackmore and organist Jon Lord would "duel," sometimes for up to twenty minutes, and the loser would get their amps blown up by the road crew afterward. Not really.

The Purps' most notorious moment came as they recorded

Hell Bent for Leather

their seminal *Machine Head* album in Switzerland. The band observed Montreux casino burn down during a Frank Zappa concert and the smoke from the fire drifting over the lake inspired one of the most famous metal songs ever, "Smoke on the Water." The riff is basic and very easy to play and the whole thing goes on way too long, but to this day "Smoke" remains the most played air guitar track in the history of rock. Not the whole song, just the opening bit, the good bit.

Blackmore and Gillan never really hit it off, though, and after this run of classic albums Gillan left the group to form his own band, which he called Gillan. The Purps replaced him with David Coverdale, who was soon to leave to form Whitesnake, but Blackmore remained unsatisfied and so left himself to form Rainbow with Ronnie James Dio, who then fell out with Blackmore and left to join Black Sabbath for a while and then form his own band, which he called Dio. Blackmore called in Graham Bonnet, but he didn't last long and was replaced by Joe Lynn Turner, who, although getting on better with Blackmore than his predecessors, was less of a hit with the record-buying public. Their sales tumbled. In the meantime, Gillan had disbanded his own band, thinking Blackmore was about to recall the Purps, but he wasn't, so Gillan joined Black Sabbath for a while instead. Only then did Blackmore phone him up, and, at last, in 1984, the Purps were back.

Then they did this merry-go-round all over again. And then a few more times after that.

Ritchie Blackmore is currently performing a mixture of folk and medieval music, playing the mandolin dressed up as a druid with a pointy black hat and a moustache with his wife in an outfit called Blackmore's Night.

They're doing quite well.

The Purps are touring the world without him.

Here are some notes on a few more big '70s bands that crossed my path.

Uriah Heep—The *Heep*. Led by the interminable Mick Box. Got through scores of drummers. Debut album was called *Very 'eavy, Very 'umble.* All nearly died of an electric shock onstage in Dallas in '76. First metal band to play in Moscow. Still going. Which album should you buy? *Still 'eavy, Still Proud: Two Decades of Uriah Heep.*

Thin Lizzy—Invented the classic "twin lead guitar" sound that I mistakenly considered Iron Maiden better at.

Budgie—This posse of Welsh stalwarts emerged from humble boogie-woogie roots. Their album covers featured images of budgerigars dressed up in different outfits. Most notably a budgie dressed up in full Nazi Gestapo gear, and another with a squadron of fighter budgies dive-bombing enemy emplacements. Which album? *Squawk.*

Nazareth—Scottish. Rumbling. Big in Canada. Which album? *Rampant.*

The Groundhogs—a trio. Invented grunge. Greasy and moustachioed. Intermittently brilliant. Album? *Split.*

Mountain—Leslie West their leader was incredibly fat. Their song "Nantucket Sleighride" became the theme music for television's *World in Action.* That's all I know.

Dumpys Rusty Nuts—didn't start until the '80s.

Jethro Tull—no.

The Five Horsemen of Armageddon

Armageddon's Ring still needed a drummer and a vocalist who could sing and whose voice had broken, and to get rid of Luke as soon as possible. My father's response upon hearing our cassette had been to walk out of the room at the first drill of Luke's solo broadside.

"I spoke to Luke actually," said Paul, soon after that first rehearsal. "Just yesterday in fact."

"I don't suppose he's decided to leave the band?"

"No, he was saying how excited he feels about our progress to date. He said he's going to go and buy a Marshall amplifier next weekend so we can hear him a bit better."

"Oh, I see."

I practiced manically. I pledged to myself that I would play guitar for at least two hours every day, and stuck to this schedule religiously. The songs I was writing now were twice as complicated as before: they had quiet intros, sultry middle-eights, spastic codas, indeed anything and everything I could squeeze in. I even began to conceive an Armageddon's Ring concept album based around a massive nuclear war, but I couldn't think of any concepts to go with it except explosions. I played in my small bedroom, trying to headbang but unable to because it made me dizzy, while my family banged on the wall.

Then, one afternoon, my eye was caught by some brightly colored, "electrocuted" capital letters on the front of a magazine in WH Smith: *Kerrang!* It looked amazing, revolutionary, so I peered a little closer. The front page was claiming a world exclusive: my hero from Kiss, Ace Frehley, pictured for the first time ever *without his makeup on*. The picture was crap though: Ace was wearing huge sunglasses and covering the bottom of his face with his hand; you couldn't see anything except a few pockmarks. But I was still sufficiently excited to snatch up the magazine and buy it immediately. Sitting on my bed back home, I devoured every revelatory word. Here was *my world* on the page. I'd had no idea such a source existed. I read every article seven or eight times, picking up vital metal information: links of different band personnel; all the different scenes; the coarse, sexist metal vernacular; and, best of all, reviews of all the new metal albums being released that fortnight. At £1.10 I considered this to be extraordinary value, especially since you also got a double-sided poster in the center pages. *Kerrang!* empowered me instantly; it became my gospel, an instruction manual. I was no longer alone. It remained by my side for the next ten years. I worshiped it.

Paul phoned again.

"I've got some even better news than before."

"Even better?"

"I think I've found a singer with a microphone."

"Shit!"

"I know. And a drummer."

"Shit! With real drums?"

"A real drum kit plus cymbals and sticks."

"Shit!"

Another weekend session down in the Bavister conservatory beckoned, this time as a five piece. Cool as ice.

Chapter Five

*E*ver since Grandpa had died when I was six, Granny had lived alone in the ground floor of a 1930s whitewashed house in Bexhill-on-Sea, a fusty resort in East Sussex where people go to retire then die. We made this horizontal trip of a hundred miles once a year, and it was usually full of incident because the dog was always carsick and my father insisted we stop at public houses along the way to "let Toby stretch his legs." My father would then tend a jug while we emptied the newspapers caked in dog vomit, and poor dazed Toby relieved himself against a wooden table in the disapproving beer garden.

In Bexhill, when we weren't shivering on blankets on the pebbled beach, my sister and I cannoned destructively around the flat while Granny cooked dinner. Once, as I was passing the grandfather clock in the hall at velocity, I looked up to find my mother and father blocking the way.

"What?" I complained.

"AC/DC are playing at the Donington Festival of Rock in a few weeks' time," said my father.

"Sorry?"

"Yes, they are," said my mother, touching my shoulder. I was fourteen so this was just about OK. "You probably want to go."

"Yes, I do!" I said. I'd never even heard of it. How exciting! Even though I was into other bands now, the idea of actually see-ing AC/DC in the flesh was the most exciting thing I'd ever heard! Angus! Brian! Phil Rudd on the drums.

"I'm sorry but you can't," said my father.

"You're too young," said my mother.

"Maybe next time," said my father.

"I see," I said.

"It's for the best."

"But . . ." The bastards! So why did they even bring it up?

I festered over this for months, and did some research into exactly what the hell they'd been talking about.

Donington, Monsters of Rock

My friend Owen and I often have this kind of conversation:

"1984—third on the bill?"

"Ozzy."

"Much too low."

"No, it was just a good year."

"Who headlined '85?"

"ZZ Top. A travesty."

"A shocking choice. Why did they do that?"

"Don't forget Marillion, on right before them."

"You could've gone home after Bon Jovi!"

"Before!"

"1989?"

"Yeah nice try. There wasn't one that year."

"Gary Moore."

"Gary Moore?"

"Gary Moore, '84."

"Runners-up in '84 then?"

"Van Halen."

"What about the tragic year? The Guns N' Roses year?"

"Easy, '88."

Had enough? Too bad.

"Whitesnake?"

"They played more than once."

"Name one."

"'83?"

"Lucky."

"Like fuck lucky—I knew that."

"Ratt?"

"Fuck off with your Ratt."

"Answer the question. Ratt."

"'87."

"'85 again."

"I don't give a shit."

"Yeah right you don't."

"Anvil?"

"They never did."

"Wrong. Answer the question: Anvil?"

"'80?"

"Actually '82."

Pretty impressive, huh?

Donington Park is a racetrack in north Leicestershire used mostly for motorbikes, and the setting for Europe's biggest outdoor rock concerts for well over ten years. The first one was in 1980 and the last in 1996. It had limped along for a few years after metal had officially been pronounced dead, and then finally went down without dignity after the 1997 festival was cancelled because no bands were deemed "good enough" to play. All the flesh had finally been picked off our previously noble beast. When the surviving

metallic stragglers (previously hordes) read about the '97 cancella-
tion, they slowly folded their *Kerrang!s*, lowered their heads and
closed heavy eyes. Donington was dead, which meant they were
might as well be dead, too.

When it started in 1980, Donington was considered an unnecessary addition to the festival landscape, as the old version of the
Reading Festival was still going strong. This annual Berkshire
knees-up had begun in the 1960s as a predominantly jazz and
blues event, but as the years caught up with the pedal steel, tam-
bourines, and hairlines, so rock barged its way onto the invariably
rain-lashed stage. So much so that by its heyday in the '70s, the
Reading Festival was rock's defining calendar event, pulling in up
to 50,000 bikers and freaks. It never quite rid itself of its traditional roots, though. There was a whiff of hearty pullovers, thick
glasses, and cat-gut acoustic guitar strings, which added a folky
tang to the center partings and Black Sabbath patches. Roy
Harper was there every year, and everybody had a moustache. The
Quo would inevitably finish up the weekend's proceedings, boo-
gieing down into the Thames night, toasted by a thousand raised
plastic pints of Ruddles.

"See you next year then, Rory."

"Aye, see you next year, Geoff. Mind how you go."

Punk broke up this hops party soon enough, but it was the
wrong kind of music to be playing to the sprawling fields. Punk
was never going to work in such a wide-open space. It belonged
inside pogoing, sweat-streamed walls, not on giant stages with
cows in the adjoining field. So the slack was taken up by the
emerging British metal bands: your UFOs, Uriah Heeps, Saxons,
and perhaps a spot of the Purpses too. However, punk had
dragged behind it a new breed of band—the postpunk and the
new wave—and these bands had begun to infiltrate the Reading
stage in a way that punk hadn't been able to. This came to a head
in the early '80s, when the indie/alternative faction and the met-

allers began to feel distinctly uncomfortable with this forced annual proximity. There were suddenly clear divisions. Projectiles with agendas were spinning out in urine-yellow trails from the throng.

Metal chose tactical retreat. It withdrew to Donington Park, which became an instant metal refuge. To this day, it remains the only annual festival in the world to have represented just the one style of music. No deviation, variation, or contamination; you came to get metal and you got it in spades. They called it the *Monsters of Rock* festival, quite correctly. The first one went like this:

August 1980. A killer lineup is waiting to perform and it's pissing down with rain. Things kick off at around lunchtime with Touch, an American bunch of pansies actually, hardly the kind of band to be inaugurating the gleaming Donington boards. This inauspicious appearance was capped in style by Touch vocalist Doug Howard, who accidentally swallowed a bee onstage while drinking a glass of water. They split soon after.

Next up were Riot, another American band that despite never being successful, were still going strong well into the '90s. Nothing in their performance that day stands out for me to mention. (I am aware that I said it was a killer lineup. Hold on.)

Then, *Saxon.*

Saxon rocked the motherfucking stage to pieces. They virtually blew the goddamn thing off its foundations. Well, not quite, they didn't have to; that had been done the night before, when roadies set off too much pyro on one side of the stage, and literally blew up the PA system. The damage totaled £18,000 but they fixed it up for the next day just in time.

Saxon (new wave of British heavy metal) were from Yorkshire and were originally called Son of a Bitch. Their vocalist, Biff Byford, was somewhat larger than life, and an early pioneer of spandex, and of *that bulge* in particular. Their second album, *Wheels of Steel*, was riding high in the charts, which brought the lads to the stage full of cocky rock star abandon. Some said their relatively lowly place on the bill that day was an insult to their chart success. Some disagreed. Thankfully everyone agreed that Saxon were on storming form that afternoon. And they were back again two years later, this time third on the bill behind headliners Status Quo and Gillan, to fulfill their Donington potential once and for all. I had a brief fling with Saxon myself, around the time of their *The Power and the Glory* album, but never got beyond that average piece of work because, to me, Biff's voice sounded fatty, like fries, and most of their songs were too predictable anyway.

After Saxon's blistering performance, the day's bar had been raised. Next up were April Wine, an unremarkable Canadian group that had been going all through the '70s. The crowd applauded tracks from their recent platter, *Harder . . . Faster!*

So far, so Saxon then, really. But hang on, what's that noise? It sounds pretty good, it sounds ruthless, it sounds well-organized. Could it be the mighty Scorps?

Yes, it was.

The Scorpions, one of heavy metal's Great Perennial Bands, were formed in Hanover in 1965. Child prodigies Klaus Meine, Rudolph Schenker, and his young axe hero brother Michael, gathered some years later, in 1971, to record their debut album, *Lonesome Crow*, which sounded like some sort of echo-prog Jimi Hendrix with hysterical operatic vocals over the top. It went on for hours. I took mine back to the shop, despite its cool-as-fuck clear vinyl.

These early feminine swirls in the ether were soon anchored to a more turgid beat when Michael left the group (for the first time). With *Virgin Killer* and *Taken by Force* it was clear that the Scorps were slowly getting the hang of what metal albums were supposed to be called. Soon though, after a cracking double live album recorded in Japan called *Tokyo Tapes*, Michael's replacement, the comedy hippy-looking Uli-Jon Roth, left the Scorps to be replaced by Michael again, whose legendary ego was suspected to already be causing havoc with every decision he made. (This rather exhausting state of affairs would continue for the rest of his career. Even his eponymous band, the Michael Schenker Group, weren't exempt from his whims.) Michael left again soon after to be replaced by Matthias Jabs, another German spandex god, who, despite a brief reappearance from Michael a year later, has remained with the boys ever since.

With Jabs on board they became one of the biggest and best metal bands in the world. *Lovedrive, Animal Magnetism, Blackout, Love at First Sting*; each sold more than the last, and they cruised to their peak after their second double-live set, the clear-as-day *World Wide Live* in 1985. Was this their eternal sunset? Was this the crest of the Scorpions' wave? No it wasn't, though it ought to have been.

1989: ecstasy; raving; the Stone Roses; Gorbachev; the fall of the Berlin Wall . . . and Klaus Meine, rapidly balding, jet-throated Scorps vocalist, singing (and whistling) "Wind of Change," a moving paean to the forces of progress. It was a worldwide sensation, going to number one in eleven countries (U.K. excepted). In the *perestroika* spirit of the time, they also recorded a version of the song in Russian, and it hit the top spot there too. All over the world, billions of people watched the symbolic collapse of the Eastern Bloc, soundtracked by the Scorpions. They played vast stadium concerts in celebration. Even if you didn't smoke you'd bring a lighter along to the show, just to hold it in the air and sway and burn your thumb along with "Wind of Change." The German government gave them a medal.

Back at Donington in 1980, the Scorpions arrived onstage having just released their excellent *Lovedrive* album. They're the band of the day so far—they kick some serious axe ass, and the first ever Donington crowd loved them and their twin Flying V attack and Klaus's impassioned shrieking. An hour later, and the Scorps have triumphed again.

I used to *love* the Scorpions. Klaus Meine's strange German accent sent exotic shivers down my spine and I bought all their records and loved every one. Their metal was the sound of *fitness*: hard, lean, not too long, simple rock melodies, raunchy sex lyrics, and striped spandex hugging every sweaty and brilliantly choreographed stage pose. True professionals the lot, except wimpy bassist Francis Bucholz, who I didn't like because he looked like one of my teachers at school.

Next up were the penultimate band of the day, the mighty Judas Priest. Here were the boys fresh from their classic *British Steel* album, and firing on every last Black Country cylinder. Rob Halford made his trademark entrance with sunglasses, leather cap, and riding a great big Harley Davidson motorbike. The rest of the band, studded up to their necks in leather, delivered the goods behind him as day gradually turned to night.

It had been a hell of a bill, but there was still more to come. The evening drew to a close with a triumphant set from headliners Rainbow, featuring Ritchie Blackmore again, and then, after a brief, rain-sodden firework display, the first *Monsters of Rock* was over.

Of the fifteen times the festival has taken place, Metallica have appeared the most. They played it four times, eventually topping the bill in 1995. Iron Maiden can also claim a rarefied position in that whenever they've been there they've headlined. They were also the loudest—in 1988—which was probably the mutha of all Doningtons. This was the year with the biggest ever crowd (over 100,000), and the one with the most rain—a Donington certainty. It was also notable for something else.

In 1988 two young men were crushed to death after a crowd surge during the Guns N' Roses performance. Had the band been further up the bill, this might not have happened (they were second bottom on the bill that year—they'd grown a lot since being booked). Should the authorities have made provision for the group's newfound popularity and predicted the crowd's response? Or should we just be thankful that it was only two young lives wasted, as opposed to the nine killed in the Roskilde Festival in Denmark in 1997 while Pearl Jam were playing? These two young men went for a brilliant day out in the rain and mud to watch their favorite bands, and never came back.

The metal world was horrified by the deaths; it was the worst thing ever to happen to the festival, or to metal in this country as a whole.

The festival was cancelled the following year. It was back in 1990, allegedly much safer. There were other attempts, if not to shut down the thing altogether, then certainly to curb the "unwarranted" tendencies of, shall we call them, the sociological cutting edge of metal's more extreme protagonists.

Toby listens to some Iron Maiden without any problems.

Do you remember Twisted Sister? I certainly do. They were on *Top of the Pops* in 1984, performing their bubblegum existential metal classic, "I Am (I'm Me)," and we watched it as a family. At that time, yeah, I was into metal, but this lot? Dee Snider, vocalist, was a blond-corkscrewed painted *demon*. We all blanched—except for Toby the dog. He'd been lying asleep in front of the fire, then Twisted Sister came on and he was rolling around on his back, grizzling and waving his paws around in the air! As soon as the song finished, he lay back down again. We all raised our eyebrows. Blimey, Toby really likes Twisted Sister!

Then some Twisted Sister

They were on again later in the week and Toby did it again. We asked dog-owning friends whether theirs had behaved in the same way but they hadn't. What a crazy dog. My mother wanted to write Twisted Sister a letter about it.

With this tale in mind and a note on how dangerous Twisted

Sister looked at the time—all ripped red rags, black face paint down their cheeks, and reflector shades—we arrive at Dee Snider's famous police warning before Donington '83. What follows is a made-up conversation, but it's based on what actually happened and what was actually said, so it's true, but also false.

"Excuse me, Mr. Snider, sir?" Detective Inspector Radish approaches Dee with his hands politely held behind his back.

"That's me," replies Dee. He's applying the finishing touches to his makeup before the Sister hit the stage.

"I'm afraid I have something rather important to tell you, sir. We've just received a ruling at the station, and I think it's probably in everybody's interest if I inform you of exactly what it entails."

"Well go on then, shoot!" Dee is American. "But you'd better hurry—we're due up on that there stage in two fuckin' minutes!"

"Well that's actually it, sir."

"The hell you say, dude!"

"I'm afraid the Leicestershire County Authority has delivered a ruling just this afternoon, stating that you, Mister Dee Snider of Twisted Sister, are only permitted to use the word—and I say this to you strictly within inverted commas, sir—'*fuck*,' sixteen times during your performance this afternoon. I really am most terribly sorry for this inconvenience."

"You fuckin' what?"

"I'm afraid it's true, sir. Say the word '*fuck*' onstage more than sixteen times and I'll have to personally escort sir to the village police station and lock you up to await the arrival of your costly American lawyers. I'm really dreadfully sorry about all this. We're big fans of yours down at the station, sir, but our hands are tied, so to speak."

"Mr. Snider?" a roadie interrupts. "It's time." His head disappears back behind the curtain.

"Sixteen times, huh?" Snider narrows his eyes.

"Yes, sir, that's right. Sixteen. I've, erm," he produces a chalk-blue notebook from his raincoat pocket, "got this notebook to count them all in, sir."

Snider brushes past him toward the roaring crowd.

Afterward Snider said he'd been tricked. He claimed that the words "*motherfucking*" and "*motherfucker*" were different to "*fuck,*" and how was he supposed to know that the police counted them all the same? Twisted Sister never played Donington again. They probably wouldn't have done anyway, but still.

Another band that appeared to wilfully court the attentions of police forces worldwide, especially at their pair of Donington appearances, were the almost legendary W.A.S.P.

W.A.S.P. (We Are Sexual Perverts) were a group of cartoon shock-rockers led by Blackie Lawless, who originated from Los Angeles in the early '80s. Their first single is a piece of metal history, frozen there in the bloody aspic. "Animal (Fuck Like a Beast)" was banned almost instantly, not least by their own record company even before its release. Not only was the song lyrically suspect, but the record sleeve featured a frisky-looking dog about to rape a woman. Quite some opening gambit, said *Kerrang!*

Even without this single, we metallers were already very impressed. Their live show was infamous, too. W.A.S.P. threw raw meat into the crowd, tied a naked masked woman to a rack, and used more pyrotechnics than anyone previously had the guts to attempt. Lawless himself was decked out in his famous buzz-saw codpiece, which shot fire into the expectant audience. In darkened auditoria, all this looked great, but in the broad daylight of the Donington stage these antics fell horribly flat.

Their albums were patchy though workmanlike. They charted but were bigger in America than Europe. As the years passed, they were forced to rely more and more on their outrageous live spectacle, and W.A.S.P.'s members fell by the wayside. Lawless ended up making a dodgy concept album staffed entirely by session musicians. W.A.S.P. are still going. They recently released an album called *Kill! Fuck! Die!* Lawless is still going strong with the first two on that list, but his group seems unwilling or unable to fulfill the destiny of the third.

Helicopters have been a recurring Donington motif. During Cozy Powell's drum solo in Whitesnake's 1983 headlining performance, two choppers hovered over the crowd with arc lights hanging down from their fuselages, illuminating his thumping antics. And in 1986, ZZ Top buzzed for what felt like hours over the audience in a helicopter, in what was meant to be a kind of "introduction," right before they took to the stage, to play "Gimme All Your Lovin" and probably "Legs."

Many bands have arrived backstage at the festival in a chopper—it appeals to their sense of macho self-importance—but only the Snake and the Top have had the guts to use them as part of their actual performance.

At Donington, there has always been a proportion of the crowd unhappy with what they're getting from up there on stage. They've been rained on all day, they're caked in mud, they've been slurping at plastic beakers of semicarbonated lager since lunchtime with only limited lavatorial facilities, and they've had to wait in line for half an hour to buy a commemorative T-shirt, which has cost them a month's pay. Not only that but they also lost their best mate fifty yards into the enclosure, mobile phones aren't due to be invented for another ten years, and you're only as high as most of everyone else's shoulders.

You're pissed off, and you're cold and alone. At least you've got all these great bands to alleviate your circumstantial woes, right? *Right?*

In pop, you scream. In punk, you spit. In indie, you stare at your shoes. In goth, you build human pyramids. In dance music, you dance. In hip-hop, you shoot people. In metal, you piss into a plastic bottle and throw it in the vague direction of the stage. The only problem with this is that the target of your projectile is usu-ally at least a hundred yards away. You don't hit the band with your dirty bottle, you don't even hit the security guys in their target-like yellow T-shirts; you hit somebody like *you*.

Here's who I would've thrown my two-liter bottle of piss at, and the year in which I would've done it.

1980: April Wine

1981: Slade

1982: Status Quo

1983: Meat Loaf

1984: Gary Moore

1985: Marillion

1986: Bad News (I wouldn't have been alone. Trust me, it was like Dresden.)

1987: Bon Jovi

1988: Helloween

1989: *pause to rehydrate*

1990: Thunder

1991: Mötley Crüe (always been shit I'm afraid, despite cool antics.)

1992: Thunder again

1993: *more rehydration*

1994: Extreme

1995: Warrior Soul

1996: I haven't even heard of the bottom four bands on the bill this year. By '96, my urine was reserved for the likes of Stone Temple Pilots and Smashing Pumpkins. Kiss headlined this year, back in their makeup with the original line-up. Like the Beatles re-forming, but thirty fucking times better.

1997: *silence*

No Sleep 'til Hammersmith

To my eternal shame, I never actually made it to the *Monsters of Rock*. This was for a number of reasons: lack of money; Donington Park's vast distance from Winchester (I kidded myself); no one else to go with. But I think the real reason was that I was always too scared; the spectacle was just a little bit much for me. Despite this gaping hole in my metal credentials, my first-ever gig earns me back a little respect. It was Ozzy Osbourne, at the Hammersmith Odeon in 1986, on *The Ultimate Sin* tour.

In actual fact I wasn't there to see Ozzy, even though I'd liked him since Marc had introduced me to *Bark at the Moon* (Ozzy dresses up as a werewolf in the video) and *Talk of the Devil* (Ozzy has strawberry jam in his mouth, meant to be blood, on the cover). I was there to see my new heroes, the mighty Ratt, who were Ozzy's support band that night.

Ratt were part of a new crop of Los Angeles bands that were brightening the scene. They were young and hungry and dressed in women's clothes. They wore chic makeup, played their instruments brilliantly, had poptastic choruses and were challenging the established old guard while appearing on the all-new MTV. They were new and trendy, a little like me I liked to think, and I was there to check out Ratt's debut U.K. performance with my friends Mark (with a wholesome K this time) and skeptical Dominic, who was just there for Ozzy and thought Ratt were a bunch of wimps.

My father was heroic that day—he drove us all the way to London right from the Southampton school gates. The three of us sat in the back and disguised our school uniforms as best we could; we removed our ties and untucked our shirts and ruffled our hair like crazy, but the bloody great crests on the blazers pockets gave us away. My father duly dropped us off on the orange-lit

Hammersmith pavement where we watched the car disappear from sight, each lit a cigarette, and with me almost overcome with excitement, swaggered up the steps and into the venue.

Our tickets were right at the back of the balcony, just two rows away from the back wall; an atom bomb could've gone off onstage and we'd have been able to chat without raising our voices—it was the very worst place to be sitting. The venue was gigantic but dark, murky, and rather solemn and, strangely, nine-tenths empty, even though Ratt were almost due onstage. People were standing about chatting casually and drinking beer out of plastic glasses.

"How come they're all talking?" I asked my friends earnestly. "Ratt are on any minute." They both just looked at me and then started talking themselves. I was hopping between both feet; the muzak (Lita Ford) was dying down, the lights were dimming. Where were all the Ratt fans?

Then it was like Obi-Wan Kenobi had whispered in my ear. I bolted and ran, hot, stale air rushing through my messed-up hair, right down to the front row of the balcony and sat politely in one of the empty chairs, just in time for the white sheet with Ratt written on it to drop dramatically and reveal the band. I folded my blazer and tucked it under my seat and ecstatically punched the air until Mark and Dominic scuttled down to join me and did the same.

We went sitting-down bonkers. We waved, thrust clenched knuckles, sang, yelled, headbanged, cheered, pointed, and clapped more than anybody else. And Ratt noticed! To be honest, we were the only ones doing anything. After each song they would acknowledge us with what was really a *Yeah, thanks kids, now button it before you spoil what's left of our London credibility*, but which we took as *You guys are the best fans we've ever, ever seen*. They must've only been able to see our bobbing heads and octopus arms above the parapet.

Warren de Martini, the better-looking guitarist (I was given the responsibility of naming two of our family cat's kittens—I named one Warren, after him, and the other Joe, after Aerosmith's Joe Perry), stuck his lit cigarette between the strings on his guitar's headstock as he played. I'd never seen anything as cool as that; he didn't attempt to actually smoke all night, just kept lighting new ones and fastening them in. I did it myself the next day in my bedroom with the window open—cool as ice.

Ratt played their one hit, their instrumental solos, and bade us goodnight. We got 'em back for an encore and afterward they linked arms and bowed at us. We almost stood up, but weren't quite sure how—we'd been weakened at the knees. Instead we smoked furiously, toasted our amazing new seats, and pooled together for merchandise but came up short. During the interval, stewards with torches gruffly led us back to our real seats at the back. The place filled up, and we were suddenly too short to see anything other than the patches on the denim jackets in front of us. Ozzy had a cape, dry ice, fireworks, twice as much stage space including steps up to the drums, and threw buckets of water over the front rows while swearing uncontrollably. The Odeon became like a church—and I was the timid agnostic right at the back.

My father had spent his evening in a Hammersmith public house. As we sliced back through the yellow-lit night in his red Saab, his sarcastic over-the-shoulder questions went unanswered as the three of us poked our ears and swallowed as much as we could, aural virginity lost, thoroughly deafened. At school the next day, my ears were so traumatized that I heard sudden snatches of the previous night's repertoire throughout the day; these ghostly sonic hallucinations lasted for several excellent days until the terrifying realization that Ozzy had, in actual fact, completely fucked up my hearing for good.

"Oh don't be such a fucking prick," said Dominic.

Chapter Six

youth gone wild

Iwhined to Paul so much about Luke being in Armageddon's Ring that he eventually fired him. By all accounts Luke was outraged, but I couldn't have cared less. We were now a four-piece, albeit with a singer and a drummer that I still hadn't met. I was convinced that the band was now so big and important that I'd need a new guitar to be able to do myself justice. Thus I informed my father when my fifteenth birthday came around that it was time for me to move on up to the next level. I needed a futuristic axe that was maybe red and had a pointy headstock. This present could be for my birthday and Christmas combined, I suggested.

"And for the next five years after that," said my father.

"That's completely fine," I replied.

"And your sister's birthday too," he said.

"She won't mind," I replied. "I'm sure this means a lot to her." She was at Girl Guides, thank God.

We drove up to Kingfisher Music in Fleet, over an hour's drive. My father had insisted it was the only place we could possibly go. I'd suggested the small music shop on Winchester High Street, but he'd cackled at the suggestion like Alan Rickman.

In Fleet we left the car in a pub car park, which my father took as an invitation to down a professional couple. We were never allowed cola or potato chips at home, so these pit stops were actually a treat for us kids; it was a cunning way of getting us to ask to go to the pub. Between sips, he bombarded me with guitar facts and things to look out for in the shop.

"Don't just pick the one that looks like the one that chappie from the Rats plays."

"Of course not." Shit.

"And don't forget, we're on a strict budget."

A what?

"And what about my poor old electric?" he said. "What's wrong with that all of a sudden?" We'd been through this already. "What's going to happen to it now? Can I have it back?" he asked.

"No! I mean, no please. I mean, I'll play them both." I could chop and change between them during a gig. How cool was that?

He stroked his chin. "Mmm, yes. I suppose you could use the spare one for slide. Good idea."

For *what*?

One thing he didn't tell me was that music shops are the single most intimidating places on earth, especially for a teenage novice like me. The first thing that hits you when you enter music shops the world over is the sound of four or five people playing extremely dextrous guitar solos at high volume with screaming feedback, all at the same time. You look at these people and do a double take. That nine-year-old girl over there . . . she's playing Eddie Van Halen's "Eruption"! That blind old man in the wheel-chair is playing "Purple Haze" at double speed! All the staff look like they're in Def Leppard!

"You alright there, mate?" a young man with massive hair asks me.

"Fine thanks."

"Ah, good man!" says my father. "Or should I say *woman*, eh? My son here is bloody handy on the old axe. And he *loves* the Iron Maidens! Take him away, I'll be back in a minute."

Oh God.

It was terrible. The assistant showed me a guitar and asked what I thought of it.

"It's nice."

"Fancy a spin on her?"

"Oh, no thanks."

"How about this beauty?" He lifted a shiny red guitar with a lightning bolt slashing through the middle of it, plugged it in, and started to play. He was utterly brilliant, his fingers blurred like a woodpecker's beak. He held it out to me, I rested it on my knee, and it started to feed back. I felt sick. The assistant smiled at me, urging me on with his eyes. He shook his hair. I played an E and handed it back.

"Nice," I said.

"How about this delightful specimen?" He took hold of a Gibson Les Paul, played a few acrobatic scales to check it was working, and passed it over. I played an A.

"Nice one," I said.

This lasted half an hour. My father returned smelling of fresh beer and asked how we were getting on. I'd run out of chords to use and had started to play "Armageddon's Ring" on each new guitar. Then the helpful assistant picked up a guitar and started playing it too. He watched my idiot fingers, but added in all sorts of whammy bar dives, trills, and God knows what. At one point another assistant came over, grabbed a guitar, and the two of them duetted pyrotechnic solos against my clunking chords. Why were they doing this?

"What about this baby?" said my original assistant, sweeping up a white and quite boring-looking guitar. He twiddled on it, and my father tutted like he could do better, which he absolutely couldn't.

"How much is it?" he asked.

It was quite cheap—it was the one I got. It was an Aria Wildcat.

"How about a distortion pedal to go with it?" said the assistant, tucking my new axe into its blue velvet-lined case.

"Yes please," I said.

"No," said my father.

"Yes," I said, grittily.

"I think it's for the best," said the assistant.

If you're a shit guitarist, get a distortion pedal: it'll cover up the majority of your shortcomings. If you're really really shit, just turn up the distortion: it's there marked Distortion on the dial. Distortion pedals are stabilizers for guitarists. Play the riff to "Smoke on the Water" without effects and it sounds terrible. Play it with your distortion pedal turned up to the max and you *are* Ritchie Blackmore. In fact, you're better, because you're you. These days, sadly, you can't play "Smoke on the Water" or "Stairway to Heaven" in guitar shops anymore. Music shop staff are so sick of those two riffs that you won't even make it to the second stanza before you're unplugged and thrown out onto the street. Apparently they won't let you play the intro to "Sweet Child o' Mine" anymore either.

I got a wah-wah pedal too. Not only did I now sound like any metal guitarist you'd care to name, but I also sounded exactly like Jimi Hendrix. There are lots of guitar effects you can buy to make your axe sound more interesting; it's a very lucrative business. The basic ones are these:

Flange makes your guitar sound floppy, and up-and-downy, like Hawkwind.

Delay is basically echo, but can be multiplied to a million cathedrals'-worth for that epic spacey vibe.

Compression cleans up and tightens the sound, but is only really for dullards and engineers.

Chorus makes your guitar sound like a sandwich, or Dire Straits.

Tremolo is only good for playing The Smiths's "How Soon is Now," so is banned.

Phaser sounds like hippies in a tin box.

I used to take the Wildcat everywhere. Here I am with it at a family friend's house. My father is lying on the floor.

Pitch-shift repeats the note you play but at any pitch you want, like a personal duet machine, so you can sound like Iron Maiden but just on your own, if you get the switches right.

Listen to musicians, to guitar players, and they always say they learned their craft by playing along to their favorite records. Play, copy, and rewind till you get it right, that's what everyone does—everyone except me. I only ever did this with one record, and it wasn't even a particularly good one. *Done with Mirrors* was the new album from Aerosmith, their 1985 big-money comeback where they declared in interviews that they were finally off drugs. Which was a lie, because they took more drugs making this one than any of their others. It was the *next* one when they stopped, when they switched from being junkie zeroes to MTV heroes overnight. *Done with Mirrors* was rubbish.

Why did I play this particular record all the way through, when I could've chosen something as seminal as the Scorpions' *Blackout*? It's because one day while practicing I accidentally played the riff to "My Fist Your Face," the second song on *Done with Mirrors*. I stuck the record on to check that I wasn't mistaken, and lo and behold the whole song seemed quite easy to play along to (I'm not dissing you, Joe—its simplicity is poetic, man), so I just carried on from there. Soon I got to the point where I felt able to perform the whole of *Done with Mirrors* in a single sitting without once lifting the stylus. I counted the band in, and off we went like wildfire. Between songs I thanked Long Beach Arena in a hoarse whisper and occasionally, during an easy bit, raised my arm to the sky to salute them. Finally, ravaged, I wiped the hair from my eyes and blew on my swollen fingers as the final notes of the final track trailed out of the catflap. I stood bold and mighty; I'd managed to play rhythm guitar through the whole bloody thing, with nary a brace of bum notes.

Bring on the groupies!

I climbed the steps from my new spare bedroom into the kitchen where my mother was washing up. She always heard everything I played through the glass door (I had a curtain so at least I could do the moves in private). I shimmied around the kitchen table, waiting for her reaction.

"I just wish you'd play in time," she said.

"Pardon?"

"You always play out of time. It's very frustrating to have to listen to."

"How can I play out of time when I'm playing along to a *record*? What do you think the *drums* are there for?" I drank a big glass of water.

"Well obviously it's time you began to pay them some attention."

"You don't know anything, Mummy."

"You were out of tune too."

Out I stormed.

I put the *Mummy* in there for effect. My parents banned my sister and I from calling them Mum or Dad because they thought it was common. It was Mummy and Father only. Father was shortened to Fa, which was fine, but at fifteen years old I was damned if I was going to say Mummy in front of all my mates. We both agreed that Mother wasn't an option, so we sat down and thrashed out some alternatives. My mother is short, so I came up with Titchy.

"OK," she said gamely.

But after a day or so, we realized that Titchy wasn't terribly affectionate.

"How about Small?" I said.

We rolled it around our mouths and it tasted OK, so it stuck. I have called my mother Small ever since, and so do my friends.

As I grew into my mid teens, relations with my father began to fray around the edges. I was becoming more outspoken and his alcohol consumption was steadily rising. His effortless charm was peeling away, and he was gradually being exposed to aspects of himself he didn't like to face. I don't think my clumsy adolescence was helping much; in fact I was starting to seriously piss him off. Now, surely, was the perfect time for me to dip a toe into Satanism.

I wanted something pithy and extreme. Something that would make me feel naughty, something I could really annoy Fa with. So after half an hour's browsing in Venus Records, I bought Venom's third record, their concept album about the man downstairs, *At War with Satan*. I thought about its title as I walked home, swinging the record bag. Shouldn't Venom have been on Satan's side in this war? Wouldn't they have been better off calling it *At War with God*, or *Siding with Satan*? It

All smiles at Small's birthday party

didn't bother me that much, though, as I already knew that Venom were extremely bad men.

I got home, drew the curtains, and stuck it on. It rumbled and was menacing and it didn't have any tunes. Damn right it didn't. It had an onomatopoeic song called "Aaaaarrrggghhh!" It's as ugly as a pit bull and twice as fast; it's brilliant. What does it sound like inside a tank during a nuclear firestorm? It sounds like *At War with Satan*.

It ended and I put something else on instead. Thank God that was over.

Now my father, despite the demons plaguing him around this time, was ostensibly a religious kind of guy. He was a member of the local church choir, a hugely talented but irregular member of their drama group, and when we'd moved to the smaller house and couldn't fit our two grand pianos into the front room, he'd lent the larger one, reluctantly, to the church. So the Church was all around us (I had been a choirboy myself a few years before), and though his lifestyle didn't exactly dovetail with its thinking, Fa maintained some sort of religious bedrock for the whole of his life. Therefore when the parent-baiting metal son brings a suspicious-looking record with an upside-down cross on the front into an already tense family home, the beleaguered head of household sniffs an opportunity to carve a fatherly line in the sand. Ever one for the easy life, I left it out one night in an unnecessarily prominent position in the living room, just to wind him up. As expected there was a showdown at sunrise or thereabouts the next morning.

"I want that thing out of this house."

"What thing?"

"You know what thing. *That* thing." He pointed to it like a preacher man. It was there to be pointed at—I'd leaned it against the legs of the piano.

"Oh *that*. But why?"

"I'm sorry, but I'm not having something with an upside-down cross on it inside this house."

"But look at it! It's not like it's real, it's just a record. And anyway, it's called *At War WITH Satan*. They're on your side!"

"Don't be cheeky. I want it out of the house."

"What?"

"If it's still here in the morning, I'm going to remove it from this house and burn it."

"*What?*"

"You heard me."

I pondered.

I decided to leave it where it was but turn it upside-down so the cross was the right way up. What a wag. And lo and behold it had gone when I got up in the morning.

A Saturday afternoon in Southampton High Street. Mark and I were there with our girlfriends. Vicky was my first-ever one and I had recently got through my first kiss on St Giles' Hill. We'd been sitting among daisies and it had gone alright. Today in Southampton we were just standing around, smoking, probably spitting too—impressing the ladies—when a glamorous young woman approached us. Mark and I stubbed out our cigarettes and prepared to dump the chicks, but it turned out she was a reporter for *Just Seventeen* magazine and wanted to take our picture and interview us for a regular feature called Spy. A cameraman shot us in a series of embarrassing poses, and asked us some perfunctory teen questions. *"How old are you?" "Fifteen." "What kind of girls do you like?" "Yes." "What are your hobbies?" "I play the guitar in an American-style rock band." "What was your best ever day?" "Going to see Ratt at Hammersmith Odeon. They were brilliant." "Worst ever day?" "Well, it was either when my dad caught me smoking in my room, or when he burned one of my records because it had an upside-down cross on the front of it. Both were quite bad."* What a little drama queen I was.

We rushed into Smiths every week waiting for our interview to appear, and a few weeks later there we were. I bought five copies and

Seb Hunter is fifteen. Likes girls in mini-skirts and playing the guitar.

hurried home with them. The photos were fine, stupid but fine, and our replies were all correctly transcribed, except for the last one. They'd mistakenly printed the answer to the worst day question as: "*The day my dad caught me smoking in my bedroom and burned my entire record collection to teach me a lesson.*"

Oh shit!

My father was still in bed. My mother, sister and I sat in the kitchen and discussed the best way of getting around this with the minimum possible fuss. Hide it from him altogether? Too risky in case he heard from alternative sources. After all, here were my fifteen minutes of fame, said my mother. Thanks. Somebody (not me) came up with the idea of telling him the truth. This sounded unusual, but they persuaded me, so I climbed reluctantly up the stairs to his bedroom with the magazine under my arm and a cup of tea as a peace offering. Fa was instantly suspicious, not least by the sight of the whole family stood around the bed making a fuss of him. He sat up and I slowly talked him through what had happened. He furrowed his brow and read the article.

"Bloody right," he said at the end.

"Sorry?"

"Marvelous stuff," he said, sipping the tea.

"You're not angry?"

"Well I think this makes me look much . . ., better, don't you?"

"Really?"

"Can I keep this? I can't wait to show all the lads up at the pub."

He chortled to himself while the three of us exchanged puzzled glances.

That taught the little fucker, I imagined him saying to everyone in the pub, which, of course, was exactly what he did.

Despite *At War with Satan*, thrash metal was never really my scene, though I did skim the surface in a dandyish fashion. I knew all about it from reading *Kerrang!*, and felt I could easily hold my own in a heated discussion among die-hard thrashers, even though I'd only listened to about three or four thrash songs ever. But I knew thrash metal was important, it was suddenly all around us—it had become metal's own punk revolution (all it lacked was the credibility). Metal suddenly stopped being Saxon singing cheerful songs about beer and knockers and turned into Obituary coughing dirges on bestial rape, necrophilia, virgin sacrifice, and injecting gasoline. And that's just the first verse.

This chapter in the heavy metal encyclopaedia is where they all went off the rails a bit, especially in Norway. It's where metal got dangerous again.

Thrash/Death/Speed/Black Metal

Thrash metal: Melodically bereft, very fast, incoherent shouted vocals.
Death metal: As above, though usually faster, but with some of the songs slowed down to snail's pace; vocals usually grunted instead of shouted; songs often thematically concerned with death and/or cannibalism and/or necrophilia.
Speed metal: Fast thrash metal, which is already fast, so this is *really* fast.
Black metal: Thrash metal played by Satanists.
False metal: Europe, Bon Jovi etc.

Who started all this?
It was Venom, of course. The godfathers of black metal.
Venom were three blokes from Newcastle-upon-Tyne: Conrad,

Jeff, and Tony. They owned musical instruments and enjoyed making a right old racket, despite an individual lack of musical proficiency. To differentiate themselves from the rest of the metal hordes they needed a concept all of their own, so they came up with the idea of black metal. In order to invent black metal, the boys needed new names. Out went Conrad, Jeff, and Tony, and in came Cronos, Mantas, and Abaddon. That's better. Then they plugged in their instruments, struck demonic, over-the-top poses, and turned everything up really loud until it became a big stinking mush.

What emerged didn't sound like the metal that had gone before. It didn't sound like punk—it didn't sound like anything. It was ferocious, foul, and feral and it bit holes out of your ears. It was a whole new sound—super-fast, super-heavy, super-Satanic. Their first record fairly leaped out of the speakers; it was the cordial *Welcome to Hell*. It didn't matter that they couldn't really play their instruments; that just got them into the occasional scrape during live performances. They spent whole gigs trying to keep up with one another. Abaddon (drums) in particular is clearly guessing all the way through their live album *Eine Kleine Nachtmusik*—he just isn't up to the task. None of them were, but that just added to their Satanic Geordie charm.

Controversy trailed behind Venom wherever they went, but soon their musical ineptitude saw them drop away behind the chasing pack. Enthusiasm alone had not proved enough for this six-legged wildebeast to remain valid in an increasingly competitive enclosure. They released a slapdash fourth album called *Possessed*, which was brutally panned in *Kerrang!* After that they were treading water all the way; the myth was blown. They were also outed as not really being Satanists—the ultimate humiliation for a black metal group, especially as it had been their invention in the first place. They retired to the metal dressing room to lick their wounds and prepare for the box set.

Actually they didn't. In the true metal way of handling one's career with as little dignity as possible, Mantas became dissatisfied and left to form his own group, which he called Mantas. Then Cronos became unhappy too and left to start his own band, Cronos. And poor old Abaddon, stuck on his own for a few minutes with his sunglasses on, pleaded with and succeeded in getting Mantas back just in time to recruit a new singer called the Demolition Man, who left soon after to be replaced by—deep breath—a *keyboard player*. Before, of course, Cronos came back and they all lived happily ever after, and are probably recording new material as I write.

Next came the Big Four, the guys who con-verted this cheap rage into multimillion dollar sales all the way from Waco to Kiev: Metallica, Slayer, Anthrax, and Megadeth. The difference between this lot and Venom could be measured in fathoms, and for one specific reason: these boys could really play their instruments. They took Venom's chaotic momentum and applied skilled musicianship, creating a frightening hybrid of flat-out aggression coupled with fluid and expressive dynamics. The results were fresh, propulsive, and exhilarating. Thrash metal was born.

Cronos and Abaddon; angry at Mantas's departure

Out of San Francisco's Bay Area via Los Angeles in 1982 came a group named Metallica. What a silly name, we all thought. They won't last long. There were four of them, beer foaming out of their mouths: snotty, spotty, a quartet of audio thugs. Their debut album, *Kill 'em All*, came on like a toolbox thrown off the Golden Gate Bridge. They'd originally wanted to call it the much more apt *Metal Up Your Ass*, but their record company wouldn't let them. They toured in Europe supporting Venom, matured, and were then accused of selling out because they'd spent a bit of money making their second album.

Their third release put all that behind them. It's as stone cold classic a record as you'll ever own: the *huge*, if–you–only–ever–buy–one–thrash–album–ever–then–buy–this–one, *Master of Puppets*. I promise you, if you put this on and turn up the volume, you can feel the force of it actually whistling by your ears. It's that thrash rarity—an album you don't want to turn off before the end of the first song. But then the band was struck by tragedy. In September 1986 their bass player died when their tour bus ran off the road in the middle of the night on the way to Copenhagen. They recovered quickly—they were a big band now—he was replaced and they grew even bigger, until in 1991 they did something nobody thought Metallica would ever do. They not only recorded a ballad but then released it as a single, produced by Bob Rock no less, *Bon Jovi's producer*. It wasn't long before they cut off their hair, recorded a live album with an orchestra, dressed in suits and stopped playing funny-looking guitars. They tried to sue their fans for downloading their music from Napster too, paving the way for its eventual collapse. I would certainly call that a demise.

Slayer couldn't do a ballad if you sprinkled their breakfast cereal with ecstasy and sleeping pills and locked them in a room with just harps. Slayer are the real deal. Not only are they sounding more brutal than ever these days, but they actually look ten times scarier than they used to. I'll illustrate this thus:

Left: Slayer's Kerry King in 1985 Right: Kerry King today. You can't see them in this picture, but he has a particularly tattooed head. You know the computer software catchphrase "Intel Inside"? Kerry likes to wear a shirt with this logo but with the words "Satan Inside" instead.

Slayer are a band I wholeheartedly respect. I don't respect
Metallica particularly, nor Anthrax or Megadeth really, but for some
reason I can't help affording Slayer the same kind of vibes I reserve
for the likes of, say, Keith Richards or Julian Cope. Slayer have never
deviated from their slovenly path and I reckon it's due 'em.

Show No Mercy, their first album, was fast and nasty and scored
them a thick notch on Satan's bedpost. Their second was a profound artistic leap: *Hell Awaits* upped the darkness ante and didn't
sound like it was recorded in a bucket. It starts off with a "microphone" in hell—you can hear all sorts of horrible goings-on
down there and even the voice of Satan himself. Then it's like the
pinging of an elastic band: the floor opens up beneath you and
you want to turn it off—the band have started playing.

Hell Awaits features "Necrophiliac," with lyrics about copulat-
ing with corpses which were quite a shock to everybody at the
time. This was the first Slayer album I heard, at the Bavisters' during a band weekend. I remember thinking, *What the hell is this?
This is terrifying! How do they do that? Turn it off! Keep it on! I don't
know what to do but I just wet myself!*

Kerrang! once described Dave Lombardo's drums as sounding
like he'd pushed his kit off the top of a concrete staircase and
recorded the results. A very accurate statement. The whole thing
gave me nightmares, or at least the three minutes of it that I could
bear, before I muffled my head in a nice feathery cushion.

After *Hell Awaits*, Slayer recorded the most sacred artifact in the
annals of thrash/death: *Reign in Blood*.

This record was hewn by the Beastie Boys's producer Rick
Rubin, but you wouldn't know it to hear it. A few months ago I
was listening to this and marveling at it from behind my sofa, and I
thought I'd get a bit evangelical about the whole thing and send a
copy to my nonmetal friend Andrew. This would sort him out, I
reckoned. Don't bother going to syringe your ears, mate, just listen
to this. When I asked what he thought a month or so later, he spoke

It's like a Satanic Guernica, don't you think?

of it with puzzlement; he'd tried to give it a proper listen a few times, but couldn't understand why the songs all sounded exactly the same. He was unable to tell one from another, which he had found frustrating and somewhat pointless, he told me. What a big girl's blouse.

"But it's aural bleach," I reasoned.

"Why would I want to listen to aural bleach?" he replied.

"Because it's aural *bleach*."

"But my ears are not a toilet," he said.

It lasts less than half an hour. It's immense. It's like being punched repeatedly with a psychedelic knuckleduster. It all sounds the same; I recommend it. The best bit is at the end of the last song, "Raining Blood," when, as the instruments fade blissfully away, all that's left is the sound of raining blood—literally. It's spooky as hell.

Reign in Blood was the peak of Slayer's creative hillock. After this they began to flirt with the occasional melody, but not so clear you could whistle it or anything. They're still going strong today.

★   ★   ★

When I say to you Anthrax, what comes to mind? I guess first of all you might think about chemical warfare. Then you might recall the actual symptoms of the disease itself. Then you might even think of genius hip-hop revolutionaries Public Enemy. If you're sitting there with your fist pumping the air in the classic devil-horn shape, then you know that this section is for you, brother.

Anthrax were from New York and their first album was *Fistful of Metal*. The sleeve is a cheap visual jibe at the band, which if you know anything about this lot, isn't fair at all. They were the ones who wore skate shorts when all of their peers were stuck in tight leather. They were the ones who shaved off their hair when they started to go bald, instead of wearing a baseball hat backward (though they introduced that into metal, too). They were the ones who collaborated with Public Enemy on a thrash metal version of "Bring the Noise." They were the ones to bring comic book street cred to the genre by obsessing over Judge Dredd and writing the thrash-crossover (you don't hear that much) hit (even less), "I am the Law."

Fistful of Metal

They got through band members like children through chicken nuggets.

Neil Turbin: ". . . quality metal vocalist . . ." *(Sounds)*

Joey Belladonna: ". . . a big improvement, vocals-wise . . ." *(Kerrang!)*

Dan Spitz: ". . . knows his riffs." *(Metal Hammer)*

Dan Lilker: ". . . headbangs well for a bassist . . ." *(Das Metal Hof)*

Frank Bello: ". . . a much better bass player than Lilker . . ." *(Metal Forces)*

"Dimebag" Darrell: ". . . hang on, what happened to Dan Spitz?" *(Raw)*

John Bush: ". . . makes Belladonna sound like the amateur he was." *(Kerrang!)*

Scott "Not" Ian fired them all, in cahoots with Charlie Benante, the drummer.

These trigger-happy New Yorkers were truly cutting-edge in the late '80s. They crossed genres. They mentioned groups in their interviews that we'd never heard of, like Bad Brains and the Red Hot Chili Somethings. They sang about social issues. What were they? Why didn't they sing about the devil, or drinking, or drinking with the devil?

They were the U2 of metal. Way too worthy. Fuck 'em.

Finally we come to the last of the thrash Big Four: Megadeth.

Megadeth's leader, Dave Mustaine, was kicked out of early Metallica for drinking too much, so in revenge started up his own band. Megadeth's records had serious, political titles, like *Killing Is My Business . . . and Business is Good*; *Peace Sells . . . but Who's Buying?* and *Rust in Peace*. (Believe me, in metal, those titles are as political as you'll get.)

Mustaine was a very gifted guitarist and thrash songwriter, and his personal troubles only added to his man-of-danger mystique. The man was a stone cold misanthrope, which did his career no end of good. Sadly, he was recently diagnosed with a type of repetitive strain injury in his left, fretboard-fingering hand. He's had to give it all up. Megadeth were quite good, though, for a while.

So far we've seen five bands. These five were all originals in the field, and also had careers long, varied, and groundbreaking enough to merit the time spent with them. Wherever these five were, they had subgenres hanging lovingly off them. The rest of the thrash metal scene was far from just a footnote—there was too much else going on to ignore, including, as ever, a couple of sub-subgenres.

Germany was hearty in its embrace of thrash. Destruction and Kreator were the first to call themselves speed metal, so let's be nice and hand it to them.

Brazil:

Sepultura. I told my friend Mark that I was writing about the Big Four. He said *No, surely you mean Big Five?* I asked in genuine ignorance who he thought was the fifth. He told me it was Sepultura. Respect to Sepultura then, and their debut *Bestial Devastation*.

Great Britain:

Slammer. First British thrash band on a major label. They failed.

Lawnmower Deth. Comedy thrash band. Qualcast Mutilator

(vocals), Concorde Faceripper (guitar), Schizophrenic Sprintmaster (guitar), Mightymo Destructimo (bass), and Mr. Flymo (drums).

Napalm Death. Probably the most influential group outside the Big Four. (Sorry, Five.) Napalm Death invented grindcore, which is less complicated than it sounds. They famously had a song called "You Suffer," which was less than a second long, lifted from their debut album, *Scum*. After that, they raised their own stakes with *From Enslavement to Obliteration*, which featured a whopping fifty-four tracks. Yes indeed, the Napalms made Slayer sound like Noddy's prebreakfast stretching.

Carcass. Ken, Jeff, and Bill. *Reek of Putrification*.

USA:

Exodus. *Bonded by Blood* almost took them to the top table. *Pleasures of the Flesh* included flashes of *pleasure*. They were ejected.

Death. Founder Chuck Schuldiner is generally credited for the entire death metal genre. Death's albums included *Scream Bloody Gore* and *Leprosy*.

Death Angel. A band of five cousins from San Francisco. Really brutal stuff. Ironically named their second record *A Frolic Through the Park*.

Voivod. They were considered slightly avant garde. *RRROOOAAARRR* is a good example of their style. They were also Canadian. Sorry about that.

Pantera. *Vulgar Display of Power*.

Sweaty Nipples. *Touch My Cum* and *Knuckle Farm*.

Nuclear Assault. Their song "Hang the Pope" was another short one—it lasted about thirty seconds. Good lyrics, this one—grunt along: *Let's go to the Vatican / Get him out of bed / Tie the noose around his neck and hang him 'til he's fucking DEAD / Hang the pope / Hang the pope / Hang the pope / Hang the pope* (repeat).

Morbid Angel. Their *Blessed Are The Sick* album has been described as "bowel-scraping."

Deicide. Vocalist Glen Benton used to repeatedly brand an upside-down cross onto his forehead, and claimed that upon reaching the age of thirty-three, he would commit suicide. Cur-rently in his late thirties, Benton now calls that threat "ridiculous."

Scandinavia: All the really scary ones.

Bathory (Swedish). Formed by a satanic recluse called Quorthorn. One of the first to take the whole death metal thing extremely seriously. In fact I'm going to be careful what I write here in case they sacrifice me to, for example, Odin.

Immortal. Again, are scary. Abath: Guitar and vocal chords. Horgh: Drums. Iscarah: Bass. Yep, good band, the 'Mortal.

Mayhem. Frightening. Their guitarist, Euronymous, was *murdered*, by Burzum's Varg Vikernes. Drummer was called Hellhammer. The singer, Dead, lived up to his name and shot himself.

Burzum. Hold on, we'll do all this in a minute.

Switzerland:

Celtic Frost. One of the earlier ones. Very influential. Until they went glam on their *Cold Lake* album and all their fans stormed off.

Krokus. Weren't thrash, but deserve a credit because they were so bad that even I laughed at them.

★ ★ ★

One of the reasons for thrash/death (whatever) growing at such an alarming initial rate (again similar to punk in this respect) was that it was so intrinsically democratic. You didn't even have to have long hair for this kind of stuff, though of course it helped. All you needed to be able to do was clench your lubricated pointy-headstocked guitar, strike a subjugated pose, and turn up at the venue. The beery moshing crowd didn't give a shit, so long as you played too fast for the drummer, didn't have any tunes, and were loud enough to cover up these alleged criticisms.

Now let's swivel to Norway. Let's swivel to *murder*.

I referred above to a pair of Norweigan black metal bands. More specifically, to a chap called Varg Vikernes, otherwise known as Count Grishnackh, who formed a band called Burzum with . . . nope, in fact he played all the instruments himself, that's how *focused* Grishnackh was. So here's Varg, a talented bloke, playing all his self-taught parts in the studio (Burzum never played live—Varg considered live performance "vulgar." Also let's face it—it would have been quite difficult, just him there on his own), creating a Satanic mosaic of sound. His albums were drenched in aural tar, ladled into the grooves with dark pagan mysticism; they sounded like something you didn't really want to be listening to if you were normal. On the surface, all appears to be well; the records sell and help to fuel a healthy Norwegian black metal "scene." The bands are rivals, quite naturally, but that just spurs them all on to creating better and better music, right? *Right?*

How come Varg killed Euronymous? Good question. The answer has to do with setting fire to churches.

Records claim that over a hundred churches have been burnt down by people who like black metal. It's what they like to do, along with ritual suicide and going for walks in the forest. Varg was in this same boat, his black clothes perpetually singed and smelling of petrol.

The frustrating truth about Euronymous's death is that it is in actual fact not only extremely dull, but everyone involved has their own meandering version of what really went down, and they're all so busy posturing about how damn important they were in the whole sorry saga that the truth is suffocated by references to people named Quiddloch, Luciferius, and Kaltoribus-Agondorhythmicus. It's hard to see through the consonants.

Euronymous was found dead and half naked, with multiple stab wounds, and to this day Varg claims he did it in self-defense.

Someone from the scene referring to Varg said, "Once he said himself to be an elf. But I look upon him as a cowardly squealing *orc.*"

They're letting him record albums in prison. Twenty-one years.

So, death metal. Here was a style of music which represented sheer extremity in both sonic and lyrical content, in which the musicians weren't the sharpest guys around, and couldn't be trusted to police their own trappings. Every month there was a new bunch further out than the last lot, going that extra 10 m.p.h. faster, whose warped couplets about butt-fucking Satan with a rusty meat cleaver inched closer and closer to the bone. I would sincerely advise those of a nervous disposition to avoid this next section—it's not much fun. They are trying to shock us, and they do a handsome job of it.

Cannibal Corpse come from New York City, and are banned from Australia, South Korea, and a list of cities as long as your arm. They are, arguably, the sickest and most unpleasant crew of a very bad bunch, although I don't want to delve *too* deep into this underbelly. Let's just say that among the "bigger" death metal groups, they come out on top (or on bottom) of the pile. We're going to cut straight to the chase and look at a few of their song titles. I'm not making these up.

"I Cum Blood"
"Fucked with a Knife"
"The Cryptic Stench"
"Meat Hook Sodomy"
"Entrails Ripped from a Virgin's Cunt"
"Compelled to Lacerate"
"Mutilation of the Cadaver"
"Necropaedophile"
"Edible Autopsy"
"Post Mortal Ejaculation"

"Addicted to Vaginal Skin"

"I Eat my own Feces and then Fuck it and Insert what's Left into a Mutilated Virgin who I also then Eat, for Pudding (then I Ejaculate into Lacerations)"

I made the last one up. It dissolved some of the tension, don't you think? All their song titles are like this—the ones above are just a few of the worst.

The controversy generated by all this delivered Cannibal Corpse a heavy dose of infamy, after which inevitably follow young teenage males. It's extremely likely that there is a whole swathe of adults in the world today whose first-ever concepts of sex developed around the principles of cannibalistic necrophilia. You wonder if the concept has stayed with them. They couldn't actually hear any of the words via the singer's mouth, though—in fact I challenge even their biggest fan to be able to pick out a single recognizable word from their repertoire—but they always helpfully printed the lyrics for you on the inner sleeve. Had they not done that, there would have been absolutely no point to their existence at all. But were they joking, or were they for real?

Everybody chooses their own moral lines to draw, me included. Cannibal Corpse were "entertainers," they were putting on a show, we were supposed to take their lyrics with a pinch of salt (and some steak sauce on that disemboweled virgin). *Hey guys, c'mon, lighten up! It's only a song! If you don't like it, don't buy it—no one's forcing you to!*

Taste and decency are entirely subjective—we feel within ourselves what's right or wrong. I happen to think that all of this went a bit too far. I don't understand what they were attempting to prove. The novelistic equivalent, Bret Easton Ellis's *American Psycho*—despite the similar subject matter and deployment, and the furor that greeted its publication—was, once the smoke had cleared, clearly a satire on capitalism. Cannibal Corpse wasn't a satire; it was there for visceral thrills only. If it was actually funny then maybe I could understand it; sick humor is sick by defini-tion, but remains "humor" nevertheless. But no matter how much I attempt to stretch my envelope, no matter how much I chastise myself for being prudish or uptight about this, I can't defend songs with names like "Fucked with a Knife." My line comes down before all of that. Me, Australia, and South Korea—we deal with this shit so that you don't have to.

Death metal continues—Kurt didn't manage to kill it. I'm guessing it's still getting more and more "extreme," as that's what usually happens in the world of pop music, with its never-ending momentum.

I'll finish this section with a photograph of one of death metal's current popular characters—a man so out there that the photo will be all you need to make you switch on your house lights, check under the bed, and turn up *Songs of Praise*. His name is Mortiis and he's completely fucking bonkers. He looks like this *all the time*.

Yes he's Norwegian. "I'm like, the King of Crap," he said recently, by accident.

Chapter Seven

on through the night

My father's Farfisa organ amplifier was broad, grey, rectangular, and incredibly heavy. He was extremely proud of it as it tended to amplify most of the neighborhood's needs when necessary. However, whenever anyone plugged anything into it, he would exclaim incredulously, "*That's* not an organ!"

"But we haven't got an organ."

"That's for *organs*!"

"But we . . ." etc.

It was so heavy that as we drove to the Bavisters for a long weekend with the Ring, the back of the Saab hung down over the tarmac, spoiling the car's fancy curves.

"It'll be no laughing matter if you break this." Cigarette smoke came symmetrically out of his nostrils. I could do that too, I wanted to tell him.

"How am I going to break it? It's invincible. I couldn't break that thing even if I wanted to."

"And don't blow the bloody speakers."

"How would I do that? We don't play that loudly. His parents won't let us."

"But you've got drums this time. Drums are very loud."

"They are?"

"Yes."

We tugged out the Farfisa in the Bavisters' tree-arched drive and the Saab's trunk sprang back into shape. The Bavisters came out to greet us and my father met them like David Niven. I was always very proud when he showed off like this.

"A cup of tea, Tony?" offered Mrs Bavister, and she stepped forward. My father, I have neglected to mention, was called Tony. Anthony on his Diner's Club card, Tone in the Golden Lion, but in the most part just Tony.

"*Tea?*" he replied sarcastically.

"Coffee?"

"*Coffee?*"

We all scrunched about in the gravel and I looked down because I knew what he was after. His face darkened, his lip curled up, and he stalked back toward the car. I smiled broad conciliatory hellos to the confused family while my father's wheels spun in the dust.

The drummer was called James and the singer was called Jez. They arrived together soon after me and as they got out of their car and started unloading their gear in the drive, I froze. They were both wearing spandex trousers and had long impressive mullets. One wore yellow-and-black leopardskin-effect spandex, the other a plain black-and-white striped affair. I'd never seen anyone as cool as them in real life before. We were in the same band! I swam in shame as I watched them. My hair was voluminous and messy, more *Eraserhead* than Motorhead, and my voice still hadn't broken. These two had soft Hampshire twangs that sounded hearty and sincere. I knew that I sounded like a twat. I guessed my axe was going to have to speak for me.

They were friendly and charismatic and I was pathetically smitten. Everything they said I grinned at like an idiot. I had to physically restrain myself from swooning as they strutted through the house in their big trainers. I knew, however, that I held some things over them. The fact that the majority of our equipment belonged to my father was one. Also, by this time I really did fancy myself as being rather handy with the white vinyl plank hanging around my neck. The songs I'd been writing featured bone-twistingly speedy bar-chord changes, and when I recited these at ear-bleeding volume in the conservatory, I felt a rush of blood to my cheeks. Even if we were utter shit, at least I could do *that*.

The tension rose as we set up the rest of the gear. Finally James was ready. He hadn't been playing long. He only had two drumsticks, one of which he snapped in half about five minutes in. We plugged everything, including Jez's mike, into the Farfisa organ amplifier; it could take it all and more. And off we stumbled like a ninety-year-old double-hip replacementee heading down to the rockery with a walker after four Bristol Creams.

For hours we patiently waited for us all to click. We even said, *OK, let's just try and get a vibe together on a single chord. Come on everyone—E.* Nothing of the sort. James had no sense of rhythm and kept flailing at pointless sub-Beefheartean fills which made him lose the beat every time he did one; Paul had no sense of much at all; Jez seemed only able to whoop atonally into the mike; and I played loud root chords out of time, with an unlit cigarette stuck vertically into my Wildcat's headstock.

Afterward we sat on the swings in the dusk until our egos returned. We discussed the more important stuff, like what we were going to be called. Paul and I looked at one another.

"Armageddon's Ring," I said.

"What's wrong with that?" said Paul.

James and Jez made adult gestures to one another which were unrecognizable to me.

"You want to change it?" asked Paul huskily. I swung, smoked, and spat. There was a grown-up pause. All this was way beyond me.

"I just think we could probably come up with something better, don't you?" said James, like a farmer.

"Not really," I said. They all turned to me for the first time. I spat and it went down my chin.

"Well, OK, let's try and think of some better names." Paul was not only being diplomatic, he was being treacherous. There weren't any better names. I tried to make eye contact with him but his face was turned toward the fields.

"What about Excalibur?" said Jez.

"That's a great name," replied James. Yeah, what a surprise.

"Excalibur," mused Paul to the fields. My best friend Paul. *My best friend Paul. Look at me for Christ's sake.*

Excalibur returned to the conservatory as the summer night fell. We upped sticks, well James did, and made some fucking noise. We even wrote a song—"City Boy"—it had three chords and was cyclical so we were able to play twenty-five–minute versions of it quite merrily, like Hawkwind or the Grateful Dead. It was pitch black outside and the long glass walls of the conservatory became mirrors. We each commandeered our own few panes and vogued on pointlessly into the night.

Although we talked up the whole thing between ourselves (we

designed logos, the works), I think we all knew deep down that Excalibur were stuck beneath the waterline. To have a commercially viable band requires at least one talented member, to drag those lacking technical ability in their wake. Sadly for Excalibur fans, we were a band full of weakest links. The strongest things we could muster were the drum kit, the spandex trousers, and my father's Farfisa organ amplifier. In order to have succeeded in the outside world, one of the four of us would've had to feature on that list, and preferably above the drum kit.

We gathered belatedly one rainy Saturday at Jez's and James's old school. They'd negotiated access to the assembly hall and we dragged our gear onto the high, wide stage. OK we were still shit, but this was exciting. A real stage, a real venue, real acoustics, real weekend delusion. I jumped off the stage at least twenty times, like Pete Townshend with a rewind button. I sprinted across the polished stage and slid yards on my knees. Paul and I did the Status Quo up/down boogie with our guitars. We all went off in separate directions, soloing for hours at a time. Jez always remembered to thank the invisible audience after every clumsy halt. We played a forty-minute version of "City Boy," and, as ever, recorded every last pathetic minute. And I finally got to light the cigarette stuck into the end of my guitar.

It was to be our final public performance.

My father had chosen not to come and pick me up this time— there was a Grand Prix on television, he explained to Paul's mother manfully. I was offered the front passenger seat in Mrs. Bavister's car because I was still the guest, albeit a mostly resented one by now. The steam inside and the rain outside were oppressive. As a band we were going out with a squeak instead of a roar, and we were all mutely aware of

our squandered dreams back there on the echoing school stage. I stared through the gloom. The music on the car's cassette player wasn't Metal.

"What's going on with the music?" I asked Paul, cooped in the back. The music was rock alright, sort of, but it sounded strange, unlike anything I knew. It had buzzing wiry guitars, a dirty saxophone, and confusing tumbling melodies. It had attitude—it sounded too good for me.

"Hanoi Rocks," he gruffed back and passed me the tape case. They looked like women and came from Finland. I wanted to sleep with all of them instantly—just cuddles, mind. The music was the most puzzling and exotic thing I'd ever heard. *Am I allowed to like this?* I asked myself, heart beating faster, waiting for the guitar solo.

Christ, talk about a Pandora's Box.

Well. Bangkok Shocks, Saigon Shakes . . .

Hanoi Rocks

I borrowed Paul's cassette. In fact I didn't even ask, I ripped it out of its plastic cradle and stuffed it in my pocket. It was their final studio album (they were about to split up), *Two Steps from the Move*: their first major-label record, their first with a glitzy production . . . their worst one—typical. But still, on the other side of the tape was a whole album's worth of live stuff, taken from their double live album, *All Those Wasted Years*.

Andy McCoy, Hanoi Rocks's leader, started out cleaning toilets in Stockholm for a while, just to pay the bills, but soon tired of it and decided to become a rock star instead. Being Finnish, he knew he'd have history and cultural stereotypes to contend with, especially if he recruited the rest of the band from Finland, which was exactly what he did next. He assembled every-one you can see in the photo ex-cept Razzle, who was a Lon-doner and joined later, after McCoy had fired original drummer Gyp Casino. Their real names were different, ob-viously. Even Sam Yaffa—yes, he's called that because he chose to be.

L–R: Razzle, Nasty Suicide, Michael Monroe, Andy McCoy, and Sam Yaffa

"*What about you, Sam? What have you chosen? Sam Dynamite? Sam Amazing? Sam Dragon?*"

"*Yaffa.*"

"*Pardon?*"

They dressed like gypsy New York Dolls, and sounded like it too. McCoy wrote the songs, which were quite derivative but coiled interestingly around. It was easy for them to become big in Finland: it took them a day and a half and a couple of phone calls. But McCoy's ambitions lay elsewhere, in the U.K. and beyond. So after a couple of urgent low-budget releases, they relocated to Tooting Bec in South London, which they instantly immortalized in the song "Tooting Bec Wreck." It goes, *I'm a living wreck and I live in Tooting Bec.*

Hanoi Rocks were only ever a cult band; they never broke out of the glam ghetto. They weren't metal enough to succeed on the bigger Donington stage; maybe they were too exotic for our denim brothers. I guess the saxophone had something to do with it too—it certainly did for me. I fell head over heels in love with them, and the buck-toothed Yaffa was, inexplicably, my favorite member. I even scratched their logo deep into the family dresser (which is still there, my mother reminded me recently).

I got my friend Ian into Hanoi, too. Ian was one of a new group of friends from Winchester I'd begun to spend time with. This group even included some girls, the first I'd ever experienced in the context of friendship. We liked to waste time in the usual way: smoking cold and underdressed in the center of town; engineering group rifts; drowning in aftershave and vodka on the weekends. Ian was my closest friend in the group. He was a young man who spent his entire adolescence attempting to appear enigmatic; he had a poker face, went for mysterious long walks, and he would keep his mouth in an O shape after the cigarette had left it. Ian wasn't completely sold on the whole metal thing; he seemed able to cherry-pick occasional songs and just like them. I think I'm trying to say he was musically *normal*. I soon denormalized him, don't worry.

Ian had gone before my mother found the camera. The lucky bastard.

On the front of *The Best of Hanoi Rocks*, the boys are all wearing suits—Mike's is gold lamé, but the others are generally straightforward—and they're all looking damn fine and sexy. I was sitting on Ian's bed one Saturday afternoon, and, as we listened to "Oriental Beat," we had a flash of inspiration. We decided to head into town and buy some suits like theirs and go around wearing them, in public. In the thrift store, everything went unexpectedly smoothly. I found an old gray suit which matched the one Sam Yaffa was wearing on the album sleeve, and Ian picked out a bright electric blue one similar to that sported by Nasty Suicide. Sam Yaffa wore a hat so I got a hat as well, and we chose some frilly shirts with ruffles on the front, and then finished it all off with some bright red lipstick. Then we sauntered down to the main street and hung around smoking and spitting.

Our friends came out to meet us, but when they caught sight of us they were so shocked they forgot to laugh. We acted aloof, but we were smoking so many cigarettes it was obvious we were nervous. They thought we had gone insane.

"You two look *terrible*. Whatever it is you're trying to do, it isn't working."

"No you don't understand. We're dressed like Hanoi Rocks."

"So what?"

We shook our heads and sucked at our cigarettes. The lipstick stained the filters bright red. Cool.

Red Hot and Heavy

I turned sixteen, and the relationship with my father deteriorated further. Our house suddenly wasn't big enough for the both of us, and silly flouncing handbag–style violence had become the norm. We had no shame in arguing, even when I had friends over. We were like some crabby old couple who liked to show off our misanthropy in public. Fa was drinking even more, and gradually losing his already fragile grip on reality, while my mother's tolerance was, after twenty years of marriage, finally reaching breaking point.

I was biding my time, waiting patiently for all this to fade away so that I could turn into the awesome guitar god I believed myself to be. Excalibur, though sadly dead, still looked good on my résumé, but a man has to keep moving, gotta keep his chops at optimum sheen. Who knew when I'd be required to step back into the metal spotlight?

Ian used to pretend to enjoy being invited round to my house and sitting in my bedroom while I practiced playing my electric guitar. I wasn't practicing actually, I was just showing off. He'd read a book or flick through my *Kerrang!s*, while I sat opposite him, pelting away at my rosewood rod. One day he was so bored he picked up my father's twelve-stringed acoustic guitar and dumbly strummed at it. He started to yelp like a sheep, at the same time. I was so surprised that I stopped playing.

"Wow, Ian, that's terrible!" I said in a nice way.

He did it again, for longer. He attempted random made-up chords.

"Jesus, Ian, alright! You can stop now, thanks, man."

He didn't get it. He was like Luke in Armageddon's Ring. He told me to teach him some chords. I showed him and it began to sound worse as his fingers choked the strings. The sheep noises continued unabated.

Ian's instant and terrifying delusion peaked five minutes later when he suggested we start a band, just the two of us.

"All the girls will be well impressed," he said between bleats.

"But it'll be shit! You're shit!" I replied kindly.

"Yeah, but you're good. You can be louder."

That sealed it. Him saying I was good, that I could be louder, and that the girls would be impressed was enough. We started a band. We called ourselves eXposed. I stole this name plus the clever way of writing it from the title of a Kiss video collection. We were a comedy band who took ourselves a little bit seriously on the side. Well I did at least—I was unable not to. We had the great idea of using Ian's musical ineptitude as a comedy selling point, and it worked. That afternoon we recorded our first album, *Parrots and Cigarettes*.

Comedy is subjective, alright? Our songs were called "She's Frigid," "Empty Vodka Bottle Blues," "Under the Table," "Ernie is a Cunt," and "Pissed in the Daytime Blues," stuff like that. We told everyone about our album and they looked at us funny. But the laughs were on them, because before long we became cult. Our friend Gabs offered us a gig in his living room. We took it. Cheers, Gabs.

People learned the words, went crazy, it was an event. The audience only numbered ten, but still.

We gigged on: my front room, Ian's basement, various rooms around the place. The crowds grew as the word got out: a metal guitar and two microphones, mine on an improvised broomstick stand, Ian a bona fide sheep Elvis. During every gig I played an unaccompanied five-minute guitar solo, like proper metal band members did. By now I could do a bad impression of that finger-tapping thing you see proper axe heroes do, but Ian would shout swear words into the mike while I was doing it, to put me off because he was jealous.

We released an EP, a one-copy-only cassette called the *Red Hot and Heavy Sessions*. This was our attempt at a jazz odyssey: ten minutes of me and Ian playing all my father's strange, unworldly instruments interspersed with hysterical laughter. And the classic eponymous track "Red Hot and Heavy" itself, which was just feedback and Ian reciting the title of the song over and over again at a frenzied sheep fever pitch. But no matter how ridiculous or awful we were, eXposed were popular. People were becoming slightly less inclined to label me simply a heavy metal loser; instead I had become that heavy metal loser who plays in the unfunny joke band with that twat Ian.

That summer I took my final exams. I did predictably badly, and without really thinking about it, followed all my friends to Peter Symonds College in Winchester. It was more miserable shit, and after one solitary term of unhappiness and confusion, I quit. The education system had finally failed me, but I was going to be a big rock star so who cared anyway, right? My mother was OK-ish about my leaving. She asked questions about my future while trying to hold my eyelinered pout, to which I mumbled half-answers and half-truths, half-assed. I think she saw how determined I was to head down this reckless path, and, being an artist herself, couldn't help but offer grudging respect.

My father hardly said a word. We outdid one another with grunts over dinner on our laps in front of the TV.

"Pass the salt."

"No."

"I said—"

"I don't care what you said."

"Pass the fucking—"

"No."

My mother, my sister, and Toby the dog ignored us.

I got a full-time job working as a catering assistant in the Scholar's Hall at Winchester College (the same one whose entrance exam I'd failed a few years before). I spooned out baked beans to revolting children in black gowns who tried to bum cigarettes off me and enjoyed throwing jam. Then after they'd done that I had to clear it all up and prepare for their next sodding meal.

One evening, after a hard day serving dinners, I came home and flopped down on my bed, only to discover a neat pile of torn-up paper sitting on my pillow. My mother had discovered the lyric sheet to the *Parrots and Cigarettes* album. I'd used a typewriter and it had taken me ages. Horrified, I spread the pieces out over the duvet and tried to place them back together. I saw that she'd underlined some of the lyrics in red before she'd ripped them up.

"*Woke up this morning, nicked a tenner off my mum*" was the first one. Oh shit. Yes, I'd been stealing tenners off my mum. She'd actually accused me of doing so but I'd hotly denied it. The shame now hit me full-on. I sat squirming on the bed, barely able to peep at the rest of her annotations. Almost the whole of "Fuck the Parrot" was underlined. This song was our ironic bestial homage to Nuclear Assault's "Hang the Pope." It went "*Let's go to the birdcage, get him out of bed, stick your dick right up his ass, and fuck him 'til he's fucking DEAD! Fuck the parrot, fuck the parrot, fuck the parrot (repeat).*" I gulped hard.

"She's Frigid" had taken quite a bashing, too.

When, later that evening, I emerged rat-like from my room for tea, not a word was said about it. In fact, to this very day, the incident has never been mentioned by either of us.

I am very pleased about this fact.

Chapter Eight

running free

I spent all my new, hard-earned money on just one thing: stacks of heavy metal records. And at last my hair was growing, too. It could now almost be called "long," though I really wanted it to be bouffant as well. I had no idea about backcombing, so instead I washed it, rubbed it vigorously with a towel, and then slept on it, which meant that by the morning it was suitably all over the place.

With the hair sorted out, I pulled on a white catering jacket with silver poppers and doled out the bread pudding with a giant spoon. Things were pretty good; good enough for me to recall this period, if I squint my eyes, as some sort of long Indian summer. Sadly, though, despite my improved big hair, eXposed were struggling. We'd begun to get heckled recently, and Ian's ego was only just

Yep. Sitting in the fireplace, watching the dog

hanging on in the face of unrelenting abuse from our audience. We decided to quit while we were ahead, and planned a spectacular farewell gig, witnessed by an audience of approximately thirty people, including a gaggle of naïve French exchange students who somehow just happened to be there, and the look on those faces all evening will stay with me forever. This was a triumphant homecoming to Gabs's front room. We made it really special, with an intro tape, curtains, and pyro (indoor fireworks). The closest example I can think of in rock history is probably Live Aid. Just before our (artificial) final encore of "Under the Table," Ian emotionally informed the audience that this was the last song eXposed would ever play and, annoyingly, the cheering drowned out my guitar solo.

On my seventeenth birthday, I moved out of home. The tension between Fa and I had become unbearable for everyone, and I'd been offered cheap housing from the college, so the timing made sense. The move brought instant relief and new excitement, and it was only ten minutes down the road from home, so it wasn't that big a deal. Winchester College owns half the city, and I got a first-floor room in a tiny leaning cottage on the edge of the cricketing fields. I dealt with independence well—I ate brown sauce sandwiches and kept leaving my front door key in the pub or down a drain—a model of self-sufficiency.

Now bandless and becoming restless, I heard on the grapevine about a local band called No Strings. They were supposed to be halfway decent, so, using some contacts, I arranged to meet their vocalist in a bar: the Black Boy. He arrived with huge curly hair, like Brian May, and appeared to love himself. His fluffy shirt was open to the waist and he was generously endowed with chest hair, tummy hair, hair everywhere.

Over several pints of lager and lime, we shook some of the shit out of the world. Say we were to start a band of our own, what would we call it?

"You'd probably want to call it No Strings," I said, used to people like this by now.

"Maybe something like Axe Attack?" he replied.

My blood ran cold.

We eventually settled on something stylish. Noise Royale. We eyed one another smugly and shook hands. His name was Owen Oakeshott, and we were about to embark on a beautiful friendship.

Owen liked *Doctor Who*, Queen and synths. You could go as far as to say that he was obsessed with these three things. So on paper we ought to have been mortal enemies. He was a year or so older, and also somehow wiser; he appeared to be one of those people who actually got things done, entirely unlike me. We met again, and this time he played me tapes of some No Strings gigs. Yeah, they sounded good. Their guitar player was a hundred times better than me. *Bound to be an asshole*, I muttered.

"What was that?" asked Owen.

"Oh nothing. I was just going to say, that guy's a good guitarist."

"Adrian. Yeah, he's not bad."

"Not bad. Right. You wouldn't want Adrian in any new band then?"

"Oh no, he's way too . . . you know." He meant way too good.

He was playing me these tapes out of a sense of mourning. No Strings were no more. The Strings had been cruelly severed by the scissored hands of fate. But Owen wasn't down about this: we were tiptoeing toward Noise Royale.

Owen started to come over to the cottage regularly, and we'd sit in my room and listen to Kiss's *Alive II* and Cheap Trick on repeat. I was trying to get him into more of my music and away from Queen, who were banned.

What was I listening to now? I was officially *glam*.

"Seb, you like heavy metal."

"No! I like *glam*."

"That's heavy metal—you like heavy metal."

"No. It's not heavy metal, it's completely different."

I used this line every day for the next five years. Of course I liked heavy metal, but I was in denial. All of us were. Wherever you were in the metal pie, you denied you were actually in the pie, because you knew the pie was as cool as dog shit.

"What? No, no! Black Sabbath were a *blues* band." . . . "I'm a rock fan. Heavy metal? No, that's not for me, that's for losers" . . . "Partial to the occasional morsel of hard rock. Just a bit. Hardly ever really" . . . "I like sleazy rock. No, you're wrong, it's not heavy metal. That's completely different. That stuff's for idiots."

You could go on forever. They'll never admit it, so let them have their little delusions. But when they've finished their inter- minable explanatory sentences, put your face up close to theirs and with a smile just whisper, *metal*.

So I liked glam now, not heavy metal. I liked (liked? I *adored* these people!) Dogs d'Amour, Hanoi Rocks, Ratt, Poison, Faster Pussycat—anyone with wide-brimmed hats, eyeliner, jet-black hair and low-slung guitars. I didn't have to hear a band to tell you if I liked them, I just had to cast a critical eye. It was the look I attempted to foster myself. I cut all the arms off my T-shirts, wore a charity shop hat if my hair wasn't explosive enough, copious neck jewelry which gave me a perpetual rash, lots of bangles (ditto wrist rash), hooped earrings (I had two holes in the left ear and one in the right; they were permanently infected), Converse sneakers, and slashed blue jeans (only because I had no idea where to buy black jeans from). I also liked to decorate myself with satin and silk scarves, tied at random around my limbs, like a Morris dancer. I got most of them from Small, and they wafted prettily behind me as I walked. Pink, yellow, and blue. Lovely.

I got my heart broken too, which I reckoned was probably par for the course for a lonesome outlaw rocker like me. Samantha was a tomboy who had come to the eXposed gigs, and I had fallen in love with her almost at first sight. My love was entirely unrequited. Weekends regularly involved me lunging at her around midnight. Not only did she laughingly bat me away, but she also compounded my hazy alcoholic grief by heavily petting with my other friends. I dealt with it dreadfully—poems, songs, tantrums, weeping, more poems, more hopeless lunging followed by being sick. Then she did something really cruel. Knowing how pathetically smitten I was, she invited me on an Interrailing holiday with another couple I barely knew. The only reason she asked me was that I had the long Winchester College holidays and was the only person among our friends who might possibly be able to afford it. She was determined to go and didn't care who with—even if it was only me—and she knew I'd fall over myself to say yes.

In shitty budget hotels all over France, Italy, and Greece, it was cheaper for us to share a double bed than to pay for two singles, so that's what we did. I went gradually insane. I couldn't sleep. I was blindly in love with this unremarkable girl dragging me miserably around the Continent, forcing me to pretend we were a couple until we were lying in the same bed together at night where she warned me not to touch. I didn't touch. I lay with my heart thumping. I'd brought along an acoustic guitar, like a Beat troubadour, which I tied to my swinging backpack. I wrote bitter love songs but refused to play them to her if she asked. She used to say that if I didn't do all that ridiculous stuff with my exploding hair then I might actually be vaguely good-looking underneath. I never even kissed her.

I eventually lost my virginity to a girl named Louise, who lived in a village three miles from town. I'd met her at a disco and my friends had pushed me in her direction because they'd heard she knew what she was doing, if you know what I mean. We soon became boyfriend and girlfriend, and on the night in question Louise and I took turns on the record player, alternating between her Terence Trent d'Arby album and AC/DC's *Blow Up Your Video*, until I summoned up the courage to proceed. It happened during "Sign Your Name." She was kind to me. We did it a few more times and then she walked me to the bus stop.

★ ★ ★

Back in Winchester, as I pored endlessly over my growing pile of back issues of *Kerrang!*, I noticed that all the bands I loved had something in common (apart from the fact that they all looked the same): they were all heavily tattooed. Hanoi Rocks had rose tattoos, as did Kiss's Paul Stanley, so I decided to copy them. I'd heard there was a tattoo parlor in Southampton's red-light district, so one Saturday I nervously headed down there with my friend Gabs. But out of all the thousands of pictures on the walls, I couldn't find a single stand-alone rose. I found one eventually, but it had a snake coiled around it. A snake? Alright, I thought, lacking the imagination to ask the guy to leave out the snake bit and just draw the rose on its own. The burly tattooist went to work with his needles while I sweated and feigned interest in the horse racing on television. It hurt quite a lot, but wasn't too bad; it was on my upper left arm and I loved it.

I rushed back home, and as I rolled up my sleeve to show it to Small, she said, "Please don't tell me you got Hanoi Rocks tattooed on your poor arm."

"How dare you!"

"Oh god, you did, didn't you?"

"Of course I didn't!"

I showed her. She peered up at it.

"The snake's got quite a big nose, hasn't it?"

"That's its *neck*. It's a rattlesnake. That's what they look like."

She was right, though—the tattooist had fucked up. The snake's hooded neck did indeed look like a giant protruding nose. She put her glasses on and peered at it some more.

"Well I'd swear that looks like a nose to me."

"It's its neck!"

Over in my Winchester College cottage, I was gradually wearing Owen down. I'd show him my tattoo and play him more glam metal records, and he'd scientifically deconstruct them and put them back together again (explaining all the while what he was doing). Then he'd tell me he thought one of them was amazing, because of some specific thing he'd heard.

"'Calling Dr. Love' is staggering," he'd suddenly announce.

"I agree!"

"The way the middle-eight breaks down to the diminished D-flat in the bridge before the final chorus works brilliantly." Yeah, he was musically trained as well, the annoying bastard.

"Exactly. Yes." What the fuck was he talking about? I cued up "Rocket Ride" with trepidation.

But at least he was finally getting enthusiastic about the music that *I* was playing him.

In order to be Noise Royale, we needed a band. Owen went on about No Strings all the time, and I was starting to feel intimidated. And the more I had to listen to tapes of Adrian, the sicker I began to feel; he wasn't just pretty good, he was bloody magnificent, and believe it or not, Owen still hadn't really heard me play. I was waiting to be unmasked as the axe fraud I suspected myself to be. I also only had a little practice amp now, having forfeited access to the Aladdin's Cave of my father's instrumental warehouse when I moved out. When I'd asked if I could take the Farfisa organ amplifier with me, Fa hadn't even bother to pretend he was laughing at me.

Doing it for the cameras— the day I moved out

Actually, a kind gust of familial wind had blown forgivingly over our mutual loathing the minute I moved out. Suddenly we got on again. We learned to respect one another, perhaps for the first time, as two dysfunctional adults. We met at the pub, holding up cigarettes like evil tweezers, and he would be sarcastic to me. Previously I would come back at him with cheap insults and big-man swearing. Now I could relax and bat his sarcasm back with some experimental stuff of my own. We settled down into a gentle barrage of pisstaking.

Winchester College had chasmlike school holidays, all of which I had off, on full pay. The rent I was paying on the cottage was less than five pounds a week; my eating was all taken care of from college "stocks," so unusually for an overdressed seventeen-year-old metaller, I had cash permanently sloshing about my untrustworthy person. Besides my hungry consumption of metal albums, I was on a diet of one new electric guitar every two months. These weren't American-made, sumptuously constructed design classics, oh no. These were lumps of balsa wood from the little music shop on Winchester High Street, crassly spray-painted primary colors, chopped into unusual metal shapes by short-sighted sweatshop carpenters, and all for less than eighty pounds. They suited me just fine, and I lined them up against my bedroom wall, a sickly parade of cheap, impossible-to-tune eyesores. I bought a big amplifier from a friend of my father at the Golden Lion; it didn't really work properly but had dazzling lights on its large-knobbed silver control panel. My father pronounced it "Absolutely fine. Stop complaining." For the first time in our relationship, I bit my lip.

While I was feeding my thirst for electric guitars and surreptitiously trying out all the different brands of hairspray at Boots, Owen was busy getting our band together. He had another friend (I type this through particularly gritted teeth), a friend who was still a better one to him than me. Andy Walter, pianist extraordinaire and general all-round nice, friendly guy, also happened to know what he was doing musicwise, since he'd been in those taste-harbingers of doom, No Strings. (Are you, like me, picturing the Strings as a band with *two synths*? You'd be right.) It wasn't all bad for me, though—Andy had short hair.

One day Owen dropped by the cottage and said we were there. Where?

Owen Oakeshott—vocals and leader

Andy Walter—keyboards and smiles

Seb Hunter—guitar and jewelry

Danny Moynard—bass plus unnecessary "attitude"

Johnny Evans—drums

I was terrified. This was my first exposure to people who could actually play their instruments. We gathered in a wooden hut for our first rehearsal, on the grounds of the college I'd recently dropped out of. The word about town was such that, believe it or not, we had five people come along to witness this significant moment in Winchester rock history. We wished they'd all piss off, but nobody was brave enough to say anything. They watched silently as we chatted, blushed, and sweated setting up our gear with the sun pouring through the plate-glass windows. Johnny's drums were seriously large and shiny (we were already in awe of this dude), Danny was showing off, looking all indie, while at the back of the hut I was having problems tuning to Andy's synth. He was patiently prodding an E with his index finger and just saying "no" over and over. Suddenly fed up with our lack of progress, Johnny rapped his sticks in the air above his head and shouted out, "One, two, three, four . . ."

Owen shrieked into his mike, I dropped my plectrum, and Johnny had to start again.

Let There Be Rock

The rehearsals went badly. Owen had taken it upon himself to record a compilation tape featuring some of his favorite songs that he'd decided we were to learn: "I Don't Want to Talk About It," the Everything But the Girl version; "Spirit of Radio" by Rush; "Home Sweet Home" by Mötley Crüe; Judas Priest's "adaptation" of "Johnny B Goode" (this is much, *much* worse than you can possibly imagine). These were all total shit! "Rock 'n' Roll Hell" by Kiss. Well, mostly shit.

Danny the bassist, who thought all heavy metal was "pathetic" and liked the Smiths (we never quite got to the bottom of what he was doing in this band), was particularly unhappy with Owen's cassette.

"I refuse to play this," he said at regular intervals. Owen tended to concede, to keep the peace. *Good for Danny*, I thought, though I disliked his aloof nature intensely.

"You like the Smiths, huh?" I challenged him one day.

"Yeah?"

"Pfff," I replied. "They're nothing on the *real* Smiths."

"What are you talking about now?"

"*Aero*smith."

Danny walked away, as usual.

Johnny was a big guy in every way, especially around the middle. He smoked Benson & Hedges like a darts player and had an iron flick that he buffed up with the heel of his palm. At random moments he'd suddenly rattle through a giant air drum solo punctuated with his mouth, which usually had a cigarette in it. He made everyone jump. Johnny was very dry—funnier than the rest of us, but gentle with it, and always enthusiastic about all we did as a group, even the terrible cover versions. He didn't take any shit, though—he was a genuine adult. He had a proper job and lived with an older woman who had a kid and government housing; guess he must have had sex and stuff as well. Respect to Johnny all round then.

The songs Owen was making us learn embarrassed even me. This selection represented the more shameful side of our genre—every song featured synths for a start (maybe I shouldn't have been surprised by that, considering we had a synth player in the band). Had this tape featured some Tattooed Love Boys or L.A. Guns then it would've been fine. We slagged the songs off while tortuously fitting rudimentary versions of them together, section by agonizing section. "Spirit of Radio," for God's sake? It's one of the hardest songs in the world to play! I started to think that Owen had chosen these songs just to make me look stupid. If that was correct, then it was definitely working. In the evenings I'd sit dejectedly in my bedroom, hands wrinkled from washing up my pupils' soiled dinner plates, wearing out Owen's tape. I'd rewind until the tape chewed up, my fingers desperately searching out obtuse, agonizing riffs, melody lines and horrendously complicated solos. I'd recently bought a really nice black Les Paul copy guitar, but it wasn't helping much. At least it stayed in tune, though, and at least my mother wasn't there to tell me I was playing out of time.

Things got worse one summer afternoon when Owen announced that we were going to cover a new "radio smash" he'd heard: Guns N' Roses's "Sweet Child o' Mine." As soon as he said it, the whole band gazed dolefully at me.

"I can learn that!"

Have you heard the guitar line that introduces that song? *Jesus.*

"I can learn that easy. Stop staring at me."

At least the chords were easy: D, C, G, D. Manageable.

Our own original material was easier for us to play, though some-times not for lack of trying. Owen and Andy went out of their way to make their songs change key at least seven times, and Owen was obsessed with inserting difficult time signatures into middle-eights. At times like these I would have no idea what was going on, and just stand there watching Johnny stagger along, while Owen tried to count me through it with his jabbing arm. We'd written about six or seven songs between us: "Magazine," my lumpen critique of the morality of the pornography industry (that I knew nothing about). Nice and easy to play, no hard bits; "Licking the Ashtray," a breathless gallop in A, with hard-hitting lyrics about poverty, and only two tempo changes; "Manhunt," Owen's epic synth masterpiece per-formed from the viewpoint of a rapist, which sounded like Europe playing "Eye of the Tiger"; "Just Because," Andy's tearjerking power ballad about nothing; "Gravity 1086," an instrumental in a pointless time signature that I got wrong every single time; "Suicide," my proudest moment and our best song, a poppy, tumbling-chord num-ber with glitter-cliché lyrics that were meaningless but sounded nice; "Gangbang," Owen's emotional celebration of gangbangs, with its chorus: "*Gangbang! Gangbang! I've got to, got to, got to have another one!*"; and finally "Under the Table," the lost eXposed classic. I could play that one. Damn right I could—it was easy!

One of the best things about being in a band is sitting around in the pub shouting down everybody else's suggestions for a name; Noise Royale had lost some of its charm in the interven-ing months, so we needed a new one. Though I wasn't the musi-cal leader, I was pretty much the visual one, so it was my dodgy aesthetic that was calling the shots. Not that this affected Johnny at all, mind; he was happy just drinking his pints in an ever more methodical fashion, slapping us down if we talked too much shit. So during these discussions, I was in possession of an unwritten power of veto, which was called upon often as Owen and Andy disgraced themselves with their silly suggestions.

"Definitely something with 'boys' in the title. The something Boys!" exclaimed Andy.

"Don't be so fucking gay," I replied.

"What about Boyz, with a z?" suggested Owen.

"Like the Dirty Boyz!" exclaimed Andy.

"Nothing with boys or zeds, forget it. Jesus, where have you guys *been*?"

"What about the Dirty Kidz, with a zed?" said Andy. "Or without."

I looked pleadingly at Johnny.

"Get a grip," he told them.

"The Dirty somethings . . ." Owen mused, looking skyward.

"The Dirty Girls!" said Andy.

I stared at him.

We ended up with Rag and Bones. *Nope, hold on,* I said. *Rag 'n' Bones please. Alright, that's acceptable.*

Once we'd settled on a name, Owen tried to talk us into playing a gig. We'd sit smoking after rehearsals, listening to tapes of what we'd just played, trying to let him down gently, but he wasn't having any of it. He was determined to get us onstage—his ego demanded it.

"And I want something big."

"What, the Guildhall?" I was joking, obviously.

"Yes!"

"Oh for Christ's sake. Can't you just—"

"Why not?"

To make a little extra money on the side, Andy played piano for a ballet class of early-teen girls every week. He'd sit there jauntily and they'd all trot along under the watchful eye of their dance teacher and her stick. *Come on girls! Come on Andy!* The classes were held in a place called the John Stripe Theater. Owen had begun to attend too, playing the recorder in accompaniment. It was a dark day for the band when he told us about his prowess on the recorder. He offered to play a solo on it during "Manhunt,"

Me and Owen, cheeks to cheeks. Stop looking for the snake's big nose.

but we hurriedly told him it was absolutely perfect already, thanks.

"Why not play a gig there?" said Owen, and we ignored him.

After rehearsals, the rest of us trudged home while Owen headed up the hill to the theater, hoping he could use his recorder playing as a way in.

Next day he had that smug look on his face again. God knows how he'd managed it but he'd got us a gig.

"There is no fucking *way* we're going to be ready."

"This is going to be the show of the year!"

"I'm not doing it," said Danny. Johnny did a loud air drum solo. Owen and Andy did a high five. I lit a cigarette and stared at them in horror.

The following morning we climbed the hill to the theater and huddled together in the doorway. Peeping through into the auditorium, it became clear that we were dealing with a bona fide theater .

"Owen!" came a thick voice out of the gloom.

"John! Aha!" Owen started along the back row of seats and bear-hugged a giant black man. Johnny and I stepped back in a cloud of Benson & Hedges smoke.

This orb of a man was John Osbourne, and he was the theater's lights and sound man. He giggled a lot, wore a flat cap, and smelled of sweat, and as the first black man I'd ever spoken to (ever been to Winchester?), I was initially very shy and overpolite. We sat in his control room looking out over the huge stage below as he showed us all his effects and demonstrated the PA system.

The stage was mesmerizing even when empty. Owen sent us down there and we wandered around whooping and flapping our arms. We jumped off the large black trestles and ground our cigarette butts onto the shiny floor with our heels while Johnny did air drum solos.

"What do you think then lads?" Owen came down to join us.

"When do we do it?" asked Johnny. Up in the control room, John was letting us have it with the lightshow again. It sparkled and flashed around us.

"I reckon before the end of the year," said Owen. It was currently October.

"*What?*" I said. The words were obliterated by "Spirit of Radio" blasting out of the monitors. Owen leaned back and gave a Tarzan roar. Andy crabbed around, nodding and grinning. Johnny played air drums (he never got bored of it). I tried saying "*What?*" again, but John had increased the volume and we could see him giving us a double thumbs-up, which Owen, Andy and Johnny all returned. Any veto I'd thought I still possessed had just been flushed down the toilet.

There was a new purpose in the air at rehearsals: the smell of terror. In between band practices, we'd all been trying to learn our parts extra properly, and it was amazing what a difference this made. I played the classical guitar solos in "Johnny B Goode" correctly, Johnny played the intro to the Zep's "Rock and Roll" spot on (shame we couldn't come in spot on), and Danny got the timing right on "Gravity 1086." As a group, though, we were starting to realize that although Owen looked good when he was going for those high notes—looked like he was taking a shit—his upper vocal register was in dire need of paper for the cracks. He came up with the solution of just screaming if he couldn't hit the note, which worked alright for now.

One day Andy innocently asked if I'd had any luck with the guitar intro to "Sweet Child o' Mine." I looked at my feet. Not a chance in hell, but I wasn't going to admit it in front of the rest of the guys. We'd been playing the song through without that bit. I'd forgotten all about it actually. But this was a setup, because Owen suddenly exclaimed, "Aha!," raised a theatrical eyebrow and pointed dramatically toward Andy, who calmly played the intro on his synth, no mistakes at all. Johnny crashed in at the right place and we went through the whole song to the end. Andy kept trying to smile at me reassuringly while playing one-handed, but I was too embarrassed to meet his eye.

My humiliation was not yet complete. Owen and Johnny were still keen to play "Spirit of Radio" and I still couldn't play it. I couldn't even play a rudimentary version of it. The intro was fingertapping, for God's sake. They were so keen to play this song that the band would run through it, Danny included, with me just standing there with my arms crossed, being grumpy. Andy would play the guitar parts with the synth, while Owen stood next to him playing the proper keyboard part on the same machine. (This dreadful spectacle at least afforded me a glimmer of aesthetic schadenfreude.)

"What we could do . . ." said Owen afterward in the pub.

"Is what?" I replied.

"I'm not suggesting this, I'm only putting it to the table. But what we could do is maybe get someone else to play guitar during 'Spirit of Radio.'"

"*What?*" The table was quiet. I was the only one who had spoken. I looked them all in the eye, one by one.

"We could, for example, get Adrian to come on for one number, play 'Spirit of Radio,' and then bugger off again."

Adrian was the axe god from Owen's last band, No Strings.

"*Adrian?*"

"Like a special guest appearance."

"*What?* Come on! What would that make me look like? It would make me look like some kind of talentless cunt! Why can't we just not play the fucking song? Is it that fucking important that we play 'Spirit of fucking Radio?' At least my education had taught me how to swear.

Johnny's face darkened. Owen swatted me away.

"You wouldn't need to lose face. You could, like, mime along."

"*Mime?*"

They called Adrian and he said yes, alright, he'd do it if we paid him. But he also wanted to do five minutes' worth of unaccompanied guitar soloing. Owen agreed to his terms.

Adrian Muckley, if you're reading this: You can go screw yourself.

Instrumental Solos

The world's first ever drum solo took place at approximately 9:45 P.M. on August 4, 1968, in the Ipswich Gaumont. It was a Thursday night and it was raining. Iron Butterfly were onstage, and the Gaumont was about four-fifths full. The Butterfly were dredging through the seventeen-minute title track of their latest album, *In-a-Gadda-da-Vida*, which was, amazingly, the world's first ever platinum album. (The authorities actually had to invent a whole new category for this achievement; once sales had raced past the gold mark, it was platinum they came up with to top it.) *In-a-Gadda-da-Vida* was Iron Butterfly's second album. Their first, *Heavy*, had performed moderately well and had featured the corking "Get Out of My Life, Woman," but *Gadda* was their masterpiece—their *Four*.

The boys were dealing it out onstage. Doug Ingle had lurched through an accompanied organ solo, Eric Brann was delivering the riffs like wrenches, and the moment was approaching for Ron Bushy's drum spot. Usually he just flapped about for a bit, bashing up his cymbals with the other guys still playing their instruments, but that night, as he paradiddled into the opening bars of this particular section, the rest of the Butterfly stopped playing. To this day nobody knows whether it was accidental or not. The scene was like a Roadrunner cartoon, when Wylie Coyote runs out over the edge of a cliff with his legs still pounding and to his horror realizes there's no cliff left beneath him. He's treading sheer air—how long can he last? Can he claw his way back onto land? This was exactly how it felt for Bushy. *Don't look down. Go for it.* He drummed on and the hall fell silent.

Eleven minutes later, Ipswich went totally nuts. Bushy got a nine-minute standing ovation. That night a musical phenomenon was born. Iron Butterfly's third album was called *Ball*.

A layman might ask: Why do instrumental solos at all? To which the seasoned metaller would shake their head, tut, and recite a list of why they are necessary.

1. Why the hell not?
2. I am a fantastic musician and I cannot express the upper limits of my extraordinary virtuosity within the stifling constraints of our songs, so I require this opportunity to show the audience what I'm capable of. Shut up and listen.
3. Value for money. That's an extra ten minutes added onto the show. You ought to be grateful!
4. It gives the nonsoloees a chance for a quick breather backstage and perhaps some oral sex and/or drugs.
5. It gives the lighting guy a chance to use his strobe lights.
6. The musician's ego: sheer spotlight hunger.
7. It gets the audience involved. You can do a bit of call-and-response. You know—*blam!*—points to left side of crowd, left side cheers wildly; *blam!*—points to right side etc.
8. Tradition.
9. The soloee may be making noises about wanting to leave the band. This is a good way to encourage them to stay.

10. An altruistic gesture from band to audience. Need a pee? Fancy a cigarette? Go on, off you go, come back in ten minutes. (But don't forget to buy some merchandise while you're out there.)
11 The support band did one so I should do one too.
12. The drummer did one so I should do one too.
13. Metal bands are superstitious, hence the absence of a number 13.
14. The other guitarist did one so I should do one too (etc.).
15. I have a new instrument/amplifier and I want to show it off.
16. They think you actually enjoy it.
17. You enjoy it.

I'll tell you right now: if you've ever been to a heavy metal concert, you'll have witnessed an instrumental solo. They all do them—they have done since the late '60s. My first exposure, of course, was at Hammersmith Odeon with Mark and Dominic, watching Ratt. It's a perfect example and I can remember it all. Here's the drill:

Ratt finish their third song, four of them leave the stage (we were thinking, *Is that it?*) and the spotlight settles upon drummer Bobby Blotzer. Bobby makes a series of dramatic descending drumrolls, crashes his cymbals noisily for thirty seconds, and then stands up holding his sticks in the air and grinning through the dry ice.

"Hooray!" we shout.

He sits down and does it all over again.

"Hooray!"

The spotlight then turns blue, but instead of the drumrolls comes the thud of his bass drum. Thump thump thump thump (twelve more thumps), cymbal crash.

"Hooray!"

He's clearly exceptionally talented. After ten or so minutes of this, I lean over to Mark and whispered my concern that seeing as

Ratt are the support band, oughtn't they to be spending less time on this and more time on playing all their ace songs? We could see the rest of the band smoking cigarettes in the wings.

Bobby ends with a big cymbal crash, and stands up again. "Hooray!"

The rest of the guys walk back to their places and carry on for a few more songs. Then the stage goes dark again and a red spotlight picks out guitarist Robbin Crosby stage right. Crosby adjusts his footing and leans forward slightly, plays some very fast scales and raises his right arm into the air.

"Hooray!"

The spotlight turns orange. Robbin puts his plectrum in his mouth and starts to do a bit of fingertapping—two-handed stuff. In between the fingertaps, he wiggles his whammy bar a lot, which makes screechy diving noises. He finishes on one sustained and piercing note, raises his right hand once more, and the spotlight turns hollow white.

"Hooray!"

The lads amble back on carrying their instruments. They get through two more songs, then, after the guitar solo in "Back for More," instead of heading back to the excitedly awaiting chorus, all the boys except for bassist Juan Croucier march off again. The spotlight glazes across from the fire curtain and turns yellow. Juan widens the gap between his knees and plays some deep scales.

He plays more scales and the spotlight accidentally drops off him for a second but then wearily swings back purple. He plays a note and points off to his left.

Somebody coughs.

He plays two notes and points to his right.

Some girls are chatting.

He plays a complicated sequence of ten or so notes and points to the heavens (us).

"Oh hooray."

The boys come back on and treat us to a brilliant pair of Ratt 'n' Roll stonkers. Then singer Stephen Pearcy tells us how much he loves London and London girls, and they all go off again except for second guitarist Warren de Martini (my favorite member; remember the kitten?).

YAAAAAAYYYYY WARREN I LOVE YOU!!

The spotlight turns green and Warren plays some rapid scales rather languidly. He doesn't even bother removing the cigarette from his mouth. Actually, they haven't even bothered to lower the stage lights. They burn brightly around him as cigarette smoke curls up through his hair. He stops to remove the cigarette and take a drag.

"Hooray!"

Finally the boys wander back, play "Round and Round," the house lights come up and they're done for the night

A thirty-minute support slot, Ratt's first ever show in the UK, and they spent half of it playing instrumental solos? That's absolutely standard metal behavior. When Ozzy came on later, each member of his band did one too, including the keyboardist. The crowd didn't mind in the slightest. You see, the fact that our heroes are so darn technically proficient is a sincere source of pride. We're extremely smug about it, as of course are the musicians themselves. When U2 first appeared and people were saying The Edge was this great guitar player, we metallers said to ourselves: respect to The Edge then, whoever he may be; respect for The Edge's chops. But then we heard this dull chiming on "Where the Streets Have No Name," and we pissed ourselves laughing. *Call that being good? It's shit! I'll show you good!*

And good was what they showed us, there in the rainbow spotlights with their legs spread and hair hanging over their faces. Good is *speed*, good is *classical scales*, good is *looks really awkward*.

Heavy metal has absolutely nothing at all to do with the liberating, chain-breaking, DIY, just-get-up-and-express-yourself blueprint of what rock and roll was invented for. In a way it was the next stage. It didn't need to rebel, or to wear jeans, or to feel dangerous about hair below the collar—that had been done in the '50s and '60s. Heavy metal took all that for granted and assumed that you were lining up for the next challenge. And far from being the clichéd, club-footed, talentless morons of popular notion (musically), these hungry thrill-seekers set about learning to play their instruments to within an inch of their lives. *You want to laugh at us? Go ahead, sucker, but I bet you can't do this.*

There was a film in the '80s, called *Crossroads*. It was about a wholesome guitar-playing teenage Caucasian American, who, with the aid of his suitably grizzled Negro mentor, was wandering around the South in search of blues legend Robert Johnson's mythical "lost song." It's an extremely tedious film, but has an ending that features a Metal Solo War between this teenager and the bad guy, played by real-life axe god Steve Vai. The pair take it in turns to spew out ever more dazzling metal solos to a whoopin' and hollerin' crowd. The way it's depicted is blues (good) versus metal (bad). Vai has a silly-looking metal guitar and long hair and sneers all the time, while the short-haired teenager plays a no-frills guitar and gives Vai and the crowd his innocent doe-brown eyes.

You don't need me to tell you who wins: Vai was robbed.

I guess my point is that although the geek won, with his more conservative axe, haircut, values, and nice black man as a friend, the crap they were coming out with on their guitars was exactly the same. In real life Vai played all the parts. The moral of the story being that long boring interminable guitar solos are the finest currency American music can buy. In other words—fuck the blues, feel the metal girth once more.

As with most things, Led Zeppelin were particularly good at soloing. Ten minutes of exhausting technical fury wasn't enough for the Zep—oh no. They took the concept of the instrumental solo and stretched it as far as they possibly could without destroying it completely. The Zep being the Zep, though, they snapped it in two every other night.

Take Bonzo's drum solo, for example. They wrote a whole song just to include it, called "Moby Dick." A clever, Trojan Horse–like device, it fooled the audience into not going for a piss when it started. They even had the guts to put it onto their second album. Think about it, they've had worldwide success with their debut platter—have they got the tunes to follow it up? Can they hit platinum paydirt all over again? Can they sustain the kids' attention for another fifty minutes' worth of spinning black vinyl?

"I"'ve got an idea lads," in a Birmingham accent.

"What's that then, Bonzo?"

"Why don't we stick a ten-minute drum solo in the middle of this song, and then put it in the middle of the album!"

"Perfect!"

It was even better live. His drum solos sometimes went on for up to half an hour. They encompassed large periods of relative inactivity: he would sit pensively under the pale spotlight, toying with the rim of a tom-tom for minutes at a time. Then he'd stop for a while, stare at his juglike floortom, and finally give it a whack, almost as an afterthought. He knew full well how stoned the audience was and he took good advantage. He petted his kit until the lads got their shit together backstage, and then they all rounded off "Moby Dick" in a different time zone from the one it had started in.

Jimmy Page's antics were even better, and even now nobody's entirely sure if he was just goofing around. Two words should jolt your memory: *violin* and *bow*.

Halfway through the heavily improvised "Dazed and Confused," when no one knew which way was up or which way was down, Jimmy would begin to rock to and fro, his dripping fringe swaying, away in his own mystical world. The rest of the group took this as their cue and legged it to the wings. Jimmy then produced a violin bow from his back pocket and proceeded to whack it against his guitar strings. This sounded really strange but he seemed to be getting into it. He carried on like this for about fifteen minutes and then did the whole pointing-the-violin-bow-at-the-audience thing, to generous applause. The ripped threads of the bow hung down and were illuminated in the dry ice. Then he added another twenty or so effects to his guitar, including the sound of flying ducks, and got back to work with the rest of the solo.

The Zep released a feature film, taken mostly from concert footage at New York's Madison Square Garden, titled *The Song Remains the Same*. The instrumental solos are all included, each in its glorious entirety. But instead of forcing us to watch Jimmy and his bow for fifteen minutes, or Bonzo and his giant gong, the Zep recorded "dream sequences" for us to enjoy while we listened. Each member's personal sequence was shown over their particular solo spot.

Jimmy Page: climbs up a scrawny mountainside at night, perhaps being chased by something out of camera shot. He reaches the top and a druid/Merlin-type character grabs his hand, then waves a lantern in the air, which trails a rainbow of psychedelic colors behind it.

Robert Plant: sails in a Viking boat to an island, where he rides a horse through the countryside to arrive at a castle. He has swordfights with some dwarves and rescues a beautiful maiden from imprisonment in a tower. They run off and cuddle as the Viking boat is set on fire. I think.

John Paul Jones: leads a dual life. Marauds around in the night as a highwayman with a pig mask, chasing black carriages and making a nuisance of himself. Then he arrives home, takes off his mask, and has a hearty meal with his buxom wife. I don't really understand this one.

Bonzo: doesn't bother with a dream sequence. Instead there are shots of him drinking beer in the pub with his mates, racing drag cars, and generally taking the piss.

The film came out to bad reviews.

Master showmen that they are, Kiss have always had slightly more imagination than most in the presentation of their solos. I use the word "slightly" only because although this is good, they've done it exactly the same way for twenty-five years.

Bass solo: Gene Simmons stands on a plinth. He hits a single deep note, then sneers and widens his eyes. He hits the note again and jerks his neck around. And again, his head jutting out in a rhythmically demonic fashion. Once more, is that blood around his mouth? *Dong* goes the note again (I should mention that he uses a flange effect on his bass when he does all this) and blood gushes from his mouth. The note remains the same but is speeding up, blood runs down his chin, and Gene appears to be experiencing spasms. The note thuds out, Gene is suddenly lifted high into the air on an invisible wire and lands on a plinth high up onstage. He stops playing the note and raises his arms with blood all over him. We cheer. He goes back to playing the note and flies gently back down again. The rest of Kiss come back on and finish playing "God of Thunder."

Guitar solo: Ace Frehley is playing scales (blues scales—he can't do classical scales), surrounded by billowing dry ice. Is it me or is his guitar on fire? The front of his guitar lights up and loads of smoke comes out of it, but he carries on playing regardless. With Ace rooted to the stage in his six-inch stack heels, his guitar begins to rise into the air, but it sounds like he's still playing it.

I am the Lord of the Wastelands.

The guitar flies thirty feet in the air above him. It swings around making whooshing noises. Then it comes back down, Ace hauls it around his giant silver shoulders, the rest of the boys come back on, and they all polish off "Shock Me."

Paul Stanley and Peter Criss do solos too, but they're not half as exciting. Stanley does a vocal solo as well. These take guts, so don't laugh.

All this soloing takes a fair amount of ego. In extreme cases, this ego spills over into whole albums of solos. Let's get this bit over with—I'm starting to feel sick.

The blame for this sort of thing, as usual, lies squarely at the door of the guitaring fraternity. Some of these guitarists were getting too good to be locked into the traditional song-based way of doing things. They felt they'd outgrown the concept of what bands were for. Or rather, knowing deep down that they couldn't completely dispense with a backing group, they went about rebuilding the focus of the band with the guitar as star. No, the guita*rist* as star.

And I command thee to kneel.

An exercise: I'll log onto the Amazon website, pull out one of these guitar albums (there are, depressingly, hundreds of them), and, using the "People who bought this item also bought . . ." facility, see what other albums these guys are buying. This should illustrate the partisanship of fans of severe instrumentalism.

I'll begin at one I actually own: Steve Vai's *Passion and Warfare.* (It's boring, in case you wondered.) I'll include a few genuine unedited extracts from one of the album's reviewers, too.

People who bought *Passion and Warfare* also bought:

Joe Satriani—*Surfing with the Alien*: ". . . essential for all fans of shredding . . ."

Tony MacAlpine—*Maximum Security*: "Tony . . . plays Chopin pieces beautifully, on distorted guitar . . ."

Vinnie Moore—*Mind's Eye*: ". . . it's incredible how fast this guy can play sometimes . . ."

Marty Friedman—*Dragon's Kiss:* "I think this is best among the best album in the Instrumentel rock of world"

Yngwie Malmsteen—*Concerto Suite for Electric Guitar:* "As you listen to this album, you will definitely know why they call him (The man with the lightning fast fingers)"

Jason Becker—*Perpetual Burn:* "His extreme melodic sensibility is very evident, even through some of the sillier wanking passages . . ."

Al DiMeola—*Elegant Gypsy:* "They say women get really turned on watching Al DiMeola on stage (because his fingers are so fast) but there is more to this brilliant guitarist than just technical ability. Be warned, first of all, that this is an instrumental album from start to finish. Some people, for some absurd reason, don't like instrumentals."

Come Taste the Band

Rag 'n' Bones officially hired Adrian to perform an extended guitar solo and to play on "Spirit of Radio." As I was distinctly unable
to perform either of those two tasks, I had no option but to swallow my pride and to live with it. But further oddities were afoot.
Owen phoned.

"I've got us some strippers!"

"What for?"

"For the show."

"Why?"

"To get their kits off! Naked girls! Rock and roll!"

"Alright then, if you insist."

Sue, the lady who led the ballet classes, got on particularly well
with Owen and Andy. One day Owen had told Sue how much
he'd like to get hold of some female dancers to stand on either side
of the stage and perform a striptease as we played. Sue said that so
long as they didn't properly strip, we could use her teenage daugh-
ter, Kate, and her friend Flora. By the time of the gig, Owen was
going out with Kate, who was just fifteen, and it all suddenly made
sense. Flora was fourteen and I left her well alone.

We (Owen) hired a PA system. It was expensive. In fact everything had begun to get expensive, and we were all being asked to
contribute to the cause, which we did with absolutely no grace,
especially Johnny. The fireworks were particularly costly, so we
decided to save them for the very end of the show.

"A skeleton next to a dustbin."

"A dustbin?"

"Maybe leaning on it. And smoking a cigarette with the other
hand, wearing a hat."

"What kind of hat?"

"A cool hat. Like my hat."

"Do you want the dustbin full of rubbish?"

"Yeah! Good idea."

My mother had agreed to design our poster. She sketched fish bones poking out the top of the dustbin. I sat next to her under the lamp.

"Cool!"

"Seb, why does the skeleton have to be smoking a cigarette? Is it because you think it'll only be a cool skeleton if it's smoking?"

"It's not my fault that that makes it cool."

"So you do think it's cool to smoke. It really isn't, you know."

"Look, are you going to draw it smoking or not?"

"I suppose you want it drinking beer as well."

"Yeah, good idea, you could draw some empty beer cans around the bottom."

"Oh Seb."

"What?"

"I really don't know if I want to be a part of this. When lovely Owen asked me, he didn't say anything at all about it being a drinking and smoking skeleton. He was charming and just told me I could draw it however I liked. And now you're demanding I turn it into a skeleton I don't approve of."

"He would!"

"Lovely Owen."

"*Lovely?* He smokes more than me!"

"I'll bet he doesn't. I'll bet you're lying to try to make him look bad and make yourself look better."

"Anyway, this wasn't his idea, it was my idea!"

"I'm sure it was, dear."

"It was!"

"I'm sure it was, dear."

"It bloody was!"

"There, alright? He's holding a cigarette. Happy?"

"Can it be lit?"

In the end we scrapped the skeleton so that there was more room for our logo. As you can see, my mother did a great job with it—she spelled it out of scruffy bones. If you look closely you can see a list of added extras. We had no plans to actually utilize any tubas, we just needed something else to stick on the poster and *Instrumental Solos* didn't sound like that much of an attraction—to me especially, in that I wasn't going to be doing any. We thought writing *Tumultuous Tubas* was amusing, somewhat vaudevillian, but it ended up confusing people. *A big fuck-off metal gig in Winchester? Cool, I'll go! With fireworks! Strippers! Confetti! Tubas? I've changed my mind.*

Owen and I spent two nights running around the town center pasting up posters in imaginative and original locations: on every pillar in the main street, on mail boxes, on the windows of Wimpy, on the backsides of statues, tree trunks, doors of banks, in our parents' windows. Rain blurred the Bones' details. We went out again at one in the morning with waterproof marker pens, to make sure our details were indelible. Owen asked Johnny for some money for the photocopying and pens and was told to fuck off.

We got our gear to the theater a couple of days before the gig, rolled it to the back of the stage, and turned it all up as loud as it would go. Wow! It really sounded like something at this crazy echoing volume! The auditorium itself was in the shape of an amphithe-

A *Night of Excess* IN THE
JOHN STRIPE THEATRE
(*KING ALFRED'S COLLEGE, WINCHESTER*)
FRI. DECEMBER 16TH

STRIPPING STRAPPERS
CONFETTI CANNONS
TUMULTUOUS TUBAS
PYROTECHNIC PIZAZZ

RAG 'N' BONES

An ear-splitting Exposé of Sleaze Culture

ADMISSION £2·00   **8·0** O'CLOCK

Tickets through association or at the door.   BAR AVAILABLE

ater, so the audience were to gaze down upon our shaggy heads while we performed; we were already anticipating their terrifying horseshoe presence. We practiced with cold hands while gales and rain whipped outside, shy under the shifting spotlights. Occasionally we would jump politely off our allocated trestles and grin at our daring. We didn't discuss any formal stage moves. Maybe we thought that with the crowd fired up and the Bones pumpin' it out to the max, we'd all spontaneously *rock out.* Whatever the case, we were too shit-scared to attempt to do anything about it. Choreography was the least of our worries.

Chapter Nine

two minutes to midnight

ecember 16, 1988: Rag 'n' Bones' D-Day had finally arrived. We applied our makeup in huge dressing rooms with lightbulb-rimmed mirrors, troweling on the foundation with help from the child strippers, covering up the bags under our sleep-deprived eyes. People were everywhere—we didn't know half of them. Johnny's mates? Danny's? All our friends were enjoying the edgy backstage vibe, sitting in sinks drinking cans of beer and complaining about the clouds of hairspray we hissed out with sticky fingers. I wiped bright red lipstick around a permanent wavering cigarette. Dominic and Mark kept poking their heads out round the velvet curtain to check how the dim auditorium was filling up.

"There's more of us back here!" sniggered Dominic.

Owen was pacing back and forth, orange rags hanging from his open-waisted white shirt, trying to memorize the lyrics to "Walk this Way," which he still hadn't learned. I'd written them out for him a few nights before.

"If I forget them again, I'll just hold the piece of paper surreptitiously and read them out. Don't worry about it."

"How?"

"Look, calm down, I'll disguise it somehow. Has anyone seen Andy? I"ve got the sheet music for *The Four Seasons*."

Instead of an intro tape, Andy was going to play a selection of Vivaldi in the dark on his synth. We'd pressed buttons trying to get the keyboard to sound like violins, but it carried on sounding synthy.

I trailed behind Owen with the lyrics that he'd put down again.

"Owen, please don't refer to the audience as 'Winchester' at any stage tonight. OK?"

"Yeah, yeah, whatever."

"As in, '*Good evening Winchester, are you ready to rock?*' Don't say that. It's cheesy."

"Yeah sure. Andy!" He surged away.

I ran into Danny looking relaxed and aloof—the bastard.

John Osbourne came down in his pajamas and flat cap to tell us we were due on in ten minutes. We could hear the audience chattering. I lost contact with my legs—they'd both turned to jelly. I needed a rock to hold onto, so I searched for Johnny. He was standing in the shadows, hiding behind a giant fog of Benson & Hedges.

"Johnny! So glad I've found you! Feeling confident, yeah?"

"I'm completely fucking shitting myself."

"Oh no, Johnny, no. You can't be."

He said he was off to puke in the bathroom.

I retired to my dressing room to stiffen my hair and smoke a final cigarette in the men's room. My mascara was starting to sting. I came out making involuntary bird noises in my throat and walked straight into my mother and father, Fa with an expression of wry amusement, Small looking nervous. Fa held his hands sarcastically behind his back, like a sergeant major.

"Look at the bloody state of you!"

"Not now, Fa. *Please* not now."

"I hardly recognized you! Thought you were a—"

"A girl, yes I know."

He said hello to Owen and the rest of the 'Bones. Everybody stopped briefly to chat politely, as one does with parents. *Yes Mrs. Hunter, we are excited. Yes, quite nervous! Oh no I don't think it'll be too loud for you! I certainly hope not! Of course you can use the ladies room. It's just this way.* My mother warned me not to smoke onstage. I pushed them out through the curtain, and then it was just the five of us; our hangers-on were slouching in their seats waiting for us to fuck up. We peeped at the crowd who filled half the theater. Was that good or bad? we discussed, not listening to our own replies.

"Right then," said Owen.

"Right," said Andy.

Danny shrugged, Johnny air drummed half-heartedly. I'd got uncontrollable shakes.

Adrian arrived. He shook off the rain and snapped open his black guitar case to reveal a stunning paisley Fender Stratocaster. Adrian was older, and had a sharp nose and straight blond hair. He didn't acknowledge me—he hadn't even acknowledged me when they'd gone through "Spirit of Radio" earlier in the day. And his guitar solo. Three times. And made a fuss about the dry ice not being right.

It was time to show him what I was made of. Surely I was made of something by now. I'd learned the solos, honed my cues, and I looked much cooler than him and his twatty fawn suede tasseled jacket, but I'd had enough of being just edifice for once. I wanted people to think that I was good.

I wanted Adrian, Owen, and Andy to think I was good.

I wanted Fa to think I was good.

I went round the back of the curtain, put on my guitar, and stood in my allotted place alone in the dark while Andy synthed out *The Four Seasons*. "Winter," I believe it was, and it sounded pretty bad from where I was standing. Out in the auditorium I could see camera flashes going off. Still in darkness, I stepped up to my trestle and felt for the neck of my axe. Judas Priest's version of "Johnny B. Goode" was to begin with a bit of whack and fizz from me.

"Winter" finished.

Right then, this is it. Red spotlight bangs down onto my head. I lunge at my guitar and don't think I fuck it up.

Straight in there, dude!

Let's Get Rocked

Here are some recollections of the following hour or so.

The two ascending key changes toward the end of "Johnny B. Goode" gave everybody an early glimpse of Owen's vocal technique and the challenges the evening would place upon it.

We played "Walk this Way" as an instrumental except for the chorus. We all gave Owen evil looks when it became clear he wasn't going to attempt to sing it, but he was busy prancing on the central trestle, ignoring us. He shrieked the chorus dreadfully. Also during "Walk this Way," my bottom E-string detuned quite severely. I was so nervous that I didn't realize exactly what was wrong until we were about halfway into the song. I gave the tuning peg a quick tug and stepped onto the old wah-wah. This was the song with the strippers. They stripped to my horrendously out-of-tune guitar and no singing.

During "Magazine," Andy suddenly came over and stood next to me. I looked at him with startled wide eyes. *You're in the wrong place! Get back behind the synth!* Maybe he'd lost his mind. No, there just aren't any synths in "Magazine" (I wrote it, see?), so Andy had chosen to enhance his personal performance by strolling around the stage, grinning inanely, and jutting his head out in time with the music during the songs he wasn't a part of. He hadn't told anyone he had been going to do this. We disapproved but were currently busy.

Owen said ridiculous, embarrassing things between the songs.

"So you want to have a good time tonight? *Yeah? No?*"

(*silence*)

"No?"

(*silence*)

"Did you like that one? Did you?"

(*silence*)

"Alright Winchester. Are you ready for a dose of red hot rock 'n' roll? Are you *ready to rock?*"

(*silence*)

"We love you, Winchester! You guys are blowing my mind! You sure know how to *rock the house down!*"

(*silence*)

"Alright! This next one's called 'Magazine.' It's about a magazine."

(*silence*)

"Let's *party!* You all want to have a party, yeah? Yeah? No? You don't want to have a party? Alright then." (*pause*) "This one's called . . ."

(*Johnny raps echoing drumsticks.*)

We all spontaneously sat down during our power ballad "Just Because." Danny started it. Johnny, playing the drums, was sitting down already.

Throughout the other songs I strolled aimlessly around the stage without rhythm, grace, or poise, thinking I was the coolest. My mother gave me a terrible time for this afterward.

"Did you like it?" Breathless.

"What were you doing just wandering round the place like that?"

"Did you like it?"

"Not in time, or anything."

"Did you like 'Magazine'?"

"I couldn't tell one from the other."

"Fa? What did you think? Did you like it?"

Fa made a big show of laboriously removing giant clumps of cotton wool from his ears.

"Pardon?" he said, and everybody laughed.

During the interval we served a selection of red and white wine in the theater foyer. I don't know why we did this. I think we thought it was the right thing to do in a theater environment. The band mingled briefly with the audience. Mostly, though, we congratulated ourselves backstage and wondered if anyone from *Kerrang!* was in attendance. Well, I was wondering that.

The second half began with a solo acoustic spot from me, sitting on a trestle with Fa's twelve-string. I played a song I'd written called "Where Have All the Angels Gone?" It's moving, and profound.

Alone at the piano for his own solo spot, Owen serenaded the audience with a self-penned ditty called "The Apology Song." Enough said, I think.

We screeched back in with our killer instrumental, "Gravity 1086," but straight away I broke a guitar string, and screwed around behind the curtain for ten minutes trying to put a new one on. Meantime, Owen chatted to the crowd. It was one-way traffic out there. When I got back, Danny played it right for a change, but we were unsure if Owen had "lost" the crowd or not during the unscheduled time they spent together.

Adrian was introduced, came on with dry ice, and stood in the middle. He had a serious expression on his face and raised his right arm heavenward at regular intervals. I donned a pair of pink sunglasses, turned down the volume dial on my guitar, and mimed along to "Spirit of Radio." I don't know how many people noticed. All my friends knew because I'd told them. They booed Adrian when Owen thanked him at the end of the song, and I sniggered at the back of the stage in my shades.

We all left the stage for Adrian's guitar solo. When he had finished, he exited and we all came back on. There were some more boos from my friends, but generous applause elsewhere. I can only imagine Adrian's family were there in force.

A few people left their seats, came down to the stage, and started dancing and playing air guitar in the aisles. Owen got "lively" with them, then called everyone else down too but they chose to remain seated. Even I was getting a little slinky by now. Shuffle, shuffle, blush.

During our final encore, a cover version of Little Richard's "Tutti Frutti," the pyro and the cannons all went off, and confetti and stuff went everywhere. It was really cool.

We came offstage and I was the happiest I'd ever been. Bring on the groupies!

Rock 'n' Roll Heroes: The Rag 'n' Bones Sessions

Rag 'n' Bones's collective cloud nine lasted for several days. We were (we really were) real-life celebrities among certain people sitting on the divider on the main street. The punks chucked empty cider cans at us as usual.

We tried very hard to be modest about our success. We graciously told our friends that without them the whole thing wouldn't have been possible—*We're only able to be so brilliant because of you.* But after a few days of soaking it all up, we realized it was time to get a grip and start to play some proper shitholes. We saw it like this: big successful band deigns to play intimate club gig for the benefit of our most hardcore, obsessive fans. In other words, we had become, in the flash of an eye, completely deluded. Though Owen, of course, was deluded already.

There was only one other place in Winchester to play: a narrow pub behind the station with a boxy backroom for bands and no stage—the Railway Inn.

We wondered whether this pitiful venue could cope with all my guitars, the drum kit, the synth, three amplifiers plus Johnny. And would its low roof have the vertical capacity required to fit in all of my hair?

We weren't, however, the only band in town. There were two other groups, in fact three if I include the magnificently dreadful Ponderosa. We all loathed one another, but pretended to be friendly for the sake of the "scene."

The Daughters of the Late Colonel (great name, boys) were a monstrous four-piece. They were a college band who played to drunk college kids, and their Quo-like vocalist worked behind the photo counter in the local drugstore. Their guitar player, Ross,

made me sound like Eric Clapton, and looked like Marge
Simpson but with slightly lower hair. We laughed openly at his
technique. Their drummer, Baz, was really good, and attractive,
and we often tried to steal him. We'd go to their Railway Inn gigs
and applaud ironically and then share beers with them afterward.
We were already a bunch of arrogant bastards.

The other rival band were Picturehead. I never saw Picturehead live because I was too scared. They were dark and mysterious and from the dreaded local art college. They had posters that
we couldn't understand. They were Indie. And their drummer,
Nick, had turned Rag 'n' Bones down before we found Johnny.
Surely it was meant to be the other way round? It was Murphy's
law then that this bunch of assholes would soon change their
name to Revolver and enjoy proper commercial success up in
London at the height of the whole shoegazing scene. They were
on the cover of *NME* and *everything*.

We had to put down a deposit for our first gig at the Railway
Inn (did they not know who we were?), and our rehearsals
became more relaxed. Our first performance there was a sellout;
the joint was jumpin' and the crowd sweated and heaved.

Unfortunately my parents were there too, and their relationship
was now more tense than ever. My mother was about to leave my
father for good, and they'd recently split the house into two
halves. This domestic situation perhaps explains what my mother
did halfway through our performance. There was a bit of a jumpy-
up-and-downy thing going on—the crowd were moshing and
pogoing at the front—and the mike stands and PA speaker stacks
were starting to wobble. John Osbourne was there in his pajamas
again (he was now our official soundman), and he happily
punched any kids who got too close to his gear. I grinned shyly
at the protagonists, but something snapped inside my mother and
she dived fist-first into the melee. She parted the scrum using her
arms and elbows, and shrieked for them to stop it. "*Shut up and*

watch. You! Stop that jumping around! That's my son up there!" They stopped jumping and stared at her. We played on and I felt the hot lights on my face as my mother stood triumphantly, arms folded, surrounded by calm.

During the interval (every gig Rag 'n' Bones ever played had an interval, although we couldn't afford any more wine) I noticed a weaselly-looking guy standing by the toilet door with a box of cassette cases. Intrigued, I went to see what they were.

"Awroit, Seb!"

"Hello."

I didn't know this person. He was selling tapes. Hang on, tapes of us! He'd photocopied one of my mother's gig posters and written along the bottom in felt-tip in his own handwriting, *Rock 'n' Roll Heroes—The Rag 'n' Bones Sessions.*

"What the fuck is this?"

"Calm down, Seb, old mate. It's tapes, isn't it? Like an album! I'm knocking 'em out for ya!"

"Owen! *Owen!* Who is this horrible little man?"

"His name's Graham, and he seems to think he's our manager."

"Calm down, Seb, mate. Look! *Rock 'n' Roll Heroes.* See?" said Graham, pawing at his slimy wares. "*Heroes*, eh?"

This odious runt had managed to get his hands on one of our early rehearsal recordings. The really terrible ones, when we'd been trying to learn the songs on Owen's tape—the ones where we'd had no real idea of what we were playing at all. Outraged, I tried to throw the whole box into the air, but Owen grabbed hold of me.

"Look, just let him sell his stupid tapes. Then hopefully he'll fuck off and leave us alone."

"But who told him he was our manager?"

"No one. He's just doing it off his own back. I think he's trying to ingratiate himself with us so that we'll let him be our manager."

"I can't believe he's selling that . . . that shit. What if people listen to it?"

"There's nothing we can do about it. Now just calm down and let's go and finish the gig and then later we can tell him not to do it again."

"I'll punch him in the fucking face."

"That too, if you insist."

"I will!"

Graham gave me a grin and a shrug and went back to his line. We were about to go back on when my sister skipped up.

"Look what I've got!"

It was *Rock 'n' Roll Heroes—The Rag 'n' Bones Sessions*. I tried to snatch it from her.

"We've all got one. They're brilliant!"

I looked back at Graham and he winked at me. We were enemies already, despite the fact he'd just created Rag 'n' Bones's first ever *live album*, a metal tradition as pure as the driven snow. But then, maybe I was being too hard on him; after all, wasn't the live album a definitive, fundamental rung on the metal career ladder?

Double Live Albums

First of all, why not just single live albums? That's easy. You need a gatefold sleeve to be able to get the full effect of the band's amazing live show. Sometimes, though, instead of this wide-action photograph, it's a collage of tour posters, scattered backstage passes, an empty Jack Daniels bottle, some shots of roadies carrying flight cases, a selection of plectrums and old guitar strings, and some informal "on the road" band photos, including one band member standing in front of a Japanese road sign wearing sunglasses. In doing this, the band are giving you a significant insight into how it actually felt during *Hell and Back: Worldwide Tour, '74*. They're offering you the chance to soak up the soiled on-the-road atmosphere, just as they'd done with *She Drinks Pee, '73*, the year before; the one with the yellow limited-edition toilet tissue sleeve.

It's not a question of whether or not a metal band has released a double live album; the question is *how many?* Who do you think has released more live albums (all but one a double) than any other band in the history of popular music?

It's Iron Maiden. Here they all are.

Live After Death

A Real Live One

A Real Dead One

Live at Donington

Rock in Rio

Not only that, but there's also a mammoth six-CD commemorative collection of vintage live performances called *Eddie's Archive*, packaged in a silver-plated casket. Gulp! Maybe there *is* money in these here hills. Maybe all these metal bands recording extended live facsimiles of their expensive studio work makes sense—fiscal sense—after all.

What you have to appreciate is that when they play live, metal bands excel themselves. An edgy twenty minutes of attitude and aloofness followed by no hour-long encores, pyro, or merchandising just won't do. Such activity contravenes the metal Law; the honest and fundamental responsibility felt toward those paying through the turnstiles (and often through the nose) is that it's absolutely necessary to give a proper show. It's what they do best.

The word "show" is important, as that's the angle from which metal bands approach the concept of gigging. They want to give their tousled hair, tiger spandex, and Flying Vs the most appropriate visual backdrop possible. And this does not mean just turning up and letting the performance speak for itself. The performance comes about sixth on the list. What comes before it? Let's go through them step by step, in the guise of a fictional band.

The tour's all booked up. We're starting with a string of dates in Germany, beginning in Heidelberg. Our fleet of buses has arrived at the venue, and roadies wearing black vests, sunglasses, and ponytails are unloading our gear into the empty hall.

First we need to unpack the Marshalls. They're easily the most important thing—number one on the list. There are loads of them, in fact there's really no end to how many you can use—the more the merrier. And a single line of them along the back of the stage won't do. You need to pile them up on top of each other like a giant dam of black nylon mesh. They're expensive, so lots of bands just use ordinary black speaker cabinets and stick a Marshall logo on the front with glue. And even if they are real, they're never all plugged in. That would be pointless, that's what the venue's PA system is there for.

Why heavy metal is so in awe of this particular brand of amplifier remains a mystery. As far as I'm aware, Marshall speakers aren't any louder than, say, Peaveys or Ampegs, but over the years they've become heavy metal's standard issue; the genre's khaki fatigues if you like, except, of course, they're *black*.

So we have our slab of Marshall amplifiers at the back of the stage—what comes next?

It's the props. Christ, where to start.

You've got to begin with the name of your last record, because that'll be your theme. Though before your imagination runs riot, we're talking about a limited number of themes here, this isn't Saatchi and Saatchi. We don't need to worry about anything that doesn't involve death, science fiction (but nothing "arty"), breasts (always good), violence, ancient mythology, or zombies. If you've given your latest album the title *Exploding Brain*, you're pretty much sorted on the props front. You just get craftsmen to construct a giant inflatable (has to be inflatable) exploding brain and hang it over the band while they play. And you can lift it up and down and side to side and make it wobble and stuff, too. Ditto if you called it *Big Steel Men, Crown of Blood,* or *Pigeon Attack.* These inflatables pretty much design themselves. But if you've given your album a more abstract title, like *Lunging Sodomy* for example, then you need to consult some "conceptual artists" (or your tour manager), and choose an inflatable that you feel will get across the essence of the album title. Remember, the audience will need to be able to make the connection between the two, or they won't understand what's going on. The *Lunging Sodomy* tour, and you've got an inflatable of a giant machine gun? *Eh?* But a massive blow-up backside being clutched either side by a pair of leather-gloved fists? *Of course. This is the* Lunging Sodomy *tour!* Everybody's happy, and we can sit back and enjoy the dramatic effect.

Since Eddie the Head features on all of Iron Maiden's album covers, you might be worrying about how the band managed to stay ahead of the game. How could they find a new way of presenting the same thing inflatably onstage every year? Did they leave him at home a few times? Did they have a spaceship or something else instead?

No, they did not. They dressed Eddie up. The *Piece of Mind* tour—Eddie's giant brain; *Powerslave*—Egyptian Eddie (as on album sleeve); *Somewhere in Time*—Android Eddie (ditto). And so on.

AC/DC, as well as always having Angus on the front of their albums, also gave their records ambiguous titles, like *Ballbreaker.* That one's easy enough: a flying demolition ball that swings around the place, and the usual giant blow-up Angus. But they have another regular inflatable, which comes out during their most famous song, "Whole Lotta Rosie" (a song about a woman with big bosoms). It's a huge inflatable woman with a gigantic pair of breasts that lumber and shift in the air while the crowd, as one, chant Angus's name. When AC/DC have finished the

Rosie

Hell's Bell

song, roadies get to work on the ropes and tug Rosie back in.

Alice Cooper, despite shunning inflatables, was undoubtedly the master of the onstage prop. He had a big snake, a dwarf that he would torture, a noose and gallows with which to hang himself, a guillotine, a sexy nurse, and more besides, depending on the funds available that year. All of them were capable of delivering serious injury if anything went wrong. He nearly died on stage many times, and in more ways than one.

For our demonstration show here tonight, we'll say we called our album *Deadly Pair*, and we'll go with a pair of giant inflatable zombie breasts, in homage to the DC. So far, so good. We've got our Marshalls and we've got our inflatable breasts. What's next?

The lights and the pyro. Lights—as many as the roof can support without collapsing. Motorhead released an album titled *Bomber*, so they designed the lighting rig in the shape of a WWII bomber. During the title track, the rig moved around slightly and gave the impression of "bombing" the group. And pyro (i.e., pyrotechnics): fireworks, flashbombs, shooting flame, glitterbombs, smoke, lasers—the kitchen sink. In metal, it's Millennium Night every night. Def Leppard even named an album after their love of the stuff: *Pyromania*.

Always use as much as you can afford to, or as much as the local council will allow you. Things can go wrong. Band members regularly miss their cues and are standing in the wrong place at the moment the concussion bomb detonates during the key-change right before the penultimate chorus. Deafened, burned, blinded, maimed—it's happened to the best of them.

What's next? Maybe this ought to have been top of the pile: *volume.* The venue's local council will have a noise-level restriction that dictates how loud you can go, and it's always been metal bands' proud duty to monstrously exceed it, thus incurring a heavy fine. Pay it. The consequences of your audience leaving the show complaining that you were too quiet are too humiliating to contemplate. The only rule worth remembering is that if you can still hear yourself think, then you're not playing loud enough. Even if you've been half-deafened by your amps over the years, you still have no choice but to stand and endure your own perpetual white noise, which is why the majority of metal musicians wear earplugs onstage. These sorts of sound levels have always been useful, because if mistakes are made, no one will ever have the slightest idea. Volume is an excellent smokescreen for any substandard musicianship.

Last on our list, just a shade more important than the performance itself, are the *ramps.*

If you think it's OK just to stand in your designated zone on the stage and get on with playing your instrument while throwing out the occasional metal shape, you'd be completely wrong. The reason you're wearing big white sneakers is to cover every last square inch of stage space that you can. The stage has to be turned into a kind of multilevel adventure playground, and to do this it needs as many ramps as possible. With its plinths, walkways, hydraulic platforms, moving-part drum risers, and those boringly static microphone stands, there's a lot of PE to get through. The ramps are needed to link up the various regions of the stage, and should be painted in garish horizontal stripes, because they reflect well off the lights.

We're finally ready. Now we can stand in the wings clutching our guitars while the intro tape plays "Carmina Burana" to an expectant and pumped-up crowd, and be confident that the Marshalls, the zombie breast inflatable, the pyro, the decibel count, and the ramps are all in place, so we can concentrate on doing our best with our musical repertoire.

In the middle of the crowd, sat next to the soundman at the mixing desk, is an engineer, his eyes running over a bank of LEDs. He's recording the performance. He'll record every show on the tour, so that at the end he can collate the most competent interpretations into a single definitive running order, which will eventually be released as the double live album.

There's a standard format, generally adhered to, when compiling your live album's endless selection of tracks. This means the band don't have to make any awkward decisions of their own. All that's required is a frustrating emphasis on songs from their most recent record, which has often been a dud, hence this double live album as an apology to their fans. To remind them that *Hey, forget that last album—the producer hated us—he sabotaged the drum sound and it was his idea to put the synths on there. It's the live arena where we really shine. Treading the boards and sweating buckets. Direct to you. Direct for you. We love you, fans. Please buy this new double live album. It's slightly different to the one we did three years ago, honest.*

Actually, that'll do just fine as your sleeve notes.

Sometimes, though, metal bands get a little above their station and commission a music magazine writer to pen a little something about how extraordinary this tour was (and how extraordinarily down to earth and *like us* the band are), in unnecessarily purple prose. It's as if the band have said to the writer, *Go on, Mark, write something really snazzy. Sum us up.* Mark no doubt picks up a hefty commission for writing something like this:

> . . . so we leave Montgomery, Indiana, under another scorching moon with the wind in our hair and the craziest

kids the band have ever screamed at in our dusty wake calling us back to play "Kill the Bitch" just one more time, like
a beer-soaked Jamez deStarlite did last night serenading just
the two of us with his trousers round his ankles and his
trusty Gibson in a Wilmslow Arena toilet cubicle at 6 A.M.,
and which I have to say whistles around my ears even now
as the bus chews up the desert miles. It's hot out here in the
desert wilderness—the moon pushes us on with its beady
eyes. "Too Hot to Rock," we want to shout and scream
again, just like the boyz did tonight up there on their revolutionary new revolving stage, with the passion of a million
desert wolves chasing the bus like "Juicey" Preztini chases
the fine busty wenches of Arizona, now only a matter of
hours away from our silver bullet of excess—the most amazing band in the world ready to explode in my face—your
face—all over the bitch's face, like a thief in the night—of
what a night . . .

Even as the band's biggest fan, you still never got past the first
paragraph—after all, there were pictures of flight cases to be looking at.

So what's the most shit-hot, definitive heavy metal double live
album of all time, in the eyes of heavy metal experts? There's only
one answer. It's the definitive heavy metal band. It's the Maiden,
of course! It's *Live After Death*.

I remember the first time I heard it. I almost wept with pleasure.
Its sheer iconic force slammed through my mullet and down into
my cerebral cortex. It was October 14, 1985, and in the space
between Churchill's speech in the introduction (". . . *We shall fight
them on the beaches . . .*"), and "Aces High," my goosebumps flared
into mountains.

It was partly called *Live After Death* because the band had "killed"
Eddie the Head onstage in Dortmund during the final gig of their

previous tour. Bruce Dickinson, vocalist, dived on him from the drum riser, Steve Harris, bass, joined in, kicking Eddie's head in (the brain rolled out), and mild-mannered guitarist Dave Murray smashed his guitar over Eddie's head repeatedly, eventually breaking it (the guitar). All this was filmed for German television, but never broadcast as the authorities considered the sequence unnecessarily violent. It remains in their Dortmund vaults today. Another thing the Maiden did in Dortmund that weekend was challenge Def Leppard to a soccer match. Steve "Bomber" Harris scored four and injured two goalkeepers severely enough that they had to leave the field. The Maiden ended up deserved 4–2 winners. The Leps never asked for a rematch.

So for this new worldwide jaunt, Eddie would need resurrecting, even though on paper he was already a zombie. *Live After Death* was recorded on the *World Slavery Tour*, which encompassed twenty-eight countries—almost three hundred shows in total. On this tour alone the Maiden played to thirty million punters. That's an awful lot of spandex, sneakers, sweatbands, vests, tires, beers, miles, and punches in the air. The album came with a booklet in which they listed everything they got through on the tour: the number of guitar strings, cans of lager, bottles of water, stuff you didn't think you would ever want to know about the on-the-road lifestyles of the five members of Iron Maiden. I found it humbling, and read right to the bottom several times. By then I'd only ever got through about three guitar strings myself. The Maiden had got through about a million just on this one tour. What were they doing to their guitar strings?

The performances you hear on the actual record were recorded at the Los Angeles Long Beach Arena and, inevitably, Hammersmith Odeon. After nearly every song, Dickinson calls out, "*Scream for me, Long Beach!*"

And oh do they scream.

They will scream for him forever.

Black Shrine

There wasn't much screaming going on in the back room of the Railway Inn. Instead, our audience mooed like a herd of beery cows.

"I can't hear you!" coaxed Owen, so they mooed some more, and when the lowing faded to mumbles we started the next song. Two gigs and two spectacular triumphs. Rag 'n' Bones were hitting their stride.

"I'm leaving this stupid band," said Danny.

"Good," we said.

We replaced him with a young man called Edward. Edward told us proudly that he sang for the King's Singers choir. He had a neat side parting and wore a magenta V-neck jersey with grey slacks with heavy ironed creases. He was all we could find. Not only was he the squarest man in the whole goddamn town but he also kept having opinions. *Shut up*, we had to politely tell him, *and just play what we say.*

We booked another gig at the Railway, and as we were setting up that afternoon, in came Andy and Owen. We greeted one another as usual.

"Hi, Andy."

"No, sorry," said Andy.

"Pardon?" I replied.

"*Trapper.*"

"What?"

"My name's not Andy anymore, I've changed it. Call me Trapper. Trapper Ragg, with two Gs."

"*Trapper Ragg?*"

"Yes, please call me Trapper and not Andy, at all times."

"God, do I have to?"

"And Owen is now called Owen Bones."

I looked at Owen, who suddenly seemed busy with wires underneath Andy's synth.

"Are you?" I asked him.

"Um, yes. I, um . . . am, yes."

"Owen Bones and Trapper Ragg," I slowly repeated.

"Right," said Andy.

"But why not just be *Andy* Ragg. What's with this Trapper?"

"Andy Ragg sounds stupid."

Johnny coughed.

"Oh, I see. So you're like the 'Rag,' and Owen's the 'Bones.'"

"That's right."

"You can be '*n*,' if you like," said Owen, hilariously.

"Ha!" Inside, I seethed.

And for the next month or two, whenever anyone called him Andy, he'd angrily correct them. We loved calling him Trapper. We thought it was the funniest thing we'd ever heard. We tried to get his girlfriend to say it too, but she refused.

It was time for Owen to leave home too, so we decided to get an apartment together, which could double up as Rag 'n' Bones HQ. One day Dominic told me that the old people's home where his mother worked had a little independent apartment off to the side which was up for rent. It was a huge old Victorian building on Sleeper's Hill, a posh, steep private road. However, Dominic's mother had doubts about our solvency (rightly so seeing as Owen didn't have a job), so we walked up there and dazzled her with our slimy middle-class charm (our hair slicked back into ponytails), and eventually persuaded her to let us have it. It was tiny: two small rooms and a bathroom with just a toilet and a shower. There was still no way we could afford it, but it was very exciting. The band now had a pad.

My father's Saab was the grumbling removal van. He didn't help with my stuff, he just sat listening to the cricket on the car radio and smoking with the windows rolled up, which was lucky really, as Dominic was lying on the floor inside the apartment wearing just a pair of pants, stoned out of his mind.

Dominic and I had recently got into smoking dope. If I wasn't sponging Marmite off a founder's portrait at the college, I was with Dominic, lying on my back in the countryside somewhere, slack-jawed and giggling. He would come round to the Sleeper's Hill flat and we'd smoke dope and listen to old-fashioned stoner music and think we were radical mystics. The rest of the band disapproved of my new lifestyle. Owen wasn't at the flat much anyway; he'd virtually moved in to our teen stripper Kate's parents' house. Bizarrely, they treated him like a son, even though they had one already. I would go around there when I needed to eat, and drank whisky with Owen and Kate's father in their front room listening to Bob Dylan and watching illegal horror films. They scared the shit out of me (the films and Bob).

Dominic and I, poised to take soft drugs

Shortly after we moved in together, Owen met a strange, short troll of a man in a pub, whose name was Badger. He was a "character," so Owen, ever one for becoming excitable in the presence of a character, invited him to join the band. Badger turned up at the next rehearsal with a cheap guitar and asked if he could plug it into my amp, which he did anyway before I'd finished glaring at him. Not only did he have the shortest hair out of all of us, but he also wore a vest instead of a T-shirt. He couldn't play the guitar properly but did this very amusing duckwalk thing the whole time, while poking his tongue out. He made cockney wisecracks and Owen thought he was a comedy genius.

For our first gig at the Railway Inn as a six-piece, Owen

decided to dress up as Captain Caveman, startling not only the audience but us too. It turned out that it had been an accident—he'd emptied Kate's makeup bag while she was out shopping and smeared himself with all he could find, completely unsupervised, and then walked up to the Railway on his own, wearing a rug he'd found in a cupboard.

It was a suitably strange performance. A few days earlier, Owen and I had asked Edward, the new bassist, if he might trouble himself by wearing a pair of jeans for the gig, but he'd told us he didn't own a single pair. So we stuck him behind a pillar at the Railway, in the hope that nobody could see him, and gave Badger instructions to keep him wedged in. I don't know why we bothered, because as soon as our first note was struck, Badger went duck-walking off into the crowd (much to Owen's delight and the crowd's surprise), while Edward emerged from the pillar and stood with his chin-high bass center stage. I pouted in my lipstick and shoulder pads, deeply ashamed of my band—of Owen's caveman getup, this new short-haired wanker with his tongue hanging out, of the King's Singer square on the bass—this whole grisly freak show. How come there wasn't anyone else in town who looked like Sam Yaffa?

Trapper did his usual rooster walk during the synthless songs, and sang backing vocals into my mic with his arm around my shoulder. I told him to get off. At least my parents weren't here this time, I thought to myself. Sulking at half time, I smoked several joints with Dominic outside the fire exit. He consoled me by telling me that he didn't think Badger was cool and that he thought I was the cool one. I held the smoke in for as long as I could then exhaled and agreed with him, and went back in to tackle the second half, eyes blinking in the light. It took the rest of the guys about thirty seconds to realize that I was playing a completely different song. Johnny stopped playing, and I turned lazily around to see what the problem was. A Benson & Hedges quivered between his angry lips.

"What?" I drawled.

"Get it together, dickhead," he shouted. I fiddled blindly with my bright red guitar. As we resumed and began the one song Badger had brought to the group, "Black Shrine," I felt a kind of muso bliss seep over me. Dominic and I smiled at one another as my guitar solo transcended the crappy little room—it felt like this wave of sonic pleasure could go on forever! Oh shit, the band have stopped playing again.

I got a stern ticking off from Johnny and Trapper and somehow made it to the end of the set list.

Our manager Graham was there again, only he wasn't out manager.

"I haven't told him anything!" said Owen. "I don't know why he's going around telling everyone that."

After the show, the harsh realities of our mediocrity began to hit us for the first time. This time around, there was no postgig euphoria. We needed something to give us a lift, to get the rock 'n' roll fire flowing back through our veins. We decided that Johnny ought to compose a drum solo for the next gig.

"How long for, for fuck's sake?" he asked grumpily.

"Ten minutes?" Owen replied.

"Ten fucking minutes!" protested Johnny.

Nobody asked me to do one.

"And another thing," said Owen, with that sick theatrical curl in his voice. We stood smoking, waiting for his bullshit. "It's about time we made . . . ," and he paused for about ten seconds, ". . . an album."

Chapter Ten

trash can junkies

Owen persuaded us that making an album was easy, even without a record contract; he said we just needed to free up some cash. He went ahead and booked a recording studio up in London for two consecutive nights at a place called Vonn's, just off Holloway Road. We rented a van and asked Edward to drive, because he was the only one who had a license. The van arrived at Sleeper's Hill mid-afternoon, and I stumbled out with my guitar to be greeted by the sight of Graham sitting proudly in the front seat, smiling at me.

"Awroit Seb, mate! Hop in!"

"What's he doing here?"

"I'm your manager!"

"Owen?"

"Nothing to do with me, honest."

Johnny gave Graham the finger behind his back. Who the hell was this obnoxious little turd?

The drive took ages. We kept going the wrong way, and having to piss out of the side door because Edward wouldn't let us stop and offload the beer we'd been drinking. When we eventually arrived, we stood starstruck in the studio reception for five minutes. There were backlit fishtanks and an unsupervised fridge with beer in it. There was a pool table too, and Johnny got straight down to a game, by himself. It was already late evening; we were to work through until seven or eight in the morning in a side studio with a junior engineer and a 16-track machine, though most of us didn't know what any of that actually meant. We'd brought along a portable cassette recorder, to keep a kind of audio journal of our exciting trip. While we were still in the reception area, Trapper cruelly pressed record while Edward asked me what my song "Suicide" was actually about. He asked me this because in the van on the way up to the studio we'd decided to change the name of the band to the Trash Can Junkies, which was a line from the song. We'd all agreed that it made us sound much more dangerous and grown-up, but now they wanted me to contextualize it. The song was about nothing, of course; I'd just strung together a bunch of words that I thought sounded cool. I looked at the whirring tape machine.

"It's about, you know, this kid," I began uncertainly.

"Mmm hmm," said Edward, placing his hand under his chin. Everybody was listening now.

"You know, a rock 'n' roll kid."

"What's that exactly?"

"A kid, who's, you know, living on the fucking edge, man."

"Meaning?"

"You know, this kid's fucked up, and there's a girl, and he's a junkie, and they're, um, rock 'n' roll sort of thing."

"I see."

"Do you? Good. That's it then. Anyone for another beer?"

"But why is he fucked up?" asked Edward.

"I don't know." I stubbed out my cigarette on the arm of the sofa.

Mark, our good-natured engineer, told us that getting ten songs done was slightly ambitious, that we were more likely to end up with three at best.

"But we're here tomorrow night as well!"

"Is this your first time in a recording studio?"

"So what? Let's rock!"

The drums took about three hours to set up, and we quickly became bored. We repeatedly sent Graham to the garage to buy us food and more beer. Eventually it was time for us to lay our Junkie classics onto some wax. We'd forgotten to bring any amplifiers with us, so me, Badger, and Edward had to plug ourselves directly into the sound desk, and I complained for ages that the distortion didn't sound metal enough.

"OK, off you go. First song, take one," said Mark, ready to record.

"What, we all play together—at the same time?"

"Yes, and get on with it. Time's ticking away."

"But I thought what we did was record all the different instruments separately and then add them together afterward."

"We haven't got time for that, not if you want to do ten bloody songs. Now come on, get on with it—you're not Bon fucking Jovi."

We smiled at one another. That was true. Bon Jovi were shit.

Despite ourselves, by the end of the session at seven the next morning, we'd recorded virtually all the backing tracks. This meant that all we had to do the next night was record Owen's vocals. Mark kindly burned off cassettes of what we'd done so far, and we sat in reception with the morning light breaking through, ridiculously excited by what we'd created. We couldn't quite believe that it was us coming out of the little tape machine. We sounded fucking brilliant! What we were listening to could've been virtually anyone! Trapper phoned his parents and played some for them. They said yes, it sounds very nice.

Graham had done something managerial. He'd arranged cheap lodgings for us in a dilapidated B&B in Brixton. We all crashed in one big room on bunk beds, except Edward, who carefully removed a folded pair of pajamas from his small suitcase and repaired to the bathroom to climb into them in private. He came back and we laughed at him for ten minutes and then fell asleep with our mouths still open.

Next day, or rather night, apart from some godawful caterwauling on "Black Shrine," Owen acquitted himself with dignity. There wasn't much for the rest of us to do, apart from some ensemble fingersnaps during the first verse of Owen's song "Striptease Louise." We all piled into the recording booth, donned headphones, and gathered around the waist-high microphone, ready to click. We nodded confidently at one another as our cue approached.

Click, 2, 3, 4, *click*, 2, 3, 4, *click*, 2, *click*, 4, *click, click*, 3 . . .

"Hold on! Hold on!" Owen turned to the rest of us. "Who's fucking up the clicks?"

Nobody answered. We all looked at him innocently, and Mark rewound the tape ready for us to start again.

Click, 2, 3, 4, *click*, 2, 3, *click* . . .

"*Who's fucking up the clicks?*"

Mark's voice came over our headphones. "Erm, guys? I think I know who it is. I was watching this time, and, erm, it was Graham."

Eh? The little bastard had sneaked into the booth and was standing round the mike with us clicking, and nobody had even noticed.

"Get out, you little fucking prick."

"Aw, lads! Come off it! Can't I just stay in here with you boys and, like, pretend to click?"

"No. Get out. Fuck off and get us a cheese fucking sandwich."

We did the clicks.

Winchester, Saturday 2 P.M. I'm surging up the stairs to the dining hall just noticing that I've got my white coat on inside out. I was supposed to be at work over two hours ago, I've missed lunch altogether, and I can't hear any noise, so they must've washed everything up as well, which means I'm probably in the shit. The giant wooden doors slam behind me and I run tangled in the coat through to the back office, dripping with sweat and not having slept since we left the studio. We'd driven back to Winchester as quick as we could, which hadn't been quite quick enough.

"Mr. Beard wants to see you."

"Fuck, when?"

"Now."

Mr. Beard reminded me that I'd already received two written warnings for lateness, then gave me a lecture about responsibility and the workplace, and blathered on about my hair being unhygienic for ten minutes.

"Yes, Mr. Beard," I replied, trying to tie my hair up with an elastic band.

"So I'm afraid I'm going to have to let you go," he finished. "Your career with us has come to an end."

"What? You mean, like now?"

"As in this very minute."

"Is there any point in saying anything?"

"No."

Winchester, Saturday 7 P.M. I'm wandering through the town center wearing a violet petticoat with a wide-brimmed straw hat, minding my own business and quietly wondering how I'm going to get another job, when a cheery greeting comes from a pair of crew-cut men on the other side of the street, both holding bottles of Newcastle Brown Ale.

"Eh! Fockin' hippie! Eh!"

Oh no. Winchester had an army barracks at the top of the main street. When you've got dormitories full of squaddies let loose for the weekend, someone more 'distinctive" in appearance knows that the town center is a place to avoid come nightfall.

"Eh! Fockin' hippie! Eh!" I was well aware that I was the fockin' hippie they were referring to, but didn't feel like stopping to chat about it.

"Fockin' hippie!" They were crossing the road toward me now. Without breaking stride, one of them took my neck in a claw and banged my head against the plateglass window of Debenhams.

"Fockin' hippie."

I tried to smile but was unable to.

"D'yas wanna fockin' die?"

This is where it started to go wrong, because I didn't understand his accent, misheard him, and through my squashed mouth I replied, "Yes!"

They became excitable. "Yas does wannae fockin' die, aye? Ya wants to fockin' die!"

"Oh. No. I meant to say no!"

"Yas wants to fockin' die!" He banged my head against the glass repeatedly. With his free hand, he pulled out a serrated hunting knife—like Rambo's—and indented my Adam's Apple with its tip. It hurt.

"Yas wants to fockin' die, aye?" We were eye to eye; his looked pearly black like a shark's. All I could think to do was blink. His friend, who'd been lingering behind, took his bottle of Newcastle Brown Ale by its neck and smashed the lower half off against the curb. Where the fuck was everybody? This was the main street! The one with the broken bottle sidled alongside his friend and playfully jabbed the bottle into my chest and confirmed that, yes, I was going to die. By this time my mind had chosen hibernation; the pain from the knife and the glass felt distant and unreal. My head was banged back and forth methodically between Debenhams and the tip of the knife.

"Fock off!"

I was miles away, had stopped listening. They stopped banging my head and said "fock off" again.

"Pardon?"

"Fockin' fock off." He let go and we all looked at one another. I frowned and said, "What now?"

"*Fock off!*"

Oh! I took off to my right like a heron. I ran for a quarter of a mile and rolled underneath a car parked outside the Wessex Hotel and lay there holding my breath for twenty minutes.

Despite our manager Graham's undoubted talents at doing nothing and being annoying, we decided to take a gamble at shooting for the big league, the premier division. The Trash Can Junkies fired Graham. Fantastic! We replaced him with my father. Oh no! Fa's pub bullshit had won over Owen and Trapper. He said he had "contacts," "people in the know," and "friends in powerful places." This was exactly the sort of nonsense talk that Owen liked best, so despite my misgivings (and not inconsiderable pride), Fa was given the job.

At our next gig at the Railway Inn, Fa stood next to John Osbourne at the sound desk, nodding seriously with his arms crossed. He occasionally leaned over the board and attempted to fiddle with the switches and faders, but John swatted his hand away.

"Great gig, lads," he told us afterward. "Some good bass work there, Edward."

"Thank you. I thought so too."

"Great drumming, John." He was the only one who didn't call him Johnny.

Fa's first big idea was to get us signed to Virgin Records.

"Nice one, Tone!" said Owen.

"Mr. Hunter, that's great!" said Trapper.

When it emerged that the bloke he'd chatted to in the pub who'd worked somewhere within the Virgin establishment couldn't be tracked down again (or rather Fa couldn't be bothered to track him down), our expectations settled slightly.

"I've got another idea," said Fa at one of our frequent band meetings in the pub.

"What is it, Mr. Hunter?" asked Trapper excitedly.

"I'll phone Richard Branson myself."

"Brilliant!"

"Jesus Christ," I said through my cigarette.

At the next band meeting he claimed he'd made the call, but Mr.. Branson was abroad or something. Fa said he'd got snotty with the receptionist when she wouldn't give him details of where exactly Branson was staying.

"But anyway, never mind all that, I've a better idea."

"Brilliant!" exclaimed Trapper.

"I'm going to get you to play in Virgin Records' head office reception area, so that everyone that enters or exits the building will see you in action. They will then offer you a recording contract so that you can cut a disc. There'll be no escaping the Tin Can Junkies!"

"Trash," I said.

My father looked at me irritably. "What?"

"It's *Trash* Can Junkies, not *Tin* Can Junkies."

"That's what I said."

"No, you said *tin*."

"I said *trash*, Seb."

"That's a brilliant idea!" exclaimed Trapper.

"Oh yeah, brilliant," I said sarcastically. Everyone looked at me sourly.

I felt the band had become a bit of a joke. We were swollen and out of shape; we needed some of our fat trimmed off, to get rid of Badger, and preferably the synth. If we needed any synth on a track then Owen could have one set up at his side and play it (if he really had to). The only problem with this was that it would mean getting rid of Trapper, too. Owen heard me out and reluctantly agreed, so we decided to act fast. We called Badger first and fired him, then paid Trapper a visit. We told him we were sorry, but we were getting really serious about the band now, and serious meant no synths, and we hoped he understood that it wasn't personal, seeing as he was one of Owen's best friends and all. We offered him an olive branch.

"If you can learn to play the bass instead, you can rejoin the band and we can get rid of Edward. That would be perfect all round. Just the four of us, see?"

"But what on earth's wrong with my synth-playing all of a sudden?"

"It's not to do with your playing."

"So what is it then?"

Keyboards

"NO KEYBOARDS" is the ultimate metal cliché, the easiest thing for us to say. Keyboards have always been our natural enemy. I can define the metal world's collective attitude to these ugly black and white slabs of sonic compromise with a single word: *Lame*.

Lame: The kind of band that feels they need to augment their already puny sound by adding girly-whirly synth fluff over the top, like chocolate fucking sauce.

Lame: The moves the keyboard player makes onstage, up there in his caged crib, with *Roland* written on his (or *her*) piece.

Lame: The keyboardist's haircut: fluffy and balding.

Lame: The keyboardist's idiotic unfashionable sunglasses.

Lame: The keyboardist's cape.

Lame: Name one cool metal keyboard player ever.

Lame: Did any keyboardist ever customize their ivory plank-axes in a metal-stylee? No.

Lame: The sound keyboards make. The sound of lettuce.

Lame: The shapes keyboardists throw, i.e., no shapes whatsoever, other than "playing the piano" shape.

Lame: Rick Wakeman out of Yes.

Lame: The shapes keyboardists' mouths form at the height of their ridiculous splurges.

Keyboards aren't metal. Metal instruments have to be natural, honest, feral. Only after achieving these criteria is it OK to spray paint them with candy stripes and lightning and stuff. Guitars are made of solid maple or rosewood—hard woods—and have strings made of wound steel. Basses are the same but heavier. Drums are wood and taut skins, and you smack 'em with more wood, as hard as you can. Cymbals are bronze. Microphones are steel mesh on top of tubular iron.

Keyboards are warm and plastic, and if you look closely, they wobble.

Motorhead don't use keyboards. If Lemmy ever saw a keyboard, he'd vomit. Slayer couldn't even pronounce the word, let alone plug one in. In the mid-'80s some clever engineer designed the guitar synthesizer, but no one was fooled because it was made out of plastic and didn't have any strings. What did this revolutionary new instrument sound like? It sounded like a synth, of course!

Shit

Europe

If your hapless synth player's ego was really out of control (like Trapper's), they'd demand one of those keyboards-on-a-strap that became popular during the late '70s, so that they could run around the stage like a proper band member. These were essentially just your standard synth, but hung round your neck in a pathetic approximation of a real guitar. You saw them on MTV all the time.

This is a Roland Jupiter 8. It's an 8-voice poly-phonic synthesizer with a 61-note keyboard with 2 VCOs per voice. VCO1 is switchable between trian-gle, sawtooth, pulse, and square waves and can be switched between 4 octaves. VCO2 has the same options with the addition of a noise generator switch. The Jupiter 8 allows the VCOs to be synced.

The Jupiter 8 voice has two filters. In addition to its low-pass, resonant VCF, it has an adjustable, nonresonant, and nonmodulat-able high-pass filter. The VCF can be modulated by one of the envelopes, the LFO, and keyboard tracking.

This is a Roland System 100 modular synthesizer. The System 100 was a modular analogue monophonic synthesizer, a more affordable version of the System 700. The System 100 with one VCO per voice (or two with an expander), the machine was con-trolled by a 37-note keyboard. The 1976 models modular units were

comprised of: 101 the synthesizer, 102 expander; 103 mixer; 104 sequencer; 109 monitors; RV800 stereo reverb; GE810 graphic eq; and PH830 stereo phaser.

The Hindenberg Klaschundt Mk IV has a large tapered pink socket, enabling you to hook it up to a Flymo 65 Grassbuster, and comes with separate wheelbarrow attachment.

The classic Yamaha DX7. Owen played one of these. He wrote "Manhunt" on it. He turned its settings full-steam onto *MAGNIF-ICENT*.

In a section involving keyboards, it's inevitable that at some point we're going to pass the door of that dreadful plodding beast known as progressive rock, the synthesizer's natural home. If we tiptoe up to the gate and rest an ear softly against its rotten timbers, we can hear the following records playing within, in their eternal pomp and resplendent majesty:

The Lamb Lies Down on Broadway by Genesis
Foxtrot by Genesis

Nursery Cryme by Genesis
Trespass by Genesis
Moon Madness by Camel
Journey to the Centre of the Earth by Rick Wakeman

In the '70s, synths went crazy. Their popularity soared as technology raced ahead. These new machines demanded whole new lexicons of synthetic parpology. Synths started to resemble castles. Was Rick Wakeman actually onstage with the rest of Yes? *Tales from Topographic Oceans* sounded familiar—swollen and interminable—so the addled nerds in the crowd assumed he must be up there somewhere, behind all those banks of polyphonic gadgetry.

In the 1980s—the decade synonymous with the very concept of the synthesizer (the decade they even started to synthesize drums)—the machines shrank in size but sonically exploded. Foaming synths and splashy bright beats came to personify the era. Think Journey, Toto, Survivor, Foreigner, Asia, Giuffria, Night Ranger, Loverboy, Kansas, Boston, Europe, Bon Jovi, yuck. It's all synth-driven rock, and most of it, sadly, was bought by metal fans. They claimed to be unearthing further shades of expression, deeper emotions in their guitar music: "*A broader palate of colors, that's all. It's still really raunchy!*" they lied. "*It's just more melodic.*"

Bullshit.

For some reason, though, pianos in metal are fine.

Cherokee

After hearing the evidence, Trapper said he'd give it a go with the bass. He managed to borrow one from the Daughters of the Late Colonel and turned up at band practice the very next day having learned to play all our songs overnight. That's how clever Trapper is, and how easy the bass is. And our songs were really complicated, so fuck off.

Now we really kicked ass. We were a mean motherfucking foursome. Owen, Seb, Trapper, and Johnny. And were gonna get signed by Virgin! We were so stoked we booked a headlining gig at a community center in Basingstoke ten miles up the road, with a support band. Look at us, eh? Support bands! We hired a photographer to take our picture round the back of the flat in Sleeper's Hill.

Although we realized that playing a show outside Winchester was a gamble, we felt sure our reputation had spread and that Basingstoke must be gagging for some Junkie action by now. Confident and cocky, we hired a van and headed up the highway, metal mercenaries come to steal their bitches, wondering whether they'd be hotter than the ones in the Railway (they couldn't get much worse). We pulled up outside the community hall and found the support band we'd booked, Cherokee,

L–R: Owen, me, Trapper, Johnny. We're all smoking.

busy unloading their gear. They'd told Owen on the phone that they weren't bad, always happy to support someone decent. But as soon as we saw them, we realized we'd screwed up big-time.

"Oh my God," said Trapper.

"Shit."

"Turn the van around! Quick!"

But it was too late, they'd seen us.

Cherokee were the real deal. They all wore spandex. They all had long hair—and not only long, but layered too. Their guitarist had a whole rack of different axes. They had flight cases with *Cherokee* stenciled on them. Their drummer had a double-bass drum and could spin his sticks. We tried to hide Johnny in the van.

"Got a lot of people coming down for this tonight then?" their vocalist Pete asked us, jogging over in giant white sneakers.

"Um . . ." I looked at Owen.

"Some. You know. Some people," he said.

"Great," said Pete. "Can't wait to see you boys in action!"

"Likewise!" we all said nervously.

The Cherokee bassist set up his effects: pedals, spare instruments, and speaker stacks to the right of the vast stage. Trapper, who had been playing the bass just three days, watched him and drank his beer slowly.

At seven o'clock, it was time for Cherokee to take the stage.

"Your fans not here yet then?" chirped Pete. Apart from Cherokee, John Osbourne, and the five people behind the bar, the only Trash Can Junkie fans in the building were the four of us in the group. Cherokee fans were thin on the ground too; in fact fans were generally conspicuous by their absence. Cherokee did have a small gaggle of groupies, however, whose low, lacy tops we eyed hungrily.

"Erm, not yet, not yet," replied Owen. We sat politely on a bench along the side of the hall to watch Cherokee's performance. They played this empty room in Basingstoke like it was Hammersmith Odeon. Pete leapt around like a crazy ape, similar in style to Iron Maiden's Bruce Dickinson. And their guitar player was extraordinary. I had no idea how he did what he was doing. He was a genius! Their metal shapes were truly immaculate; had there been judges present, they'd all have held up signs with perfect tens. Their songs about dragons were epic; their songs about sleazy chicks were sleazy; their songs about the night were mysterious.

"Aren't they great!" said Johnny.

"They're fucking awesome," I returned. "That's the problem."

"Thank you, Basingstoke!" said Pete, with his foot on a monitor as "Demon Slut" halted on a sixpence.

We applauded from our bench.

By now it was obvious that nobody was going to show up and pay money to watch this kick-ass gig, but we were all too polite to mention it. Cherokee replaced us at the bar and we shuffled up to the stage and began. We were dreadful. We were clunking amateurs compared to them. I wanted to play facing the curtain behind us. Between our songs Owen said, "Thank you, Basingstoke!" too. We stopped after our sixth song and then the two bands mingled. Cherokee said nice, placating things to us.

"You boys rocked, yeah."

"Thank you." We'd never been so embarrassed in our lives.

"Yeah, you boys sure know how to rock like a motherfucker."

"Well I'm not sure we did, but thanks anyway."

"Oh you did." Yeah alright, shut up.

Their smiling guitarist came over to talk to me but I ran into the toilet.

As we drove home, we slagged them off.

"They were so unoriginal."

"They'll never get anywhere playing like that."

"The drummer had a stupid nose."

"He sang with an American accent."

Oh for God's sake. We *all* sang with American accents.

We decided that to become more competitive, we needed to make our songs more labyrinthine and difficult to play. Owen and I sat cross-legged in the park, in cut-off T-shirts and tight jeans, composing with acoustic guitars and Owen's notebook. I'd strum random chords, trying to come across as breezily talented, while Owen sat watching until I made a mistake. As soon as I did, he'd pounce.

"Stop! What was that chord you just played!"

"Sorry about that."

"No, it was genius! Do it again! It sounded sort of like a minor ninth on the augmented G. God, that was fantastic. Play it again!"

I'd stare at my fingers. "I can't. It was a mistake."

He'd pick up the other acoustic and fiddle with it. Owen couldn't really play the guitar but he sometimes liked to give it a try. He'd make a stab at a G chord but with wrong bits in it. I would do the same, moving my fingers into slightly different positions, until Owen would explode, "That's it!" I'd freeze my fingers, Owen would pronounce this bastard chord's official name, and there we were, ready to begin the song. Invariably, we were now in the hardest possible key for a guitarist to play in. The same process started all over again in the search for the following chord, then the next one, and so on, until the verse was finished. Now we just needed a stadium-sized chorus, but it would have to contain another weird twist in the middle. And a couple of time changes. Nothing could be straightforward. We did all this pointless stuff to show people that we were clever. *We're musos, see? Proper musicians. We sneer at your risible A to G to F to Gs. Feel the weight of a proper chord progression, bitch.* C#dmin to Eb7sus9th to D6minhangingbasket. Owen would top these technical masterpieces with a cutting, bitter lyrical critique of something he didn't know much about—the situation in El Salvador, say, or anal sex, if he was feeling lazy. He was a bad lyricist. He tried to be wry and postmodern but it never worked. Here are the lyrics to his "satire" on strippers, "Striptease Louise":

> *Don't want no, love and affection*
> *Don't want no, domestic confection*
> *All I wanna do, all I want from you*
> *Is my daily dose, of sex injection*
> *Put your leg up on a chair*
> *Run your fingers through my hair*
> *And gimme a sleazy piece of your striptease . . .*
> *LOUISE!*
>
> *When you work your way, through the all-male section*
> *And you point your finger, in my general direction*

All I can do, all I can feel
Is my King Kong, Eiffel Tower, steel-built erection
Put your leg up on a chair, run your fingers through my hair
And gimme a sleazy piece of your striptease . . .
LOUISE!
(GUITAR SOLO)
LOUISE!
(GUITAR SOLO)
LOUISE! YEAH! YEAH!
(REPEAT FIRST VERSE)
LOUISE! YEAH!

With Fa stuck indoors on the phone to Richard Branson, we killed time by playing yet more gigs at the Railway Inn. We were getting better, and tighter, and introducing our dazzling (and complicated) new songs into the set, but it was always the same collection of tragic metalheads who showed up. Just them, nobody else, except by accident. They weren't exactly a critical audience, but at least they could sing along to the catchier stuff now that they knew it so well. Owen loved getting everyone except Johnny to stop playing, and leading a crowd singalong on a chorus, working them up to fever pitch.

"C'mon Winchester! I wanna hear you *scream*! C'mon! Sing after me! *Steeeamroller!*"

"STEAMROLLER!" bellowed the leathery peasants, their plastic pints of lager spilling over excitedly.

"*Louder*, Winchester!"

"STEAMROLLER!"

"That's more like it! *C'mon!*"

"STEAMROLLER!"

"*Louder*! I want you to bring the fuckin' *roof* down!"

"STEAMROLLER!"

They could've gone on all night. I would stand to the side and enjoy a quick ciggie and despair at our knucklehead fans. Where were all the girls? I mean, my girlfriend Louise was there, but I was kind of sick of her by now and treated her like shit because it made my mates laugh. I'd casually insult her in front of them all, and she took it on the chin because she really liked me. When we played she stood over on my side where I could see her, and I rolled my eyes to illustrate my frustration with her constant attention. I was an asshole. But then Owen yelped, which meant it was time for us to crash back in, and time for me to step up to the mike for some "STEAMROLLER"s of my own.

To make matters worse, our album was still "unfinished," meaning that although it was pretty much ready for public consumption (for selling at our gigs and stuff), the ten songs were still rough around the edges. We paid for two more overdub-and-remix sessions in recording studios, but our songs would always sound worse at the end of a remix than they'd done at the start. And the bloody thing was beginning to sound dated. Richard Branson wasn't going to want to invest his life savings into that, we muttered bleakly, bent over rerecorded backing-vocal playbacks at 3 A.M. in deepest Portsmouth, running out of money yet again.

Even though the Trash Can Junkies were stalling badly on the release-date front, and we were getting bored of our fans instead of the other way around, there was one thing I could feel suitably proud of. I had thrown myself wholeheartedly into the belief that taking lots of drugs turned me into one supercool motherfucker.

Dominic and I had started hanging out with a guy named Bob, who took about a hundred times more drugs than we did, so we thought he was pretty grown-up and sorted. He was also the only person we knew that could be relied upon to always have some on him, so bumping into him in the town center was a pleasant, if graceless, experience. Bob eventually took us under his pharmaceutical wing because we were so complimentary about his stuff. We were, I guess, acceptable to hang out with for a little while, if he was bored, and we were cynical enough to laugh along at everything he said, so that he'd occasionally hand over his large, conical joint.

Back at the Sleeper's Hill apartment, stoned and listening to the Doors, Bob would regale us with tales of other drugs. We sat mesmerized while he span urban myths about acid and angel dust, mushrooms and mescaline. Then he'd turn up at the flat with fifteen-year-old punks we didn't know, who'd tell us how good sex was on acid and show us needle marks on their arms. The punks sat on my bed, which I didn't like, but I didn't say anything because they were from rough neighborhoods and had three-foot-high green mohicans and CRASS painted onto their lapels with correction fluid. Then they took advantage of my befuddled state by trying to steal all my stuff. But I believed this was an important part of my education, the price to be paid for ending up a cool drugs person, like Lemmy or Keith Richards.

We played another gig at the Railway Inn, and afterward somehow sneaked a whole case of Newcastle Brown Ale back to the Sleeper's Hill apartment for excessive aftershow consumption. Bob, Dominic, and I were the first ones back, and we started on the beer.

"Right," said Bob. "Tonight's the night!"

"The night for what?" we asked. I still had all my makeup on. I never took it off after a show, not even in the shower. I just let it rub off over the week, until my face looked half-clown, half-tramp.

Bob flipped open his infamous drugs tin and handed us both a tiny square of clear plastic with a little black dot in the middle.

"Black microdots," said Bob. "Acid."

"Ah!" We peered at it. "At last!" Bob had been promising us acid for ages, but kept telling us he wanted to wait until he got hold of some stuff that would blow our fucking heads off.

We chewed on the microdots and waited. Owen came back and had one too but promptly fell asleep.

Fifteen minutes later, I could feel it kicking in. We all laughed uproariously for a while, slightly out of control. Then Bob demonstrated a clever trick that added trails to a moving hand, which we all repeated while cooing. Then Bob did a trick where he slowed his voice right down, so it was like we were all talking in slow motion. Wow! It was amazing!

Then he said, "But this is what it's really all about." And suddenly there we all were. The three of us and a new level of consciousness. The fifth dimension. It was quite staggering. Dominic and I said, *Yes of course! It all makes sense now! I can't believe we never saw this before!* Dominic's aura was green and Bob's was orange, and I couldn't tell what color mine was, but maybe it was blue. We pointed at one another, and said *Yeeeeeeessssssss* a lot. Then my brain began a roller-coaster ride. I had no idea where we were heading but my neural momentum was unstoppable. My eyes were open but I was suddenly racing down multicolored tubing at a million miles an hour; my consciousness blasted down thick metaphysical cables, going somewhere at terrifying velocity. Until suddenly, *blam*—a valve severed. There was a muffled nuclear explosion inside my head.

Shit.

My eyes were wide and Bob and I were staring at one another. *Something really bad has gone down. Hasn't it?* Bob could see into my head—he was horrified. "That's not supposed to happen," he said.

I began to flush with panic as the scale of my fuck-up reverberated between us. I was an LSD disaster already. Bob shook his head in despair and turned away, saying that I was going to have to start all over again. Start what? He seemed to be suggesting that what had just happened meant *everything*, but I had no idea what this everything really meant. I wanted to ask him a zillion questions, but he'd turned away and was grimacing meaningfully at Dominic.

Meanwhile I was getting steadily worse. I couldn't move. The aftermath of this grisly roller-coaster ride was running cold through my synapses. I was alone. Bob and Dominic seemed fine, slack-jawed but fine. I wanted to die, was desperate for it to end, but Bob said we had at least five more hours to go. I would have killed myself at this point if I'd been able to physically do so. That would've been a relief. I ought to have been hospitalized—I went right off the end of the psychotic scale, right down the fucking drain.

Somehow I inched through it, and a few miserable hours later I banished myself to Owen's room, where I lay sprawled on his bed. What did he mean I was going to have to start all over again? What, my whole life? Why? I didn't understand.

I must've fallen asleep as the morning sun clawed through the trees and into the curtainless bay windows. I woke up later to find Dominic and Bob smoking dope in my room, listening to Guns N' Roses. I went in to join them. I asked dazed questions about what had happened the night before, but Bob deflected them all, and soon we were all stoned and back to normal.

Round at Bob's house a few days later, they persuaded me to do it again.

"It's much weaker this time," said Bob.

"OK," I said, like a complete dullard.

It was worse, if such a thing was possible. After about a half-hour of it, I staggered upstairs and lay thrashing about on a double bed. Bob followed me to try and bring me out of it, but after an exploratory word of comfort he saw quite clearly the circle of hell I was operating in, and went back downstairs, muttering doomy prognosis over his shoulder. Later I tumbled back downstairs but the others had left, so I watched television through burning corneas. I can't remember anything else about it.

I didn't take acid again after that. It kind of ruined me. I was a Grade-B casualty, like the ones in Bob's urban myths we used to laugh about. I was Winchester's very own little Syd Barrett. I slowly pieced my head together, and I'm OK again these days, but the subsequent ten years had paranoia and mental anguish in spades. It hangs over everything you'll read from here on like a hair-triggered shadow, informing every move I made. What had happened back there on the roller-coaster? What did I do wrong? Why the atom bomb? Afterward I had trouble meeting people's eyes. I changed. It was a specific type of phobia: I became scared of my own consciousness; scared of my own cannibalistic thought processes—thought process*ing*. I would quite literally attempt to flee from my own neurological pulsing, to mentally outrun the gaping black hole that had taken over my every waking thought. It was extremely hard work and it pretty much took me over.

I stopped smoking dope. I stopped taking anything psychoactive. And I drank more alcohol, which dulled it slightly.

Can't Stop the Rock

The Trash Can Junkies wanted their revenge on Basingstoke, and this time we planned our assault like master tacticians. This time we were going to *kick ass.*

Owen hired a coach and we filled it with our Winchester fans and provided them with cans of cheap lager. The Junkies sat importantly at the front with the grumpy middle-aged driver, and we all partied hard through the short trip up the highway, with our fans at the back chanting "STEAMROLLER!" and waving their cans at other drivers.

Twenty minutes later we arrived at the Royal Oak public house in Basingstoke, where we set up our gear while our coachload of fans got shit-faced. My sister had come up with us, she was going to tape the show for another live album—a just-for-the-hardcore-fans sort of thing. We began, and the six Basingstoke natives stood on one side of the room, while our lot fell about spilling their beer and singing all the words slightly wrong. By now, we were a well-oiled, well-drilled machine, and our shows were reasonably professional (I'd even learnt how to play the introduction to "Sweet Child o' Mine," after a much younger rival guitarist had shown me how). Onstage that night, I made a complete mess of it, but hey, they got the gist. We'd also started to cover AC/DC's classic "Whole Lotta Rosie," which we did well, although it was too high for Owen to sing properly. He hollered and squealed his way through it as the audience winced. If you're a DC fan, you'll know that on the live version on the *If You Want Blood, You Got It* album, the crowd chant out "Angus!" in the riff gaps at the start of the song. It's famous. When we played our version, the whole crowd chanted "Trapper!" instead. Trapper glared at them angrily.

At last we had conquered Basingstoke. Bringing the fans from Winchester had proved a masterstroke. Swollen with regional pride, we considered our next move. A nationwide tour? Bring out a range of Trash Can Junkie merchandise? Record another album? Yeah maybe, especially if Fa could get us that recording contract. We decided to consult our manager for his suggestions as to what we should do next. I wasn't holding my breath.

On paper, Fa was still managing us, though so far he hadn't done anything beyond the alleged Virgin phone call. We still met him regularly in the pub and listened to him babble on, and Trapper still grinned at him enthusiastically, but then he did that with everyone. This time, Fa suggested that we try for some support from local radio. He had a mate at Radio Solent who might be able to pull some strings. The only problem this time was that Radio Solent wasn't really a music station.

I was getting tired of this messing around. It was slowly becoming clear to me that the Trash Can Junkies weren't, after all, the true saviors of rock and roll that we'd originally assumed it would take us a few months to become. There had been no record labels rushing to sign us, no A&R men sniffing around at our gigs—in fact the only buzz surrounding us came from the flies in the filthy Sleeper's Hill apartment. My mind was turning to bigger things— things involving megastardom, fame, and significance. My glimpses of glamorous London—even Basingstoke—had made me realize that Winchester was small town, a backwater for nobodies. I began dreaming of bright lights, being in a kick-ass band where everyone wore make-up and hats and looked as cool as me, and nobody liked Rush or played the recorder.

"In the meantime, I think one more gig at the Railway Inn might be a good idea," said my father. "You never know who might be there."

Chapter eleven

night train

A week later, Owen and I were evicted from Sleeper's Hill for not paying the rent. In a desperate attempt to try and scrape together some cash, we decided to go busking on Winchester High Street. We sat crosslegged outside the Halifax Building Society with two guitars and Owen's brand-new mouth organ, and played half-hour boogie-woogies. In between his amateur honking, Owen yelled about his hard drinkin' woman, his mojo, and his lemon. We also played some of our own songs, but they didn't go down well with the passing shoppers. At the end of the afternoon we'd made just over three pounds. We bought some cigarettes, two packets of potato chips, and a copy of *Kerrang!*, and I walked home and spent the night at my parents' house.

I turned eighteen with my prospects in a considerably worse state than they'd been the year before. I was now homeless, getting welfare, poleaxed by the acid, and in a band that I didn't believe in anymore. To make myself feel better about things, I dyed my hair black, which looked very stylish and made me officially the coolest person in town. Owen and I spent more and more time talking about a glamorous life up in London—a life of chicks, Jack Daniels for breakfast, and glam metal dudes wandering around in Shockwaves hairspray and fishnets. But, we glumly agreed, there was no way we were going to get there without money.

I was starting to operate on a level of heightened delusion. My growing obsession with the glam rock bands I so aspired to was taking me over, to the exclusion of everything else. I began to resent the rest of the band for their lack of glam credentials: Johnny's short hair and beer gut, Trapper's short hair and nerdy enthusiasm, and Owen's complete lack of a stylistic cutting edge. Deep down, I knew that the Trash Can Junkies were rubbish. *They're holding me back*, I muttered to myself. If I left the band, then maybe Cherokee would pick me up, or I could advertise my services in *Kerrang!* Or, best of all, I could move up to London and finally join a band that actually took itself seriously.

Two weeks later, at a peak of aesthetic despair and desperate self-dramatization, I suddenly quit the Trash Can Junkies.

"Seriously?" asked Owen.

"I'm just too . . ." The moment was loaded with poignancy. ". . . cool."

"You can't just leave like that! We're the bloody Trash Can Junkies, for Christ's sake! What about all our fans?'

"Our fans are dickheads."

"Yeah, but they're *our* dickheads."

"They're yours now," I said dramatically. Owen phoned Trapper and Johnny. They were pissed off.

The Winchester grapevine immediately went into overdrive. *Did he jump or was he pushed?* I jumped, you stupid bastards! Don't say that! *Who'll replace him?* No one! I'm irreplaceable! All this was fascinating, until a week later, news emerged of something genuinely exciting: a proper rock festival was being staged on the outskirts of the city. It was the first Homelands Festival (a tradition that has continued to this day). And to compound my perfect timing, the organizers phoned up Owen and asked him whether the Trash Can Junkies fancied playing—third highest on the bill.

Oh that's fucking great.

"You probably regret leaving the band now, don't you?" said Trapper.

"My line is, officially, no comment," I replied.

"You dickhead," said Johnny.

One of the Trash Can Junkies's biggest fans—he'd been on the coach and knew all the words to "Magazine" (he thought they were profound)—was a young man called Simon. Simon had tight mousy curls, which he dyed platinum blond, and dressed in the latest metal fashions with lots of tasseled leather. Simon demanded that everybody call him Vince, because he considered himself the very likeness of Mötley Crüe's obnoxious vocalist Vince Neil, which he wasn't. He looked like a peroxide sheep. We called him Rinse.

Rinse said there was a spare room available in his house, which happened to be on Battery Hill—the roughest road in the roughest housing projects in town. Desperate for anywhere, I took it, moved my records and guitars in, and sat on the little single bed wondering where the hell I'd gone wrong in my behemoth career. I listened miserably to Rinse and family eating dinner downstairs at the dining room table. Rinse's mom pitied me and left a plate of food on the carpet outside my bedroom door and I gulped it down like a dog.

Later that evening, Rinse came into my bedroom for a chat. He was a few years younger and I was a bit of a hero to him, poor boy. He was a little starstruck that I was living in his house. I was just sitting on my bed, practicing my guitar. There was no Dominic or Bob anymore; they'd all gone off to take psychedelic drugs for a living, and I was suddenly socially alone.

"Seb?"

"Rinse?"

"Can I come in, mate?"

"I suppose."

He'd changed out of his work clothes, put on his metal clothes and some eyeliner, and given his hair a quick crimp. He sat on the floor below my window.

"Seb. Re-form the Junkies, mate."

"Oh, Rinse. How many times have we talked about this? I want a proper band, a London band, a band of serious rock 'n' rollers who all look like me. Johnny's never going to look like me, is he?"

Rinse looked down and nodded sadly. "But the Junkies were a great band though, Seb. Remember "Magazine"?"

"Yeah, Rinse, of course I remember 'Magazine,' man. But I need to move on. I need a new set of challenges." I needed to be in Hanoi Rocks, somehow, even though they'd split up about five years ago.

"Why don't you come and join Ponderosa?"

Ponderosa were Rinse's new band. They were appalling. Rinse was the singer. He talked into the microphone with a nasal American accent. Their guitar player was very widdly-widdly. Their drummer was a policeman with a moustache. This wasn't the first time Rinse had asked me to join. Each time I politely declined.

One day Rinse called a Winchester band summit round at his house—in fact it was in my bedroom. Thanks, Rinse. Owen arrived first, followed by the whole of Ponderosa. Owen and I were still close, despite the band's split (I was still trying to per-suade him to come to London with me, claiming it would be easier as a pair, but really because I was terrified of going alone). At that evening's inaugural Winchester band summit were Ponderosa, myself, and Owen. No other bands chose to participate, which was a shame for the summit, but fortunate for Rinse's mom's supply of biscuits. Rinse started proceedings in a suitably portentous fashion.

"OK. Who wants to go first?"

Ponderosa collectively eyed their shoes. Owen and I sat smirking.

"Anybody?" asked Rinse. "Or shall I begin myself?"

"You start," said Owen.

"Alright. I'd like to suggest that we, Ponderosa," he looked at me and Owen, "and not you two, ex-Trash Can Junkies, purchase a Filofax before the next meeting, for use for official Ponderosa band business."

"Hear hear," said Owen. I shushed him.

"Is everyone OK with that?" asked Rinse. We all nodded. Rinse, happy with the carried motion, wrote it into his diary. "Who's next?" he said.

Ponderosa looked back at their shoes.

"Nobody?" asked Rinse incredulously. "Nothing at all?"

Owen and I tried to look quizzical out of politeness, but eventually shook our heads.

"I've got a question," said Steve, Ponderosa's extremely butch bass player, who dyed his receding hair platinum blond and had a penchant for bright blue eyeshadow and weight training.

"Yes, Steve?"

"When's the next Winchester Band Summit?"

"Ah!" said Rinse. "Good question!" He flipped through the empty pages of his diary and eventually suggested a date approximately one month on, which everybody, after discussion, was fine with.

"Right. Excellent," said Rinse. "I've got a question to raise, actually."

The expectancy was palpable.

"Do the Trash Can Junkies have any plans to re-form?"

Owen and I looked at one another seriously for a moment, and then back at Rinse.

"No," said Owen.

"No plans," I said.

"No *plans*?" said Rinse, eyes narrowed. "So it might happen some time in the future then?"

"No," said Owen.

"What, *never*?" asked Rinse.

"Never," I said.

"Is that your final answer?"

"Yes it is."

"Definitely?"

"Definitively," said Owen.

Rinse transcribed the exchange and the summit petered to a close. Later that night Rinse came into my bedroom wearing his pajamas.

"How did you feel the Summit went today, Seb?"

"I thought it went fine, Rinse. Like clockwork."

"Good. Yes, me too. Productive."

"Yep."

"Good. I think the next one will be good as well."

"I do too."

"Good."

"Excellent."

He closed the door behind him and I went back to obsessing over what had happened with the acid. I was starting to worry that maybe my musical career had already peaked.

I half-heartedly tried to look for a job. I turned up at employment agencies looking as unemployable as I could, but the bastards would always send me on the same bloody mission—to the most terrifying old people's home in town, where everybody—staff included—was mad.

"Got any plans for tomorrow, Mr. Hunter? We don't want to interfere with your social life do we, Mr. Hunter?" They already hated me, the sarcastic bastards.

"No. I'm here because I want to work," I'd reply defiantly.

"Know where Woodlands is, do we, Mr. Hunter?"

"Oh, right, there again, huh?"

"Don't think you'll be feeling 'ill' again tomorrow then, Mr. Hunter?"

"I'm feeling fine, thanks actually."

"Because it would be nice if you could actually be bothered to show up, for once. How many times is it that you've not shown up at Woodlands due to these 'sudden illnesses'?"

"Is it twice?"

"*Six times.*"

"Like I said, I'm feeling fine. Woodlands it is!"

"Eight A.M. sharp. Can you remember where it is? Do you need me to draw you a map, Mr. Hunter?"

What a wanker this man was.

If you've seen the film *The Shining*, Woodlands was like the giant hotel in that, but on the flat and surrounded by acres of shimmering dew. It was very imposing. The journey involved a vicious dawn bike ride through outlying villages and gagging frozen fog, and every day I was nearly run over by speeding trucks. It felt like I'd done a whole day's work just getting there. I smoked Marlboros in the mist until I got my breath back, and hooked my hair into a contractual ponytail for my morning's wage.

I sweep the upper floors first, mesmerized by stark forest views from the single-glazed windows, and help myself to boiled sweets from the bedside tables until I make myself sick. The old people never smile, they never move, but their eyes follow you around the room. I discover that my broom is a better air guitar than my mop.

I take the smell of dying as a challenge, and strive to make it smell of fern and ice instead, and then I cycle home, warming in the midday sun, happy to go slow, and look forward to whatever the afternoon is to bring.

Next day I can't be bothered to get out of bed and get fired with *extreme rudeness*.

Fuck it. Owen and I decided to move to the capital the following week. Money be damned.

London! Take me!

With a week to go before we were due to leave town, I finally caved in to mounting pressure and the Junkies re-formed for the Homelands Festival. It would be an epic farewell performance. Rinse and his pals were joyous. The Junkies were back, and our egos swelled to fill the historical gap. A few hours before we were due onstage, I was still obsessing over which hat to wear for the show. I was torn between a floppy black felt hat and a red peaked cap like Izzy Stradlin from Guns N' Roses. Remembering how to play our songs was something I'd deal with later.

We arrived at the site (a field next to the recreation center) mid-afternoon, and observed the turnout with dismay. It was just a bunch of punks and hippies, drunk on cider with their dogs on the loose. There was a bunch of young trendies gathered around the edge of the field, and Rinse and his friends, but that was it. And it was raining. And the stage was very high and a good thirty feet away from the front-row barriers, which were empty. And, as if by fate, the band onstage were Cherokee.

"Hellooooooooo WINCHESTER!" boomed Pete, with a giant white sneaker perched on his monitor. "Are! You! Ready! To! ROCKANDFUCKINGROLLTONIGHT!!!"

"Fack orf!" shouted the hippies and punks.

Rinse and friends hurried down to the deserted crush barriers and started to headbang.

When we hit the stage at 5.30, the audience was slightly bigger, but only because they didn't want to miss headliners the Senseless Things, who were due on soon after. We filed onto the gritty, duct-taped stage and assumed hopeful positions. My floppy black hat flapped in the wind as I hit at my guitar, unable to hear anything except Johnny's warm-up thundering out of the monitors. There were some feeble yellow lights dangling above us. It was still raining. From the side of the stage we were given the signal to begin. All I could hear were some punks yelling, "Wankers!"

Suddenly there was some screaming feedback and Owen punched the air.

"Alright, Winchester!" he bellowed. "Say hello, and *goodbye*, to the Trash Can fucking Junkies!" He turned to me and frantically mouthed "start."

We played five songs. I couldn't hear anything except Johnny's bass drum and squalls of screaming feedback. I thought I could make out some isolated smatterings of applause between each number, but it might have been the wind.

At the end, Owen shouted, "GOODNIGHT!," dramatically threw down his microphone, and we all trooped off waving. Johnny threw his drumsticks into the crowd and they landed on some gravel. He went round and picked them up again.

The Trash Can Junkies were officially over.

Of all the Winchester goodbyes that followed, saying goodbye to Johnny was the hardest. Drunk, we all sat on a bench at the bottom of Sleeper's Hill and reminisced about the old times, even though they'd only been six months ago. Johnny sat between me and Owen with his head in his hands and wept, and we awkwardly patted his big back. We'd represented Johnny's best chance of making it, and here we were leaving him to a lifetime of Saturday night TV and "Spirit of Radio." We told him not to worry, that we'd come and see him from time to time, but he said, no, that would make it worse.

I loved Johnny so much. Even his drumming. I loved Trapper too, but he was always going to be OK. In fact he'd recently been offered a scholarship at the Royal College of Music, which he'd turned down in order to remain a Trash Can Junkie. To this day I still feel guilty about that. But Trapper was destined for something, so none of us really worried about him. Not least because we were extremely selfish.

So goodbye Johnny, farewell Trapper, and so long Winchester. And hello squalor.

Heavy Metal London

In 1990, heavy metal London was in full swing. It had its own landmarks, tourist spots, pubs, clubs, gig venues, and shopping, mainly based around east Soho. Here's a guided tour.

Shades was an underground record shop in St. Anne's Court, just off Wardour Street. It was a heavy metal institution. In this dingy, barely lit cellar lay racks and racks of (mostly imported) rare and collectible metal vinyl. The staff all looked like they were in Poison, and the volume level down there was needlessly extreme. When I'd visited London for odd weekends over the previous years, standing timidly in Shades was the closest I'd ever come to a sense of tribal belonging. Anybody else in Shades was a fellow soldier. There were no thrash/glam wars down here.

The Intrepid Fox pub on Wardour Street was one of two London boozing Meccas, especially for German and Scandinavian tourists. Again, frighteningly loud music was constantly played, and it doubled up as a haunt for goths, grebos, and general undesirables. On a good night, it looked exactly like the bar scene in *Star Wars*.

The Royal George, just off Charing Cross Road, was the other metal pub. This place was always popular on Saturday nights, right up until closing time, when the metallers headed into the late-night rock clubs. These days it's a sports pub.

Gossips was a chic Soho glam metal nightclub. Ray Zell, a *Kerrang!* writer, used to run it and DJ there, too. It was a regular hangout for girly bands like the Quireboys and The Grip.

Denmark Street, otherwise known as Tin Pan Alley, was where all the guitar shops were, and still are. Just off Charing Cross Road, this street was invaluable for selling your instruments when more drugs were required but royalties weren't forthcoming. Every shop window on Denmark Street was loaded with a mix of stunning antique and modern axes, which would attract countless drooling, daydreaming teenagers. All the staff in all the shops played in heavy metal bands, except the grumpy, balding owners.

Carnaby Street was where foreign tourists came to buy their metal T-shirts, bandannas, and other general accoutrements. Metal fans would wander up and down Carnaby Street at weekends if they had nothing better to do. You could buy anything from cheap bracelets to all-in-one yellow leather bodysuits to ten-inch stack-heeled boots, often all in the same shop.

The Great Frog was a tiny jewelry shop on Carnaby Street that specialized in heavy gothic-style silverware. Their best-known product was the giant silver skull ring. With a fistful of rings from the Great Frog, you'd never lose a fight in your life. Their jewelry has been proudly sported by the likes of Motorhead, Aerosmith and Metallica.

Kensington Market was a ramshackle indoor market opposite Hyde Park, where everybody bought their clothes. There were a lot of tattooists in the basement, and some secondhand record stalls around the edges.

Camden Market was a sprawling weekend version of Kensington Market, only without the specialist metal stalls. There was, however, plenty of jewelry up there, and many, much younger foreign metal fans. The more rarefied metaller wouldn't be seen dead in Camden Market at the weekend, unless he was buying a pair of cowboy boots in one of the few good shops along the east side of the main street, or he wanted to fuck a sixteen-year-old Japanese rock tourist.

The Marquee Club had recently opened in its new location on Charing Cross Road, moving a few hundred yards southeast from its original home on Wardour Street. Kiss inaugurated the new venue in 1990, deigning to play a club-sized venue instead of a stadium to honor the Marquee's special place in rock history. Other club-sized venues that regularly featured metal were the Borderline and the Camden Underworld.

The Hippodrome. This giant, sleazy nightclub on the corner of Leicester Square and Charing Cross Road hosted a heavy metal night once a week throughout 1991. I don't think the metal fans' beer-swilling antics sat well with its fancy ownership, so it was only a few months until the project was cancelled and the place filled up with losers once again.

The Walthamstow Royal Standard was the mangy dog's ass of the London metal scene. It was a pub in northeast London that put on shitty metal bands, but they used to advertise all over the place so you couldn't avoid hearing about it. If your band ever played the Royal Standard, you knew it was all over. Almost as bad was the Rock Garden in Covent Garden, which catered solely for tourists and had a cynical pay-to-play booking policy, at least for most of the bands, which meant you'd never heard of any of them.

But the music London was humming to in 1990 was the music I had come to play. The city was overrun with the skinny androgyny of glam metal. You couldn't escape it and, for five minutes, we were actually in fashion—before Kurt annihilated us all.

Lewd, Crude, and Tattooed: Glam!

Glam metal split everyone—you either loved it or you hated it. I thought it was the most exciting thing ever to happen to heavy metal. The problem was its shameless androgyny: looking like a woman wasn't very high up your average metaller's list of prorities. Inspired by the New York Dolls, Aerosmith, Kiss, Alice Cooper, and (don't yell at me, historians, you know it's true) Hanoi Rocks in the 1980s, clusters of pretty young things emerged; vampiric molls determined to express their stack-heeled angst with garish axes and charcoal smeared down their cheekbones. This new glam rock was bigger, (much) better, louder, sexier, more outrageous, more dangerous (was '70s glam ever dangerous? Gary Glitter, maybe), faster, thinner, more stylish and with flashier guitar solos. It was, however, just as technically dreadful as before. Often considerably worse.

When Mötley Crüe landed centerstage after their second album, *Shout at the Devil,* in 1985, many dismissed them as crude Kiss copyists, failing to anticipate the deluge of groups that were to follow. Although Mötley Crüe became huge, they really weren't very good. All they had going for them were their über-cool drug fiends Nikki Sixx and Tommy Lee, whose lifestyles were excessive enough to divert attention from their simplistic, barely competent music. They just about got away with their career.

The Los Angeles glam scene exploded in 1985, and, for a while, L.A. became the center of the heavy metal universe. Everybody moved there, especially Scandinavians. Record labels signed anyone that vaguely looked the part, which was, of course, relatively simple.

Poison were arguably the definitive hairspray band. Brett Michaels (vocals), CC Deville (guitars), Bobby Dall (basses—everything was always plural, to signify bogus multi-instrumentalism),

Poison

and Rikki Rocket (drums) pranced out in 1986, prompting sackfuls of hate mail before anyone had heard a note of their music. Here were four guys who decided to completely dump their masculinity. Even impressionable glam fans like me found them quite shocking to begin with. Not only were they the most feminine-looking men we'd ever seen (and we'd seen a few, believe me) but they winked in all their photos! Why did they do that? It was incredibly exciting, but we had to wait months to buy their debut album, *Look What the Cat Dragged In,* on import in Shades.

When Poison finally reached people's ears, the hate mail increased tenfold. *They can't even play their instruments!* raged the thrash metal fans. They had a point. CC Deville was terrible, that much was clear from the start of track one. The record sounded very cheaply made (which it was), and full of strange echo; it sounded raw, bare-boned, and there was yet more winking on the record sleeve. Despite this, it was, almost inevitably, a masterpiece. This cut-price neon bubblegum summed glam up. It was slightly embarrassing, but to me it was the ultimate voice of teen rebellion. Tears would form in the corners of my eyes as I grasped hard at my roll-on deodorant microphone and bellowed along with the highly emotive choruses. I could play all the songs on the guitar as well. They were an utter piece of piss.

Poison made it big. Americans like their tunes nice and simple and Brett, CC, Bobby, and Rikki sure did them proud. But then their much-delayed second album turned out to be crap. Their third was slightly better, and they had a worldwide smash with the soppy-assed ballad "Every Rose Has Its Thorn" then began—like everyone else—to take themselves much too seriously.

After Poison, but before Kurt, came a glut of limp-wristed pansies. Probably the most infamous was the frankly one-step-too-far Pretty Boy Floyd. Musically, they didn't even show up. They looked amazing, looked too good, but their record, *Leather Boyz with Electric Toyz*, was a mistake. Bands like the Floyd had run out of ideas (not that there were many in the first place), so they went for the biggest hair instead and hoped that would be enough. It wasn't. We're not that stupid.

There were all sorts of different types of glam band; it was like a giant pick 'n' mix. There was tattooed biker glam (Circus of Power); east coast glam (Vain and the Throbs); prog glam (Queensryche); porn glam (Easy Action); junkie glam (Faster Pussycat); junkie vampire glam (L.A. Guns); guys, it's not working glam (Jetboy—which was what Sam Yaffa was doing these days, for his sins. Oh Sam, *why?*); perv glam (Uncle Sam); thrash glam (Pantera); muso glam (Dokken); blues glam (Cinderella); Beatles glam (Enuff Z' Nuff); synth glam (House of Lords); knucklehead glam (Keel); charts glam (Warrant and Winger); and U.K. glam, which was just warming up, but was mostly rubbish.

There were, however, two great U.K. glam bands in the late '80s: Dogs d'Amour and Tigertailz, both at opposite ends of the genre. Tigertailz were a high-energy explosion of color, fizz, and melodic frivolity. They were Welsh and their bassist was named Pepsi. (On one of my first subway journeys on arriving in London, there he was, sitting reading *Sounds*. I clung to a hanging strap, staring down at him. He noticed, became disturbed at my attention, and changed cars at the next stop.) Tigertailz made one stone-cold classic single, "Love Bomb Baby," which lived up to its name and bombed. They were generally excellent but never really made it beyond the pages of *Kerrang!*, which was a shame. Their guitarist Jay Pepper looked exactly like a raccoon.

The Dogs

Dogs d'Amour were a different matter. The Dogs were possibly the coolest band in the history of the universe (at the time). They singlehandedly squared all of my outstanding circles. They looked amazing—no one anywhere in this book looked cooler than the Dogs, except late period Hanoi Rocks and Tyler/Perry in the late '70s.

Everyone was trying to pull off the Dogs's distinctive gypsy chic when I arrived in London. And they had cool names, too: Tyla (singer, songwriter, and sleeve artist); Jo Dog (guitar—not very talented); Bam Bam (drums—the coolest one); and there's always one, Steve James (bass). When we first saw their picture, we thought they looked too good to be true. They were *perfect.* All that the U.K. scene had thrown up before the Dogs had been dreary Rod Stewart copyists the Quireboys, dogged two-chord pantomime fools Wrathchild, and a pathetic trickle of nobodies from Coventry with a Z somewhere in their name. We held our breath as we dropped the needle onto debut Dogs single "How Come It Never Rains," and three-and-a-half minutes later, knew that our prayers had been answered. They had, indeed, come to save us.

Tyla sang about wine and women and blood and rain and death and empty bottles, much like Bob Dylan would've, had he been wearing cowboy boots, a stovepipe top hat, polka-dot shirt and been from Wolverhampton. Tyla was a poet of the times. Their music sounded authentic and lo-fi and carried knockout tunes. One of the stranger moments of the period was when the Dogs tumbled briefly over into the mainstream, and into Q magazine, which at the time was just a Dire Straits and Van Morrison newsletter. I had a friend named Geoff who methodically filed all his Qs in his bedroom and thought I was the saddest thing in the world, but when Q suddenly said that the Dogs had some merit, he was all over me and my records like a man without a soul dressed in black, which he was.

Their acoustic 10-inch EP, *Graveyard of Empty Bottles*, even got into the charts. Get off! They're ours!

And goddamn it, this brief fame went to their heads and quality control went down the drain. Tyla soon became a parody of himself—the new album sounded the same as the last one only worse, and his previously inspired vocabulary descended into repetitious cliché.

We wandered off. We still dressed like them, though. I dressed like the Dogs d'Amour for approximately four years. Once in the bathrooms of a West End rock club I was standing poised at a flooded urinal when in came Bam Bam, who took up position next to me. Oh my God it's Bam Bam! I couldn't piss. I stood there like a freak. He finished and departed while I stood disconsolately holding my jammed penis, deeply ashamed.

The Dogs re-formed a couple of years ago but it didn't go so well. So now Tyla, off the booze which had once defined him, is a solo artist. Q don't like him so much any more.

Lost in the City

Owen and I and our two bags of possessions arrived in London in February 1990, and crashed, unwanted, at Owen's sister's house in Wimbledon. From there, we decided, we would hone the final details of our advance toward the center of town. Owen used this time to book us two beds at a cheap backpackers hotel, round the back of Notting Hill Gate, while I didn't do very much at all except play my guitar. Exactly two days later, Owen's sister boot-ed us out and we headed to the hotel, where we were led to a large dormitory with rows of iron bunk beds. Unfortunately, I was only able to afford one night's stay, and on the second night I got caught sleeping under Owen's bunk and was kicked out. Owen congratulated me on becoming homeless within three days of our arrival in London.

I snuck back in later that evening and locked myself in a toilet halfway up a stairwell. I sat in the dark examining my options, which consisted of a) living on the street (but I knew deep down I was too much of a coward for that), and b) running back home to Small, and Johnny, and some yummy cheese on toast with black pepper on top.

Back in Winchester I'd started going out with a pretty girl named Anna. She was naïve but cute, and was attracted to my hair and my local celebrity status. When I informed her that I was off to chance it in the big city, she was distraught, and I had to sit with her while she cried into my necklaces. *Oh well, I'll be back sometime,* I said, half-heartedly stroking her hair. *No you won't!* she cried.

Anna was option c. On a lovesick whim, she and her friend Nicky had decided to follow me up to London. They'd organized jobs and accommodation in the time I'd spent in the lavatory and lying secretly under Owen's bunk. They'd both worked part-time in the Wimpy on the main street in Winchester, and now they had full-time jobs at Burger King on the corner of Oxford Street and Tottenham Court Road, and had rented the whole ground floor of a house in Leytonstone, East London. Jeez, that was quick. *Can I move in too, please?* They made me beg. *Please?*

Their landlord lived upstairs and didn't like me. During my first day in the flat, when Anna and Nicky had gone off to work, he banged endlessly on the door, calling out, "I know you're in there!" like a broken record. I sat curled up on the bed, out of view of the keyhole, clutching my unplugged electric guitar, terrified. He stayed pressed against the door all morning, and when he heard the girls coming back home, he clattered down the stairs and barged into the flat behind them and tore into me, spit bubbling around the edges of his mouth. Anna and Nicky tried to calm him down but he was determined to get rid of me. He gave me a week to leave and stormed back upstairs.

Instead of doing anything helpful, like trying to get a job, I decided to learn all of Jimmy Page's Led Zeppelin guitar solos, starting with the album *1*, and moving through them all in sequence. This went relatively well until I encountered the dreaded "perfect solo" in "Since I've Been Loving You" on *3*, which I'd been struggling with for years. There's an amazing downward trill he plays halfway through, which I eventually chose to ignore, and moved onto "Tangerine," which was a pleasant C, G, D.

In the evenings, after the three of us had sat down to ten burned fish sticks each, served on rented plates with cornershop ketchup, I would play more Jimmy Page while the girls nattered on about Burger King politics. We rigged up a curtain between the beds, so that although Nicky could hear Anna and me enjoying noisy sex, at least she couldn't see us.

Nicky bailed out before the end of the first week and headed back to Winchester. The landlord wanted lovely ladies only, so Anna rented us another apartment in Leytonstone and suggested that I get a job to help pay its rent. Yeah, whatever. She went off to work and I picked up my guitar.

"Any luck with a job?" asked Anna later, smelling of chips.

"No luck," I muttered, having gone to all the trouble of buying an *Evening Standard*, opening it at the Classifieds section, and putting a pen down next to it on the floor to make it look like I'd actually tried.

"How about McDonalds?" said Anna. The fast-food industry had been working well for her; she had three stars on her badge already, after only a month. There was a gigantic drive-thru

McDonalds just up the road, by the Leytonstone subway station. Next day I went up there and sat for an hour watching the place, smoking. I couldn't afford cigarettes, so I'd resorted to picking up discarded butts from the pavement, pinching out the remains of the tobacco, and constructing thin secondhand roll-ups that tasted like car exhaust. I eventually strutted into the building and filled in the application form at a brightly lit plastic table. I was sure they wouldn't want me, but two days later I got a letter saying congratulations, they did.

"Any luck?" said Anna that evening.

"*Luck?*"

She picked up the letter and grinned. "Ooh, that's great!"

I look back on my ten days' employment at McDonalds with some kind of warped fondness. God knows why.

Day 1. 5:30 A.M. and I can't get into the building. The front doors are locked and I've been waving at the milling counter staff for five minutes now. Time is everything in this business, and frankly, this is already inefficient. The staff door is apparently around to the side—and unmarked—and after pushing in behind somebody who felt it unnecessary to hold the door open for me, I learn that harsh first-day lesson, which is that nobody says hello, ever.

"Hello!" Except for me.

I'm told I can choose from any of the unoccupied lockers.

"Which ones are unoccupi—" *Bang.* A passing uniformed gentleman slams one open in my face, so that's the one I choose for today. I notice all the lockers have name stickers on them.

"Hi! Where do I get a name sticker for my lock—" *Slam.* I'm handed my uniform, wrapped in plastic. I shuffle toward the bathroom, smiling at my new colleagues. I start to change into my green uniform, fully expecting somebody to *slam* my cubicle door open, which as I'm squeezing out of my tight black jeans, someone does.

"Put this on too." It's quite exciting—it's my green learner's badge with SEB written on it, with holes for the stars I'm gonna earn 'cos I'm gonna be so fucking kick-ass at this shit.

"You did clock in, right?" he spits at me.

I hadn't clocked in but I smile politely with my trousers still down.

"Tell me you clocked in."

Exasperated, he tells me how to clock in, but I'm more concerned about him liking me than trying to take in his tedious McTalk. I don't even know what clocking in means.

Then I meet the branch manager, because suddenly he's standing inches away from my face, watching me trying to tuck my hair underneath my small green cap. It's not going well, but he neither offers me advice nor concedes an inch of my personal space, as I push cute black loops behind my ears and smile at him and say, "Hell—"

"*Quarters,*" he barks, then turns on his heel and walks away.

Quarters? Are we quarter friends?

When I worked at Winchester College, we all sat down for a nice half-hour cup of tea and merrily shot the breeze before we got down to work. The only breeze in this god-awful place was coming from the racks of frozen fries to my left.

"*Quarters!*"

Oh shut up.

Quarters are Quarter Pounders, which are what I'm going to be making today. I'm led around giant lumps of hissing stainless steel and placed before a frightening contraption with bars on the front as thick as my arm.

"This is the quarters griddle," my reluctant and bitter trainer informs me like I'm a moron. I stand politely aside with my arms behind my back and watch him make four quarters. It's like magic!

"Go on then. You have a go," he says.

I stare at the machine.

"What do you need first of all?" asks my trainer. "What's the most important thing?"

"Is it burgers?"

"Correct."

Clever me. I stare at the machine.

"So where are the burgers?" he asks.

"I don't know."

"Well where did I get my burgers from just a minute ago?" He's annoyed.

"I don't know."

"I got them from the freezer, didn't I?"

"Oh yes."

"So get the burgers."

"Where's the freezer again?"

He whams open the freezer and says, "*There.*"

I put my hand in the freezer. "How many burgers would you like?"

"Six."

"*Six?*"

"Come *on.*"

I pull out ten all stuck together and he grabs them from me and whams them down on the work surface so that exactly six are sheered off. It's an impressive move. I wham down the remaining four, and they scatter, so we have to go around and pick them all up. Half an hour later, I'm able to make two quarters at a time, but very slowly. You put your buns in the toaster (complicated toaster, not normal toaster), stick your burgers onto the cooking surface, haul down the lid and fasten it, give your work surface a good wipe, sweep your two square feet of standing space, retrieve your hot buns, spread them on a tray, pick up your condiments gun, two squirts of ketchup, one squirt of mustard, two slices of pickle, a sprinkle of rehydrated onions, react to the beeping cooker, lift the lid, scrape off your burgers, lay them on your prepared buns, fetch your bun tops, stick them on top, pick up your full tray, take it to the man in the shirt and tie and acne by the chutes, and shout, "Quarters!"

"How many with cheese?"

"None!" (Everyone shouts, all the time.)

"How many quarters with cheese did I ask for?!"

"I can't remember!"

"Four!"

"Oh dear!"

"You useless dickhead!"

"Sorry!"

He throws away my fresh quarters and when I'm back at the griddle barks out, "Eight quarters, two with cheese!"

Eight?

I have to ask someone how the cheese goes again. It's two bits of cheese, one over the pickles on the bottom bun, and one laid over the burger. After some time, I deliver my full tray.

"Quarters!" I yell.

"Kill the cow yourself, did you?"

"Pardon?"

"*Six quarters, four with cheese!*"

Oh Christ.

You are allowed a free burger for lunch, but a manager follows closely behind you as you choose, and makes you take the oldest and most disgusting one in the chute. I eat my burger in exhausted silence in the staff room.

"*Clock out!*"

"Sorry!"

I do quarters all day, and by the end my fingers and thumbs are burned, my arms are scalded, I'm covered in cold, slimy sweat, and I stink. I walk home in the dark like a zombie and Anna tells me I stink. I tell her I know. I'm supposed to wash my uniform myself, but as we haven't got a washing machine I can't, so I'm going to have to wear the same stinky shit again in the morning. I don't practice my guitar. I watch snooker in a sulk instead.

Day 2: Quarters again. I can do them without getting shouted at now.

Day 3: I'm the King of the Quarters! I anticipate imminent receipt of the first star for my empty badge.

Day 4: Disaster. I get put on the Filet-o-Fish machine. It takes me ages to get it right. It involves painful hot oil, which I manage to splash everywhere. Most confusing of all is that the Hot Apple Pies are made on the same machine, so there are two vats of oil side by side, one for each menu item. Unsurprisingly, I keep putting the fish in the apple pie oil and vice versa. I receive a complaint from a customer that their apple pie smells of fish, and the supervisor comes around to the back and yells at me in front of the rest of the guys. It's humiliating. I see my debut star vanishing in front of my eyes.

Day 5: I make the mistake of asking the manager if I can have a go on the drive-thru, or even serve on the main counter. As punishment for being so cheeky, I am sent to work in the giant freezer all day. It's a freezer the size of a large family garage and you can only stay in there for five minutes or so at a time before you start to freeze to death. I lump heavy boxes of fries into complicated storage patterns that I don't understand, and I'm yelled at again for not getting the system right. I steal frozen doughnuts out of opened boxes and scoff them whole. They're actually quite nice frozen—nicer than when thawed. I eat about ten in my first hour, and at ten-thirty I have to rush to the toilet to vomit them back up again. Somebody then locks me in the freezer for a laugh. *Hahaha!* I shout through the foot-thick door, dying.

Day 6: Fries room duty. This means getting boxes of fries from the freezer, tearing open the plastic pouches, pouring the fries evenly into racks that I've just cleaned and then dried with blue paper toweling, and then rolling the racks over next to the fryer (on which they didn't trust me enough to be stationed). Also in the fries room you have to make up the fresh orange juice, which means getting a large frozen carton of concentrated orange juice, splitting it open, squishing the frozen orange lump with your hands over an old bucket, running hot tap water over it while squishing, and then adding cold water up to the top while stirring the mixture with a scrawny plastic spatula. Then you pour the bucket into the fresh orange juice machine while standing on a chair. I'm sure it's not made like that in all the branches, but I wouldn't risk drinking it if I were you. Despite the regulations I didn't even wash my hands before I squished it up.

Day 7: Quarters again, but I've forgotten how to do them. Just as I remember, I'm moved to the machine that makes Big Macs, Hamburgers, and Cheeseburgers. It's genuine rocket science, and after nearly wrecking the entire restaurant, I'm mercifully put back onto Quarters for everybody's safety.

Day 8: I still haven't washed my uniform and I stink like pure evil; I even make myself want to puke. My hair bulges out from my pathetic undersized green cap, but they're so fed up with me that they've stopped mentioning it now.

Day 9: Pay packet! Is that all? I hate London. Where's Sam Yaffa?

Day 10: I check my bank balance: £2,741.58. I'm puzzled. I enter the bank and ask the assistant if this large figure is in fact my account, since I was expecting my balance to look more like £1.58. The assistant informs me that yes, that's my balance, that's why there's a pound sign in front of it. I walk calmly back out to the ATM and try to withdraw £30 as a tester. I am astonished when the notes pop out, and I buy five packs of cigarettes and a giant bottle of cider and walk home confused, wondering how that happened. It's May 4. The next day is my nineteenth birthday. I fall asleep wondering if it'll all still be there in the morning.

Chapter Twelve

breaking the law

*I*t's a sunny Thursday morning and I'm standing in a line in the Leytonstone branch of Barclays Bank trying to stop my body from shaking. I'm supposed to be at McDonalds, but instead I'm attempting to withdraw £2,711.58. It's nearly my turn.

"How can I help?" asks the cashier as I step up to the glass.

"I have a problem," I reply. The clerk pretends to smile and I plunge on. "I'm a musician, and I'm supposed to be buying an amplifier today, and it costs two-and-a-half thousand pounds, and unfortunately the account I have with you doesn't allow for me to have a checkbook (it was an account for little children). The thing is, I don't really want to be walking around London with all that cash just sitting in my pocket, you know? I wouldn't feel . . . um . . . safe. Do you think there's anything we can do that wouldn't involve me having to walk out of here with two-and-a-half grand in my pocket?" Reverse psychology. I was a genius!

She furrowed her brow and went through my limited options.

"We could prepare a bankers' draft?" We talked it through but I managed to think up a few reasons why it wasn't practical, thank God. She *ummed* and *ahed,* but eventually was forced to concede that I was going to have to bite the bullet and take the cash.

"I'm really sorry about this," she said.

I tried to look sad. "Oh well," I replied. "Thanks for trying."

She took my bank card, prodded its numbers into her computer, picked up the phone, and turned away from me. This was it. I held my breath. I was ready to bolt. Anna was standing at the Leytonstone subway station with our bags, waiting for me; we were heading to Winchester for my birthday, whatever the outcome. The cashier was on the phone for ages. She eyed me covertly as she spoke to what I presumed was the head office on the other end of the line. I was looking more innocent than I'd ever done before: positively angelic with my eyeliner, tangle of black hair, and a Marlboro wedged over my ear. The phone went back down into its cradle. I eyed the door.

She turned to me. "How would you like the money?"

"As it comes."

"Are fifties OK?"

"Fifties are fine."

I stood in the sunlight at the door, wedged the envelope stuffed with fifties down the front of my pants and lit a Marlboro. I blew the match out with my nose, and for half an hour managed to fool Anna into thinking I'd failed in my mission, before pulling the hot wad triumphantly from my underwear somewhere near Chancery Lane.

Back in Winchester I discovered that Small and Mel had moved out of the house. Fa had crossed the line and half-heartedly threatened them both after coming back drunk from the pub one night, so now they were holed up at a neighbor's for a few weeks, until Fa calmed down or they found somewhere else to stay. Or, preferably, until Fa found somewhere else to stay so that they could move back into the house. The split was wreaking mental havoc upon Fa and, as usual, he was burying his options in alcohol and denial. Despite our sympathies, my sister and I knew he only had himself to blame. My mother had stayed too long as it was, mostly just for the sake of me and Mel.

Fa and I sat in the pub and he swore bitterly at the injustice of it all. I was just pleased that he didn't ask me how things had been going in London. I paid for the drinks at least, which I thought was very magnanimous of me. I told Fa about the money and he thought it was brilliant. He'd been merrily ripping off banks for decades; he often told us the tale of a letter he'd once received from one of his confusing array of financial "backers" demanding repayment, to which he'd replied by scrawling "PISS OFF" on the bottom of the letter and posting it back. He'd always seemed to get away with it. He considered my Barclays windfall as following in the family tradition, as did I. Small would have been horrified, and indeed was when I dared to tell her about it several years later.

I bumped into Rinse on the main street, although I didn't recognize him at first. He wasn't wearing his usual tight leather and makeup; instead he was dressed in a shiny grey double-breasted suit and a shirt and tie. He greeted me solemnly. Something wasn't right.

"Rinse? Is everything OK?" His hair wasn't platinum blond anymore either; it was cropped short and back to its natural mousy color.

"Seb, I've let God into my life."

"You're fucking kidding me, Rinse. Do you mean you've . . . ?"

"And you can still be saved by Jesus, too."

"Rinse, is this just you, or are all of Ponderosa involved?"

"I've renounced Ponderosa."

"Well I suppose that's not such a bad thing."

"Seb, I'm serious. You might think it's too late for you to be saved, but I'm telling you, it isn't."

"Rinse, you've turned your back on metal, man."

But he hadn't. Not quite. Rinse had been converted to Christian metal, and he'd already begun spreading the word.

White Metal

From a purely moral standpoint, it could be argued that heavy metal needed Christian metal to come along to help realign a listing ship. Apart from Tipper Gore's (Al's wife's) fledgling cabal, the PMRC (Parents' Music Resource Center), founded in 1985 by a bunch of concerned wives of American politicians demanding that something be done to combat the sick antics of the metal community, there was no one in a position to stem the tide of metal's increasingly depraved behavior. The PMRC did manage to install the Parental Advisory stickers on the front of albums that we still see today, but as an inquisitive adolescent, can you imagine a better carrot to lead you into the shadows? After a while, if your latest album *didn't* feature one of these stickers, you knew you had to go straight back into the studio and pepper your tunes with some more swearing, sex, and/or Satanism.

By the late '80s, metal was getting the blame for everything that was wrong with America's youth. The conservative establishment's contempt for heavy metal had reached fever pitch. The stickers weren't working and metal's various excesses were on the rise. But instead of investigating the ultraviolent nature of films, television, cartoons, computer games, comic books, and government policies, everyone heaped the blame onto the subliminal effects of Blackie Lawless's flame-spewing crotch.

This town needs cleaning up, said the U.S. Bible Belt, someone to take matters into their own hands and lead these sinners to the Promised Land. We needed someone to come save our souls from rock 'n' roll. Hot diggedy-dawg did we need redeeming.

They infected us from the inside.

Stryper were the first. Their name was an acronym.

Salvation

Through

Redemption

Yielding

Peace

Encouragement

(and)

Righteousness

Stryper wore only yellow and black clothes, like bees. That's two gimmicks already and we haven't heard any music yet! Their debut mini-album was called *The Yellow and Black Attack*. It was heavy metal with high harmonies—not too bad actually. Then it was onward to their first full-lengther, *Soldiers Under Command*. Stryper's live shows were already making headlines; they turned the house lights *on* when they played, in a direct challenge to live music's traditional darkness. They threw Bibles out into the crowd as they performed, and their drummer, Robert Sweet, played his kit facing sideways so that the audience could get a better look at him as he drummed. Robert didn't like to be called a drummer; he preferred to be referred to as the "visual timekeeper." Their second album was the much more successful *To Hell With the Devil*. It sold over two million copies—double platinum! Who's laughing now, eh?

But they took their foot off the gas for the limp-wristed *In God We Trust*, which was altogether too poppy. Then, out of desperation—much like when Kiss ditched the makeup in '83—they took off their yellow and black clothes; and after that they even dumped the biblical lyrics. Finally, bowed and beaten, they released a compilation called *Can't Stop the Rock*, which effectively stopped the rock.

They recently held a prayer meeting in a motel, and re-formed.

But Stryper had opened the floodgates. Behind them came wave after wave of bands playing what quickly became known as white metal. The rest of us wondered what the fuck was going on. Couldn't we all just get on with pretending to worship Satan?

First and foremost, these people were Godfearing—they worshiped Jesus Christ; he was their priority, before any of the music. These were honest, morally upstanding folk, getting through life doing as much good as they could via their own patronizing agenda. So what was it that attracted them to metal? You didn't get Christian hip-hop or Christian techno, so how come they wanted a piece of *us* all of a sudden?

Some just loved the way it sounded—its occasionally uplifting nature, the power ballads, the anthems, the drive, which was what they endeavored to harness to their bandwagon. Loud axes, big heavenly hair and pumping fists; but no devil signs, please.

Not this: *But this:*

They delighted in the irony of having hijacked the Devil's music for their own pious devices. The coup required nerve; and these Christians had nerve in reserve. But why not go and listen to Cliff Richard instead? pleaded the traditionalists, sick of their preaching already, and their tedious, self-regarding interviews.

Christian metal was, almost exclusively, an American concoction. There were some European bands who outed themselves after Stryper's leap of faith, but not many. If a band happened to contain a believer in their ranks, then they tried, more often than not, to keep it quiet. In America, though, they preferred to stand wide-legged on the roof of the church and bellow about it for ages. In their eyes they were the white knights arrived to rid the earth of the forces of evil and darkness: W.A.S.P., Alice Cooper, and Venom, to name but three.

White metal bands sang about positivity, light, values, education, love, honor, charity, ethics, strength, baby Jesus, the liberating power of rock, and adult Jesus. And when we snickered and scoffed, they pointed out God's own endorsement of their behavior via the Bible.

Psalm 33: "Praise the Lord with a harp; sing unto him with the psaltery and an instrument of ten strings [an Ibanez]. Sing unto him a new song; play skillfully with a loud noise!"

Psalm 98: "Make a joyful noise unto the Lord, all the earth: make a loud noise and rejoice and sing praise."

Psalm 150: "Praise him with stringed instruments and flutes [Jethro Tull]. Praise him with loud cymbals!"

Psalm 166: "Rejoice unto the thundering drums! The everlasting roar of the people! The blazing lights, the crashing of the cymbals . . . *Are you ready to rock and fucking roll, Long Beach?*"

White metal bands dressed in white and played white guitars with their white teeth and white consciences. It was a good way of getting across Jesus' message from the inside. Little Johnny could relate to the awesome riffs and killer solos while being surreptitiously fed the dogma. Delinquent youths across America were given White Cross records at Christmas and encouraged to "Listen to the words."

Although Stryper were easily the most successful, there were other Christian metal bands out there determined to kick the Devil's nefarious ass with power chords and spandex.

Petra won loads of Dove Awards (White metal Grammys) and are still going after almost thirty years. They play traditional uplifting metal and have a broad international fan base. *Beyond Belief* is pretty cool, while *Love* is based upon the first book of Corinthians, chapter thirteen.

Sacred Warrior sounded like Iron Maiden. Clearest Christian message: "He Died" (Jesus).

Mortification played Christian death metal. Clearest Christian message: "Monks of the High Lord." I personally feel that Christians playing death metal is wrong and sort of hypocritical, and I think you would too if you heard what death metal sounds like.

WhiteHeart: "Sing Unto the Lamb" and "Carried Away (Safe on the Wings of the Lord)" will make you feel better about yourself.

Third Day's "Your Love, Oh Lord" is a live favorite.

Barren Cross were good, they sounded like Van Halen.

P.O.D. (Payable On Death) are nu metal. They love God but don't love homosexuals. "I'm not going to treat somebody different because they're like that . . . just don't bring it into my house," they said recently.

I was in Texas a few years ago, by mistake, and I saw a bouffant rocker striding out of a gas station back toward his red pickup truck. I thought at the time this guy seemed to have something of the Stepford Wife about him, a deadness in his eyes, and I happened to trail him along the road for the next half-mile or so. He drove extremely slowly and erratically. I deduced that he must've been on drugs, or very drunk, until he slowed right down to turn left. I saw a long sticker covering his entire back bumper, which read: METALHEADS FOR CHRIST.

Cool Hand Luke

Owen phoned from London. He said he'd found a squat in Olympia, West London, and we could move in tomorrow—in fact we could move in whenever we wanted, because it was a squat. I told him about my money. He told me to buy a Gibson Les Paul and a Marshall stack, and I replied, "Well what the hell else was I going to do with it, dude?" I'd already bought a copy of London's classifieds magazine *Loot*, and phoned a number of Les Paul owners and got them to describe their axes in glorious fret-by-fret detail.

Back in London, Anna and I tiptoed into our bedsit, and there on the doormat, as expected, were ten increasingly threatening letters from Barclays, informing me that they'd made a slight mistake with my account, and that I had made a more serious mistake by removing all the money, and could I please contact my local branch as soon as possible to discuss this urgent matter. Oh yeah, right.

Owen and I caught a tube to East London and picked up a Gold Glitter Top Les Paul Standard, whose owner claimed it had once belonged to Marc Bolan. I loved Marc Bolan! I paid him £500 for it, and off we went to pick up the Marshall stack, which we then wheeled down suburban streets and onto the tube. The Les Paul didn't have a case, so it looked like we were down there to play a gig. With the guitar slung around my neck, and Owen being Owen, we strummed the odd antique Junkies track as a treat, but mostly we apologized for getting in the way of the doors. We wheeled the stack and the axe through Shepherd's Bush (via an off license), and down dim-lit yellow streets to the address Owen had written on the back of an envelope: the squat.

We didn't really know what squats were, other than they were supposed to be edgy, and free of charge, and you had to hook up your electricity from a streetlamp. Anna was waiting with a friend of hers who was in London for the weekend, and Owen's guitar-toting cousin from New Zealand, Patch. The lock was all smashed in, everyone was milling around in the stark white doorway, and it was, indeed, very edgy.

Inside our new and apparently straightforward Victorian ter-raced house we discovered a suburban *Marie Celeste*. Everything one would expect in a normal bustling household was in place, but covered with a thick layer of dust, as if its owner had run down to the shop to buy a pint of milk two years before and never came back. A slippery wash of unopened letters were piled against the broken front door, plates and cutlery lay primed on the kitchen table, and cold, green food sat in the still-humming fridge. As we rifled like children through cupboards and drawers for booty, we convinced ourselves that wherever the owners had sud-denly gone (we decided they were on the run), they weren't going to be back tonight, and we felt safe enough to crack open the whiskey, crank up my stack and new guitar, and jam drunk-enly until the early hours. We all agreed that squatting was fun, until, at four in the morning, we heard a sudden banging on the front door downstairs. We inched open the broken door to a flus-tered young bloke who told us he was paid by this house's absent owners to keep an eye out for squatters, and that although he had no issue with us personally, he'd already called the police. We stood there and weren't sure whether to be rude to him or not.

The cops arrived twenty minutes later, and we all swayed drunkenly in the flashing blue light as the neighbors' curtains twitched. Ten minutes later, the cops left again because we smiled and were polite and there were five of us, compared to the lone guardian and his overeager protestations, and we headed back indoors and fell asleep on dusty, itchy beds, uncertain whether our collective bravery was going to see us through this.

The next day, while Owen, Patch, and I were out and the girls were tidying up, a brick came crashing through the bay windows, missing Anna by inches. It had been thrown by the man from last night; he stared at her through the glass with blazing eyes. Anna ran upstairs to hide until the rest of us returned after dark. All night we sat around and discussed unconvincing threats we could use on our tormentor, until finally we heard knocking on the front door once more. We all froze. It was our friend again, and this time he had more dire warnings. He told us that the house belonged to the deputy head of the Israeli Secret Police, and that he'd notified the landlord of our presence in his holy abode, and that as we spoke here on the violated doorstep, this gentleman had boarded a plane to London with an extremely violent sidekick to personally kick our asses out of his house.

"Honestly?" we asked him.

"Yeah. And his plane lands in," he checked his watch, "twenty-five minutes."

"Oh fuck!"

"And I ought to tell you, last time squatters broke into this place a few years ago, he flew back, came round, and shot one of them as he tried to jump out the upstairs window."

We gazed at him in horror.

"It was never clear how he died, whether it was from the machine gun fire or the fall."

"Oh Jesus!"

"Stay and have a chat with him if you like. Nice geezer really. He's just a bit touchy, that's all."

Like idiots, we panicked. We ran back upstairs, trussed our possessions into bulging bedsheets, called a bunch of taxis, and booked ourselves into the backpackers' hotel again.

We weren't scared, it just wasn't the right kind of place for us, we told various Australians the following day, as we drank warm beer and shot bad pool. Owen could afford to stay at the hotel, as he'd gotten a job selling dodgy paintings door-to-door, but I'd already frittered away most of the money, which meant Anna and I could only manage another two nights. In the dormitory after lights out, she suggested I go back to McDonalds. *I've still got forty quid*, I hissed back. Anna eventually persuaded me that we ought to put it toward a deposit for somewhere halfway decent, i.e., somewhere not in Leytonstone, so we found a spacious bedsit in Finsbury Park in a big house full of other young people, and Anna got a job working on the tills at the Tesco supermarket just round the corner.

So it was just me and Anna again, only a few miles further north, but this time I was all set to join Hanoi Rocks. I had a genuine Gibson Les Paul that glittered magically in the light and weighed a wonderfully satisfying ton over my shoulder, and a Marshall stack (well, half a stack—an amp and a 4' x 12' speaker) that even turned a quarter up still made your teeth hurt. I knew as I stood in front of my Marshall with the Gibson round my knees, black jeans squeezed on, petticoat ripped to shreds, and raven hair flicking around to my every stylistic command, that I was ready to run with the big boys at last. I scanned the Klassifieds section of *Kerrang!* for bands in search of an axe hero, but the ones that were looked crap, and all the cool-looking bands were looking for drummers or bass players instead.

"Any luck finding a job?" asked Anna each night. Well no, of course not. I've been too busy standing in front of the mirror again. For Christ's sake woman, give me a break.

Desperate for cash, my eye was drawn to a quadruple vinyl Led Zeppelin bootleg sitting proudly in the corner of the bedsit. It belonged to a fat bloke I'd met in a pub in Winchester a few months ago, who'd been foolish enough to let me borrow it. He'd told me to take extreme care, because it was worth well over a hundred quid. I stuck the box in a plastic bag and headed down to Soho to flog it. I did, however, tape it first.

Later that afternoon, wandering down Charing Cross Road, I found a snaking hairy line outside the Marquee Club, waiting to see controversial new American band Love/Hate. This lot seemed as good a bunch to try as any, so, beginning at the back, I tapped a bloke in a leather jacket on the shoulder.

"Excuse me, do you like Led Zeppelin?"

"No."

"OK." I shuffled forward in the queue. "Excuse me, do you like Led Zeppelin?"

Giggles. "You take photo!" I took the Japanese girls' photo, and then they took a photo of me, and then we all had our picture taken together.

"Excuse me, do you like Led Zeppelin?"

"Might do."

By the time I got to the front of the queue I had three bids, all shit, the best being thirty quid, so I headed over to Carnaby Street instead and accosted everybody with either long hair or wearing a metal T-shirt. A tall, arrogant-looking, red-haired glam chap strutted by, squeezing at a cigarette.

"Excuse me, do you like Led Zeppelin?"

"A bit."

"Oh."

"Why."

"Do you want to buy this quadruple vinyl bootleg?" I held up the plastic Tesco bag.

"No."

We stood awkwardly.

"Do you play the bass?" he asked me.

I cursed my decision to switch when I was thirteen. I cursed Paul Bavister. "No, I play the guitar. I play a Les Paul. Marc Bolan used to own it actually."

He squinted at me. He really was extremely cool. He had a long, pointy nose and was even thinner than I was. It looked like he'd never eaten a meal in his life. Cool!

"That'll do. You any good?"

"Yes, I am." How does one measure?

"I'm the vocalist in a band called Cool Hand Luke. At the moment it's just me and another rhythm guitarist. We're looking for a bass player and a drummer, but thinking about it, I suppose we need another guitarist as well. Can you play lead?"

"Yes, and I can play 'Sweet Child o' Mine.'" Wow! I'd seen Cool Hand Luke's advert in the Klassifieds.

"Do you want to come round and meet the other guy and have a jam and shit like that?"

"Yes, thank you, I'd love to." I sensed I was being too eager. I lit my own cigarette, to compete, and tried to look as moody and unimpressed as possible. My heart was beating fast. He wrote down his address and we fixed a date for the following week.

"I'm Pat." He offered his jingling hand.

"Seb."

"Zed?"

"Seb."

"Sid?"

"Seb."

"Right."

"You don't want to buy this bootleg then?"

"It's nice, but I prefer the Dead Boys."

"Me too actually." I'd never heard of them.

We parted. It appeared that I was in a band. I returned to the Marquee queue to pick up the thirty quid, but he only had a check so I had to take twenty-five quid cash from the other guy.

I changed my outfit at least eight times, but still wasn't happy with my hat/shirt combo; I cursed the fact that I didn't own a bigger

■ **COOL HAND LUKE**
*seek Pussycat/Hanoi/Stooges-
influenced drummer. Call 081-888 7389.*

stock of women's clothes. In the end, I rang on the doorbell in Manor House wearing every piece of jewelry I owned. I was sweating like a pig, with eyeliner caked black around itchy wide eyes. Pat opened the door and led me upstairs where I was introduced to my other new bandmate, Martin. Martin was even thinner than Pat: hollow cheeks, throttling scarves hanging maypole behind him, and no ass whatsoever. I thought they both sounded northern, and though I couldn't distinguish their regions, I could tell they weren't from anywhere near Winchester.

We sat on stained sofas and I was handed a can of strong lager which I sipped at noisily. We politely discussed how much we all liked the New York Dolls and Iggy Pop, and boasted immodestly about our technical abilities. Unfortunately, I had the highest pitched voice, and sounded idiotic and posh; I kept saying things like *crikey*. I also came last in the who's-wearing-the-most-bangles competition. These guys looked like a pair of bona fide anorexic gypsies. It felt like I'd struck gold; I could hardly wait to hear evidence of their obvious songwriting abilities. The stuff they said they wanted to play was the same stuff I wanted to play: lowdown dirty sleaze-rock with smart poses and silk scarves—the Rolling Stones circa 1971 but without Charlie Watts. Martin produced a cassette of a song they'd been talking about, called "Rocket." As he rewound, they warned me it was pretty rough, and featured a drum machine, and that it wasn't Pat singing, it was Martin, and that this was just an example of the sort of stuff they were currently working on.

We listened to "Rocket." It was the worst thing I had ever

heard in my whole life; worse than Bon Jovi, worse than eXposed, worse even than the Daughters of the Late Colonel. Martin was clearly completely tone deaf and he talked drunkenly through the clichéd lyrics much as Rinse had done in Ponderosa. The drum machine wasn't synchronized to the rest of the music track; it rattled clumsily in heart-stopping fills in the middle of the chorus. It was god-awful, incompetent shit. As I listened, I couldn't help myself and started to laugh. I looked up at them from between my hands, but they had their heads down and were nodding along and listening hard.

"Can you manage that?" They asked at the end.

"I reckon so." It had two chords, with a novelty third that came in to surprise you about halfway through. We picked up guitars and had a bash through it, only Pat was too shy to sing so Martin did his drunken mumble again. His fingers on his guitar weren't making sense, so I had to watch his lips, and I added some simple lead frills and counterpoints which they didn't seem to mind, though Pat did raise his eyebrows.

We got drunk and I agreed to join the band. Fuck it. I could teach Martin how to play properly and shape these dudes into whatever they'd have to become; they looked so cool I couldn't resist them. I'll be in charge of the music, though, I thought to myself, as we clambered through "Rocket" again. At one point it looked like Pat was about to start singing—he opened his mouth and Martin respectfully desisted his muttering—but Pat filled his mouth with more beer and carried on knocking his cowboy boot spurs out of time against the floor.

Halfway through, Martin's girlfriend arrived. She had white blond crimped hair and was stunningly beautiful, and for me it was love at first sight, right down the drain, *blam*, hello, goodbye, she's the one for me for the rest of my life, oh dear, whoopsy-daisy, that's not supposed to happen.

But it had. My heart had exploded.

"Hello," said Faye.

"Hello," replied Pat and Martin.

"And hello," she said to me, but I couldn't even look at her. I'd turned purple. She kept chatting to me and being friendly, then sat down on the sofa opposite and politely watched us lurch through the rest of "Rocket," but I'd completely forgotten how it went. I played a dying cat solo and then dropped the guitar onto the carpet with a thump.

"I need to go to the bathroom," I said.

"I'll show you where it is," replied Faye, kindly.

"Oh, please no!" I ran blindly from of the room.

When I came back she'd gone, and Pat and Martin were looking at me strangely.

"Everything alright?"

"Oh yes, fine, just took a piss."

I picked up my guitar and ran out.

Chapter Thirteen

cocked and loaded

Although Anna was pleased about my new band, she was getting impatient about my contribution to our basic domestic needs. My income was precisely zero, as I couldn't even be bothered to sign onto the dole. I bought the *Evening Standard* again and flicked through the Classifieds, slightly sated that I didn't need the Klassifieds anymore. In desperation, I went for a few interviews to become a security guard. I assumed it would be easy—lots of sitting around holding a flashlight in an empty warehouse—but the interviews were humiliating. I sat among rows of ex-policemen and servicemen with heavy moustaches, dressed like a transsexual prostitute with three elastic bands holding my hair back. The policemen just stared.

Then one day an ad said it was looking for fun-loving people to work outdoors on the streets of London, with women. With women? I could do that.

This was Fratton Finance, just around the corner from Paddington station. They sold financial services—banking, insurance, savings etc.—exclusively to women, and I got the job just by turning up. Each group of new recruits received fifteen minutes' worth of basic training before being sent out into the field. A bunch of us would spread out over a busy street corner in the West End or the City, and then as soon as the women started to stream out of their offices during lunchtime, we'd pounce.

"Excuse me, do you work in London?"

They're heading toward Boots drugstore, power-dressed in business suits and heels.

"Yes, of course."

"All I want to do is give you a leaflet," you'd say, walking beside them, trying to keep up.

"I don't believe you."

"It's true! And then we'll give you a quick call in a few days' time, just to ask what you think of the leaflet."

"You're not selling me anything?"

"No, I promise. Just give me your name and your work telephone number."

If they did, we got 50p. Then, later in the week, one of the hawks back in the cigarette-stinking office would phone and hound them until they finally agreed to sign away their life savings into one of Fratton's special "schemes."

On a good day, we could easily clear fifty slips each, even with half of them giving us false numbers. The whole thing was dodgy as hell, and I loved it. Especially since we were paid in cash every Friday morning, which meant we were all in the pub by lunchtime and thunderously drunk by two-thirty. When Anna asked me how much I'd made the following morning, I'd often realize I'd spent my entire salary the evening before.

Things were brighter, though. I was settled in London, earning money, living somewhere safe and with someone who really cared for me, and I was in a band with a bunch of guys who looked like chicks. The one thing I was in desperate denial over was the fact that I was in love with my fellow guitarist's girlfriend, to whom I'd spoken no more than a couple of words.

Cool Hand Luke gathered a drummer (Baz) and a bass player (Ricky) from the Klassifieds. Baz was a professional drummer from Essex and was in about seven other bands and had a double-bass drum. His hair was an extreme bottled blond, necessary because underneath he was ginger; he even painted his red eye-brows with bleach to lighten them. Baz was friendly and wore giant white sneakers, as drummers do. Ricky, the bassist, was cur-mudgeonly and sounded like Peter Cook (minus the humor), and always, I mean always, wore a bright green bowler hat.

The best thing about us, though, was that we all had long hair. The five of us walked down the street like a hermaphrodite *Reservoir Dogs*. I phoned Owen and told him of my good fortune and he said he was very happy for me. We taught Baz and Ricky "Rocket." Ricky had a song too, "Mystery Girl," which was alright. Pat had a song, "What You Gonna Do," which was actually pretty good. Someone had a song called "(I Don't Want) Another Lover," and it was shit. My own song, "Lay Me Down," was a cracker, a masterpiece of light and shade featuring a countrified breakdown halfway through, and everyone kindly considered the tune my own personal "Good Vibrations"; a pocket symphony in E with four chords and lots of frenzied soloing. It was dropped from the set soon after.

We rehearsed once a week in rehearsal rooms under a railway bridge off Holloway Road, and Martin would give me a lift down there in his battered Vauxhall. We became friends, slowly, and I taught him little tricks on his axe, such as how to tune it. We went to Camden together and got our noses pierced. We discussed Hanoi Rocks; he inspected my *Self Destruction Blues* picture disc. Martin was a good four or five years older than me—he must've been around twenty-four to my nineteen. Perhaps it was this age gap that made it hard for him to deal with the fact that I was a better musician than him. He was never comfortable with it, but then he wasn't really there for the music; he was there for the shapes, and the kudos, and the scarves round his neck, and soon the drugs too—the drugs over everything. But we're not quite at the drugs yet.

For now we were working hard to knock Cool Hand Luke into shape, God knows we needed it. I'd discovered that Pat couldn't really sing after all, but his microphone was so low in the mix that it took a long time for me to realize. We could see he was sneering, though, which was good news from a vibes point of view. At least he was trying.

He was secretive with his lyrics.

But then, strangely, our rehearsals suddenly flipped over and we became completely kick-ass. It all just gelled. We blasted through our eight songs with swagger, gusto, and precision tooling. Hairs started to rise on the backs of our necks. We even went ahead and booked a gig in Bedford as a warm-up before we hit London. We were taking this extremely seriously.

All the other guys in the band had rock chick girlfriends. Faye (Martin's)—the apple of my eye—was like Stevie Nicks: wispy and thin, all kohl and white blonde. Caroline (Pat's) looked the same only scarier and with acne. Ricky was single but hungry for love, and Baz lived in Essex with his girlfriend Shaz. Surrounded by all these glamorous chicks, Anna felt left out. Her plain, student clothes didn't fit in with the company she was now being forced to keep. She came over to Martin's house and everyone was nice to her and listened politely to her tales of life at Tesco, but I could see in my bandmates' eyes that they considered it time for me to replace her with a more suitable appendage. Someone a bit more slutty.

Anna had no idea what was going on. Our rules for women existed outside those of normal society. She had a clearly defined role to play if she wanted to run with us big, bad, macho rock gods; a role involving humiliation, sycophancy, and disenfranchisement.

Women in Metal

Ask a male heavy metal fan if he believes there's a place within its walls for women, and more often than not he'll scrunch up his face and reply, "Yes. On her knees with my cock in her mouth."

And then if you're lucky, "The dirty bitch."

And if you don't laugh, he'll think you're gay, or even worse (because he's never met a real homosexual and isn't sure if they really exist), politically correct. Metal doesn't like politically correct. If politically correct was forced upon metal, all there'd be left would be the makeup bags and the scorch marks on the walls.

Heavy metal has traditionally demanded just two things of its womenfolk: (1) look after us, cook our dinner, and wipe the sick off our leathers; (2) please look nice so that we'll want to shag you later on.

It was only when women tried to break out of this perfectly reasonable box that problems tended to occur. Metal took as its gender template the way of the caveman. The rule of the bone.

Why? Because this was Real Man's music. In other words, it was so overwhelmingly masculine that there was literally no space within it for women. It wasn't that metal didn't want chicks in it, it was more a case of *Sorry ladies: genetic necessity. Where can we put you, darling? Ain't no space here, love. Now go on, be a good girl and grab the lads a couple of burgers, chop chop.*

Women realized that to fit into this landscape they would have to strip away as much of their femininity as possible. They wore greasy leather, didn't wash their hair, got pimples on purpose, and swore and drank strong lager. This meant they were allowed to pull up a stool to the edge of the table. Everyone was happy with this arrangement—the women were playing at being like the lads, how sweet. They even learned how to play pool.

First, in the mid-'70s, came Suzi Quatro. A blonde American dressed from head to toe in leather and dwarfed by a huge bass guitar, her impact was considerable, if brief. She made it on to *Top of the Pops* and sang how she wanted it "Too Big." Then she disappeared into television. But, for the first time, a woman had punched a hole in rock, and others followed tentatively behind.

The Runaways, who came out of Hollywood (again in the mid-'70s), created the template for women in heavy rock music: women taking control—moving most of their own levers. They were the ones that blew open the doors, only for the resulting trickle to never really settle properly into the new space. But you can't blame them for trying. The Runaways came blasting out all spunky and loud, full of pop hooks and thick eyeliner, but it didn't work. No one was watching, and they spluttered through to their apt swan song, "Little Lost Girls." Afterward, two ex-Runaways made metal waves of their own with patchy but worthy solo careers. Joan Jett and her band the Blackhearts went on to record heavy metal disco classic "I Love Rock 'n' Roll" (later covered by Rag 'n' Bones and Britney Spears), while Lita Ford became an almost lone woman-in-metal flag-bearer for much of the '80s, constantly tipped for success which ultimately never came, despite a tempestuous and high-profile relationship with baddest-of-the-bad-boys Nikki Sixx from Mötley Crüe.

Disillusioned by what they'd seen so far, aspiring female rockers waited on the sidelines, preferring not to dirty their hands any further. Back in the U.K., though, in the early '80s, a couple of bands emerged who didn't give a shit what their male peers thought of them—they were out to have a few laughs, slug a few beers (pints not halves), and submit their little shoulders to the weight of some seriously heavy guitars.

Girlschool (a fantastic name for a female metal band) formed in 1978, put in the hours and the touring, and soon found themselves under the dubious patronage of Motorhead's Lemmy. Lemmy took them on tour as his support band, and the girls matched Motorhead's infamous hard livin' blow for bitter blow. *Anything you can do we can do better!* they cried from Lemmy's stinking coattails, sinking glass after glass of meths, swallowing everything that confronted them, except Motorhead drummer Phil "Philthy Animal" Taylor's suggestions of strip poker. They stayed the course and were soon being touted as metal's Next Big Thing, touring with the even more dubious Ted Nugent (extremely right wing, hunts animals with a dazzling array of weaponry, recently released a hunting-then-eating-little-animals cookbook called *Kill 'em and Grill 'em*).

An album, *Demolition*, followed, and it was looking increasingly like the 'School were on their way to an unprecedented seat at metal's top table. But then Lemmy overstepped the mark. He came up with the notion of Motorhead and Girlschool uniting under the banner Headgirl (can you see what Lemmy did there?) for the infamous *St. Valentine's Day Massacre* EP, which amazingly went U.K. Top 5 in 1981. Although this did wonders for the 'School's profile, Motorhead's guitarist, "Fast" Eddie Clark, thought all this hanging around a bunch of chicks was beneath him and resigned from the band.

Girlschool also hadn't bargained on Rock Goddess. The Goddess were a young female British threesome with a twelve-year-old drummer, and they landed on the scene after an eye-opening session on Tommy Vance's essential *Friday Rock Show*. *Kerrang!* nurtured a bitter rivalry between the competing groups, and showered us with Girlschool and Rock Goddess posters, which sadly weren't very exciting as both bands resolutely kept their clothes on (and were ugly). These girls weren't selling sex, they were selling kick-ass rock 'n' roll. Damn, we said, in our bedrooms. Girlschool and Rock Goddess eventually merged.

Women in metal have always had to fight the entire system before fighting for gigs and record contracts. Every interview a female heavy metal musician has ever done has involved interrogation over whether or not they believed they could cut it in such a male-dominated world, and then gone on to patronizingly suggest that maybe it's possible, if the girls play their cards right (*wink wink*). Why weren't they allowed to just play their music? Debbie Harry got the whole sex kitten treatment, sure, but she was respected as an artist in her own right, too. Ditto Nico. Ditto the Slits in their own twisted way. Ditto the bleeding Ronettes to a degree. And Aretha Franklin, Janis Joplin, Joni Mitchell, Billy Holiday; these women suffered at the hands of the industry's in-built sexism and double standards, but achieved artistic recognition nonetheless. I'll bet Nina Simone wasn't asked in every interview whether or not she'd consider stripping for *Playboy* magazine—like every female metal artist has been asked at some point during their grinding journey through these pimply hacks' fantasies. Maybe the blame for the press's sorry treatment of women does lie squarely at the feet of the likes of *Kerrang!*. Though if the female metal bands were crap—which most of them sadly were—what were they supposed to do? Lie to us? Some of the women didn't really help themselves, though. They shouldn't have listened to their manager's advice quite so . . . closely.

Lee Aaron was a Canadian metal singer, and pretty much the first thing she did in her career was to pose naked for a disreputable magazine. It was hard for the press to take her seriously after that, and each photoshoot was seen as a potential repeat performance by the photographer. Lee's reaction was to put on more and more clothes, until by the time of her halfway decent *Metal Queen* album, all we could see was her determined face glaring out at us from the record sleeve. She toured with Bon Jovi, became more and more commercial, and is still around, though these days playing smoky jazz.

Pluky Brit Lisa Dominique had a particularly hard time of it, despite getting more free publicity than anyone else in heavy metal, ever. This was because she looked like a porn star and got her kit off whenever anybody asked. Lisa started off in her brother's eponymous band, Marino. They received awful, shaming reviews, but from the get-go the metal press took one look at sexy Lisa and said to themselves: poster girl! Every week, one of the metal magazines would give away a giant full-color poster of a half-naked Lisa with her finger in her mouth, while on the other side would be, say, Death Angel covered in chicken's blood. This constant attention meant that Lisa soon announced her own solo career. Her first album, *Rock 'n' Roll Lady*, was panned, and the record-buying public ignored it. Lesser chicks might have called it a day, but Lisa plowed on, despite being dropped by her record label. Another company picked her up, dusted her down, and paid for her to record the back-to-basics, stripped-down *Lisa Dominique* album. Do you need me to tell you what happened?

Women often appear lost behind the paraphernalia of the heavy metal musician, almost apologetic as they struggle with a triple-necked portcullis design signature Charvel limited-edition axe, with floating Floyd Rose whammy system. But, no matter how technically proficient they might be, the majority of the patronizing male crowd will never allow them to take credit for their musicianship. The guys will always say that you're miming; the real parts we can hear are being played by a male session musician off to the side of the stage, while you clatter unconvincingly up and down the ramps in your high heels like the pathetic puppet you know yourself to be.

So to deflect this mild banter, it has always been best to let men get on with playing the instruments, while the female sticks to the singing. This means that the inherent sexism of the audience is, at a stroke, deflected by the musicians at your side, while you get on with screaming true metal into the microphone. And the final, vital piece in this jigsaw is that you must make sure the band has a proper name, and isn't just named after you. Something like Warlock, for example.

Warlock consisted of potent, screeching blonde banshee Doro Pesch out front, plus five Johnny-no-marks behind her on the gear. They sounded very similar to the Scorpions (most German metal did), so when Warlock burst forth with *Burning the Witches* and *Hellbound*, they were so busy headbanging that nobody thought to ask Doro to take her top off. She eventually fired the rest of the guys, though, and these days has a solo career under the name Doro.

Women never really infiltrated the world of thrash, death, or black metal, though a few had a shot at glam. It was easy—they had the makeup and the hairspray already on. The most notable of this breed were the vaguely successful Vixen, who emerged in the middle of the craze for big hair. The girls realized that the way to get themselves onto MTV and therefore the charts was to go straight for the commercial jugular and release three consecutive slo-mo power ballads, the videos for which were interchangeable: fish-eye lenses, arena stanchions, bouncing hair, pointy headstocks, leopardskin headbands, and the drummer twirling her drumsticks in slow motion through beads of sweat. Perfect. They smashed into the American charts, but fatally cut themselves off from their essential grass roots. They'd sold out before they'd tried to sell themselves in. They backtracked desperately in their interviews, but for us it was too late—they'd blown it.

"We didn't want to release those songs as singles, we wanted to release 'Fucked up on Heroin (Again, at Midnight).'"

"Come see us live! We're completely not like that live at all. We rock!"

Nope. Too bad. Shouldn't have done those videos, should you?

Their second album was raunchier than the first; only half of it was ballads. It was called *Rev It Up*, and they wrote some of the songs themselves. It did less well, and they split up, until they re-formed again when it was safe, after Kurt was dead.

These have been the most prominent and influential women in heavy metal. Although it's hardly the most illustrious roll call, we shouldn't forget the female influence elsewhere within our genre, which in some cases is as important as that of its men. For example, most people assume that the majority of consumers of heavy metal music are male, and although that might be true, there's a huge number of equally passionate woman metallers out there giving as good as they get, despite their unfortunate lack of civil liberties among us. Women feature in essential roles and positions throughout the entire metal food chain, too. Who is the best, most respected, most feared, most influential, and most kick-ass rock manager in the music business today? It's Sharon Osbourne, wife of Ozzy. Even Mötley Crüe called her "terrifying."

Finally, we can't leave this section without a few words on the Great Kat. Originally Katherine Thomas, from Swindon in Wiltshire, she was a classically trained violinist who moved to New York in her teens, and then at some key strategic point, switched over to axes. She specialized in rocket-fueled classical scales, and barged explosively onto the scene in 1987 with her debut album *Worship Me or Die*, which, she claimed, was "the first real revolutionary music since Beethoven." She was photographed half-naked with whips, fake blood, and hooded gimps, and was consistently offensive to all who crossed her path. She was supremely egotistical during her interviews, and often walked out halfway through. Sadly, *Worship Me or Die* remained unsold in the

Rossini's
Rape

Bloody
Vivaldi

Wagner's
War

racks, while Kat frothed at the mouth, raging against the injustice of the album's failure and urging us all to worship her the whole time. Next came *Beethoven on Speed*, featuring more of the same, only more so. Again, nobody bought it. Then she vanished—or so I thought.

She hadn't. She'd just disappeared underground, busying herself recording these. *Wagner's War* was inspired by the events of September 11, 2001. It features Wagner pieces played on the electric guitar at dizzying speeds.

Band on the Run

Cool Hand Luke headed up to Bedford for our first gig. Fucking Bedford yokels, they didn't deserve us; we were way too cool for that crappy place. At the venue, we drank bourbon and shook our bracelets as we watched the local pub-rock support band with barely disguised derision.

Up onstage half an hour later, yeah we had nerves, and the modest size of the audience was a concern, but this somehow felt different from how it'd been before. It felt like we were all incredibly tall. It felt like we were giant multijointed lizards bedecked in hats and necklaces and cigarettes and shiny vintage guitars. We teetered around the stage and played very loudly, and it nearly fell apart time after time, but whereas in Winchester such a musical shambles would have been a disaster, up here we were somehow beyond all that. We were just fucking cool, so who gives a shit what we actually played like.

We left five-second gaps of screaming feedback between the songs—accidentally, but still.

One thing that particularly surprised us was Pat. As soon as Martin scrubbed at the punky opening chords to "What You Gonna Do," Pat's previously immobile and apologetically shy frame sprang into spasmodic flailing life as he spat tortured bile out over the front row of our shuffling girlfriends. Wow! He was really going for it! We played ferociously—flashing angles, fluffed cues, sprawling feedback, and sudden surprise endings. By the time we came offstage, we were a gang. A band. A unit. And we all knew it.

Bedford didn't get an encore because they didn't ask for one, but we wouldn't have given them one even if they'd begged us. Pat didn't say a word to them all night. We're not fucking cabaret, you bunch of fucking farmers. I missed Owen's knock-knock jokes a little, but not that much. I was a grown-up now.

★   ★   ★

My job was going well; in fact Fratton had recently promoted me to team supervisor. I took this opportunity to branch out into Soho and lead my posse of terrified leafleteers down to Berwick Street, Argyll Street, or Carnaby Street, wherever I might bump into some strolling Wildean ragamuffins in my casual line of duty. After lunch the working women would dry up, so I was free to familiarize myself with all the important local metal landmarks.

Pat and Martin were crucial figures on the London glam scene. They were my passport to the entire network. It helped that they'd started their own Saturday night rock club in an underground bar on Oxford Street, which they'd christened The Hellfire Club. Pat and Martin and a short, coarse, podgy Yorkshireman named Tommy were the main guys—the club's trustees. They ran the show each week and took it in turns to DJ. Various girlfriends manned the door and the coatroom, while the men hung banners outside and carted dog-eared boxes of records around. Inside it was dark and oppressive. Perfect.

Before my first night down there, we sat around at Martin and Faye's flat in Manor House, drinking tall cans of lager, listening to trashy music, and talking about the band, the future, and world domination. Martin, a polite young man sometimes, asked if I liked to take drugs. *Well,* I said, *I used to, but not any more. But I'm not a pussy, I used to take loads.* He told me they'd recently got into taking speed. I'd never taken speed and didn't really know what it did, except, I guessed, sped things up somehow. I watched Martin and Faye put some white powder into their cups of tea. I'd been wondering why they'd made themselves cups of tea.

"Do you want some?" Martin asked me.

"What's it like?"

"It's cool, man."

"Yes, but I mean, what's it actually like?"

"It gives you energy all night. Makes you feel amazing."

"Amazing?"

"It's just really good fun. I promise it won't do anything bad," said Faye, and I blushed and couldn't meet her eye.

"I don't like acid, you see."

"It's nothing like acid." But they'd never done acid so how would they know? I went on with these boring questions for a good ten minutes before agreeing to a cup of tea with a dollop of white powder in it. It tasted like tea. In the minicab heading into the West End at about 9.30, I suddenly got it.

"Yay!" I shrieked.

"See?"

"Yay!"

"And it lasts for hours!"

I rolled down the window, goggled at passersby, and chewed rabidly at the insides of my cheeks. This drug was brilliant. It was a complete no-brainer!

The Hellfire Club

I must've gone to The Hellfire Club a hundred times. Most nights it went like this:

9:30–10:00 P.M.: Moping, changing tables a lot for no reason. Checking hair in the bathroom. Checking makeup in the bathroom. Trying to borrow some money off Pat or Pat's girlfriend. Martin DJs; he plays what he likes because there's no one here yet. The speed kicks in and I'm excitable like a puppy. I smoke cigarettes furiously and annoy everyone I come into contact with, especially Pat.

10.00–11.00 P.M.: Scandinavian girls trickle down the stairs and line up at the bar. I let them buy me drinks and then run away to hide until later when I'll hit them once again. Members of all the major London glam bands arrive. We discuss what drugs we're all on. Usually it's speed, but ecstasy is becoming popular. The crazier ones are on acid, and many more are stoned or doing poppers. There's never much heroin—at least not that's acknowledged. There's a few comedy drunks by now, usually metalhead Germans, who, we all mutter, shouldn't have been let in in the first place. Damn bouncers. Pat takes over the DJing. He hates this slot as he has to play "the hits" to get all the Scandinavian girls up to dance. He plays Bon Jovi, Poison, and Mötley Crüe, scowling.

11:00–midnight: The place is full. Martin and I are amphetamine-rushing, rammed into a corner, screaming into each other's ears about how spectacularly fantastic our band is. I try for eye contact with four or five girls I like the look of. I repair to the lavatory to tousle my hair and wipe off any smudged eyeliner with the end of my little finger. I lose my beer and try to get Martin to buy me a fresh one. Ricky arrives. I talk to him for a while but he's boring so I zigzag through the crowd while trying to maintain eye contact with the five girls. I feel like a god. I stand at the top of the stairs by the door to the street and arrogantly eye the queue of German metalheads and Scandinavian girls waiting to get in. They all either want to be me or have sex with me. I spit on the pavement, head back downstairs, and score another beer.

12.00–1.00 A.M.: Martin's DJing again, playing arcane glam, and I stand in the booth with him, looking arrogant and flicking through his records. We blow smoke out through our noses and suck our cheeks in, lights glinting off our hooped earrings. German metalheads approach the booth and request the Scorpions. We pretend we've never heard of them, and are then requested to play Metallica. We shake our heads patronizingly. Fucking idiots. The dance floor is full. Martin is taking all the credit but I feel my presence here is also valid. Martin chooses all the records. I sometimes put them back but I don't really understand the system.

1:00–2.00 A.M.: People do bad things: blowjobs in the toilets; heavy petting with fifteen-year-old Scandinavians in the cloakroom; doing drugs; vomiting. *You're my best mate—no you are!* Now it's the Stooges, the MC5, the Sex Pistols, much harsher. Everyone agrees to join everyone else's bands. Some band members fight. There are scenes with girlfriends. Only warm cans of beer are left behind the bar. Who's that on the floor in the corner covered in blood? A rumor that Hanoi Rocks' Andy McCoy is here. He isn't. He was a minute ago, I promise.

2:00–3.00 A.M.: The German metalheads are either asleep on the floor or have been chucked out. The Scandinavian girls who caught my eye are still here, waiting for me to come and take them somewhere to have sex. I would if Anna wasn't here. *Hang on, where is Anna?* She left two hours ago. Oh. I approach a Scandinavian girl. Tommy is DJing and playing some complete crap, but everyone's so out of it that it doesn't matter. He could play the Barron Knights and no one would notice. The lights suddenly go up and the music stops. Oh my God, look how ugly the Scandinavian girls are in real life! Hide behind DJ booth. Find

German metalhead there, passed out. Kick him. Stagger out onto street. Buy hotdog from a vendor. Still speeding so give it to tramp. Get on night bus. The windows fog up so I've no idea where we are. We pitch and rattle up toward North London—I hope. Anna's asleep in bed; I'm relieved she's not dead. I lie wide awake coming off the drugs, disintegrating inside.

King of the Night Time World

One evening at the Hellfire I met a raven-haired girl named Charlotte. She had a boyfriend, named Rick, who lived with Pat and played in another band, but the eye contact between us was intense. Late in the evening, Charlotte and I whispered things in passing, like *yes* and *when*? and *I'm desperate to.* Very naughty, very grown-up, I thought. Poor Anna appeared to be coming to the end of her usefulness; she had no desire to compete with the powders, the trinkets, and all this exhilarating midnight oil. I'd led her too far from her natural path already, which ought to have been college and then onward, but instead here she was. The very least she deserved was an honest amputation.

We screamed and cried and Anna moved out. Charlotte came round within the hour and we copulated fiercely and then discussed her moving in. Over the following few days, the sex moved up through the gears and my heart started to pop little bubbles—my own warning signs of l-u-v. Then Anna came round one evening for a friendly "catch-up" while Charlotte and I were busy. She knocked on the bedsit door and I opened it with Charlotte in the shadows behind me. The two girls stared coolly at one another, and then *blam*. Anna punched Charlotte in the face. Charlotte reeled backward but took it pretty well, swung back and lamped Anna straight on the nose and she crumpled, her glasses hanging of her face. Then Anna whooshed up into Charlotte's midriff and they both toppled flailing onto the floor, squealing through clenched teeth. They pulled hair and called each other bitches, fucking slut, fucking slut bitch, while I stood watching in horror. I eventually managed to separate them, but it wasn't easy. They'd ripped each other's clothes and Anna's glasses were smashed up on the floor. They both lurched again, but I was ready, and I tugged Anna away down the stairs and escorted her down toward the subway station. She was so dazed that I wasn't asked for explanations—not that any were needed, the situation was so pathetically plain. We hugged and I was deeply ashamed and she went off down the tunnel in a zigzag. I went back to Charlotte bouncier, but the light in her eyes had been switched off. Standing there on my threshold in her torn clothes, she said she wanted to go home now, thanks. *Why?* I just do, OK? *Do you still want to move in?* Another time. *Can we talk tomorrow?* I'll call you. *Promise?*

She didn't call. I waited by the phone in the Fratton office all morning. I eventually called her, but she was frosty and dismissive. She was back with Rick and I was dumped, and that night I sat down alone with my Les Paul and wrote a song called "Waste of Time." The chorus went: *I thought I saw you smiling / I couldn't see through your lies / I thought I could write a love song / It's all a waste of time.* That'll teach her, I muttered to myself. Postmodern, dude.

The boys liked "Waste of Time." They respected my bitterness. Charlotte was part of our scene, friends with Faye and Caroline, so it always felt very chewy and grown-up whenever we played it. (I learned later, however, that they were only pretending to like it—they actually thought it was "depressing.")

Martin had done photography at Wolverhampton Polytechnic, so was therefore in charge of the group's artistic direction. We all had to submit any cool photos we possessed of ourselves in previous incarnations into a communal band pool. He used them to make flyers and posters and stuff. And we changed the name of the band, because we all thought Cool Hand Luke was stupid. We were now Cat Ballou, named after the Jane Fonda and Lee Marvin '70s comedy Western. For a band like us, any name featuring "Cat" (or "Dog") was acceptable (like Faster Pussycat, Cats in Boots, the Cathouse, the Great Kat). Martin designed a logo and it was agreeably faux-Western.

Next, he set up a photoshoot in his back garden. We huddled, semiclad, in front of a white sheet, as Martin fixed his camera on a tripod, set the timer, then ran round to join us. The photo session was taken very seriously; we'd each brought at least ten changes of clothes—I alone turned up with seven different hats. Ricky had

just the one, his trademark green bowler hat, and matching green velvet jacket. Baz had turned up in a cymbal-manufacturer's T-shirt, so we had to dress him in some of our clothes instead. Never in my life had I taken myself as seriously as I did that afternoon in Martin's garden.

L–R:
Me, Baz,
Ricky, Pat,
Martin

We pouted, preened, and winked into the camera without shame or shyness. We weren't playing around anymore.

There were lots of other London glam bands on the scene, but we were contemptuous of all our rivals. They included:

The Silver Hearts. Cheap Trick copyists (i.e., quite good) with a short-assed pretty boy frontman with stupid dreadlocks. The Silver Hearts always got reviewed in *Kerrang!* Didn't help them in the end, though, did it?

Carrie. The eponymous Carrie was an infamous geezer who ran a clothing stall in Kensington Market. Carrie's band always consisted of the four longhairs he'd most recently bumped into—

always very young, naïve, and new to the city, and dreadfully underrehearsed. I was lucky not to have met Carrie before I met Pat, otherwise I would've gotten drafted. There's only one word I can think of to describe Carrie, and that's *hooded*, like Fagin.

The Pleasure Victims. All the shapes, very pretty (actually acne-ridden), thought they were the bee's knees but were actually shit. Bad AC/DC copyists. Lived the lifestyle to the max. Probably our chief rivals. They never made it. Bad luck, lads.

Suicide Blonde. Everyone felt sorry for them after INXS hijacked their cool name for one of their crappy songs.

So far we hadn't put a foot wrong. It was only a matter of time, I mused, before *Kerrang!* noticed us and stuck us on the cover, or at least included us on a poster. I already knew what I was going to wear for the photo shoot: *not much.* Then, out of the blue, we were offered two Central London support slots. One at the Borderline, and one, amazingly, at the Marquee Club. This was some seriously heavy shit.

The Borderline gig flashed by; it was OK—we supported the Silver Hearts and played timidly, but well enough. We were only allowed to play a twenty-minute set, and unfortunately quite a lot of that time was spent waiting for Ricky to recover after he got a nasty electric shock off a microphone halfway through "Waste of Time." Despite this slight setback, we went down well. Nobody walked out. But even onstage at the Borderline, all we could think about was our forthcoming Marquee gig.

The Marquee

Dressing rooms are strange places to be before those last few steps into the spotlight and potential humiliation. The drummer is annoying everyone by whacking the walls with his sticks, the bass player is talking to three people you don't know, one holding a joint, the singer is contractually AWOL, and I'm trying hard to speak to my fellow guitarist about something important and technical, only he's deep in conversation with his drug dealer. He spins round annoyed.

"What do you want, for God's sake?"

"Oh, sorry, I was just . . . I just wanted to check that you were in tune."

"Who fucking cares if I'm in tune. I'm busy."

"Right."

But it was fair enough; Martin was rarely in tune anyway, so it was naïve of me to expect him to suddenly start caring now.

There were a lot of people waiting to see us out in the audience. There was a genuine buzz, and I was shaking so much that I couldn't put my eyeliner on properly. Suddenly it was time for us to go on. *What, already?* It seemed terribly early—hardly even tea-time. We were shooed up the steps, carrying our instruments (only I'd left mine on the stage for the audience to admire) toward the cheering. Whiteout.

I'm onstage at the Marquee. I'm onstage at the Marquee.

The lights were so bright.

I'm onstage at the Marquee. I'm onstage at the Marquee.

My guitar is over there.

Do something, fuckwit.

I'm onstage at the Ma—

Shit! Martin's started already!

For the first couple of songs, I stood on my side of the stage like a doped-up orangutan, messing up my parts and staring droopily out into the fire of the spotlights. Stagefright, you see? But I gradually acclimatized and got used to the fact that the onstage sound was so awful I couldn't hear my skewed guitar solos anyway.

That night, for the first time, people actually came to watch *us* play. We'd built up a reputation as a band of lean, mean, devil-may-care motherfuckers. Not a metal band either, thank you very much. No, we were punky, spiky, with dirt under our fingernails; we were a raw antithesis to most of the Day-Glo stuff that was currently prancing about town. I'd also learnt the requisite rock 'n' roll poses. Gone were the days of the Trash Can Junkie shuffle; now I arched and lashed about like a pro. We were loud and angular and flashy, and fired wild malevolence into the crowd, guitars bouncing off our spindle knees. We were whippet thin and our instruments screamed feedback, and at the end we dropped our guitars on the floor where they clanged and fedback even more, while the house lights went back up. Afterward, we took girls (but sadly no journalists) into corners to listen to them tell us how truly kick-ass we were. Actually I think we'd outgrown the adjective "kick-ass." Patronize us with an adjective and we'd give you a withering look.

After these two shows, I was convinced we were standing on the very cusp of celebrity. I phoned Owen to gloat. He was back in Winchester.

"Back for good?" I asked.

"For now."

"What happened?"

"I needed this town back."

"You ran."

"I came home."

"I'm still up here fighting."

"So I hear. I saw Anna the other day. She's back too."

Silence

"How is she?"

"She's had it hard. And, well . . ."

We'd both been listening to Bruce Springsteen's *Nebraska*.

"Well what?" I asked, feeding coins.

"It's hard to say."

"Say."

"I accidentally shagged her."

"I see."

We paused.

"When are you going to come and visit us again? I've got something to show you," Owen continued

"Show me what?"

"It's a surprise."

I caught the train to Winchester, mostly to gloat about our Marquee gig, and met Owen alongside the recreation center. He'd cut off all his hair and grown a heavy black beard. I'd already guessed that he'd gone and done something ridiculous like that, but now I suddenly felt all stupid in my frilly shirt and dressage. We went to the pub and he told me that he'd written a concept album. Christ.

"What's the concept?"

"Aha!"

I sipped wearily at my lager and lime.

"It's a concept album about everything that happened."

"What happened where?"

"A concept album about the Trash Can Junkies story."

It was true. Not only had he already written an album's-worth of material, he'd also wangled himself a government grant to fund it. He'd even had a feature about the stupid project, and his photo, in the local paper, the *Winchester Extra*, smiling and holding an acoustic guitar.

Some of the songs for the concept album were: "Fire on Kingsgate Street"; "Tracks in the Snow"; "When We Were Junkies"; "Sleeper's Hill"; "Twelve Minutes 'til Rock"; "I Love Rock"; and, "Johnny."

I went to see my parents, to inform them of my unprecedented success in London. Small was seeing another guy, slightly older, who was soon to become my stepfather, Pete. And Fa, to everyone's delight, was doing much better for himself. He had a new place to live and was much happier. He even had a new girlfriend, and he enjoyed embarrassing Mel and me by graphically describing his latest sexual experiences.

"She grabbed hold of my crotch and—"

"Stop! Please stop!"

"And then I took off her bra and—"

"Noooooo!"

He'd started playing the organ for a local jazz band, the Burning Jaspers. I went along to the pub to watch them play, and they were pretty damn good, though Fa was turned up louder than everyone else, which seemed slightly unfair, though inevitable, as he was blasting out through his trusty Farfisa amp. After the gig he showed off all his new hepcat bandmates and handed me a demo tape they'd recorded.

"The organ's not loud enough on this, though. It needs a good remix, with the organ much louder."

The hepcats rolled their eyes, and Fa instructed the young percussionist to pack up all his gear for him—there's a good lad. Then, over a pint, he began to spell out his plans for the Burning Jaspers's conquest of the entire south coast.

"It's all about contacts," he confided, and we all laughed.

Chapter Fourteen

round and round

Damn it, Baz left the band. He wanted to devote more time to his other, better bands, he told us. Martin got angry and stalked around the room, whacking the remote control against the sofa. We waited for London's drummers to form an orderly line, but, to our surprise, they didn't. In fact, over the next few months we got through more drummers than Spinal Tap. Drummers were supposed to be stupid, everyone knew that, but we were still amazed at the consistent stupidity of the countless

■ CAT BALLOU
*urgently seek drummer with good
image. Influences Pussycat/Stooges.
For details call 081-888 7389 or
081-802 1299.*

drummers that kept on leaving Cat Ballou. I lost track of the number of times we had to put this advert into *Kerrang!*

We went through lots of bass players, too. Ricky moved to L.A. to be famous. Sadly, he never made it. From here on in, Cat Ballou was basically just me, Pat, and Martin—the all-important core of the band. The other two (and they changed by the month) were there to fill out the ranks.

To Pat and Martin, the Hellfire Club was almost as important as the band itself. Our lives revolved around it. One night down there, I was totally in there with two hot chicks, one on either side of the room. The first was Oriental-looking, with multicolored hair down to her waist and a very large chest. The other had long, black Medusa ringlets and oilslick eyes that I couldn't escape; they quite literally followed me around the room. She was indescribably beautiful. My attempts to chat both of them up sagged when I discovered they were best friends and, worse still, thought everyone in the club was stupid except for them.

"It's just a bunch of heavy metal saddos," huffed the one with the eyes, whose name, I'd discovered, was Kathy.

"I've never seen such a crowd of assholes," continued her friend.

"Are you sure?" I replied, confused.

Despite her contempt for the Hellfire hippies, Kathy liked me. I went home with her that night. She lived with two gay guys in Kensal Rise in North London, in an apartment over a carpet shop on a railway bridge. We didn't have sex because she thought there was something really special between us and she didn't want to cheapen it by shagging straight away. "Yes I agree," I said, sitting on her bed grumpily with my arms folded.

Kathy was riddled with angst. She was over from Montreal on

a temporary work permit and was working as a hairdresser on Sloane Street. She was half-Jewish, but in total denial about it. She told me she had a history involving bad drugs.

"You mean acid?"

"No, don't be stupid. Acid's *fantastic*. I'm talking about proper, serious drugs."

I had no idea what she was talking about.

"Look at this horrible nose. It's got ugly Jew bitch written all over it!" She'd clench her nose with thumb and forefinger and angrily tweak it from side to side. "Stupid fucking Jewish nose!"

I mean, it looked great, she was beautiful, what was she on about?

"My dad, you know?" Her folks were divorced; her mother was Catholic and her father the Jew. "He's like, '*Oh, you marry a nice Jewish boy!*' My gran's trying to get me into all this Jewish shit. It's . . . fuck off, you know? Leave me alone!" She gesticulated wildy.

"Right, yes."

"I'm so close to my mother," she said.

"But not your father?" She'd told me he was a millionaire. He sounded fine to me.

"He's just so fucking *Jewish.*"

Kathy was a good hairdresser, but her work permit was due to expire in six months' time, so unless she could find a friend or some other kind soul to marry, she'd be deported back to Montreal.

"Is it nice in Montreal?"

She looked at me hatefully. "It's a shithole."

"Oh, I'm sure you'll find someone to marry you. Just offer a bit of cash, a divorce in a year or so. It'll be a piece of cake!" I said after we finally got round to having sex, which was the next day. Kathy was into handcuffs and being tied up and licking food off the body and stuff like that. She was depraved.

I moved in with her. The gay guys didn't mind, they liked me. I practiced the guitar and used their bathroom products and smelled much nicer than before.

One of the first things Kathy and I did together was go to Wembley Stadium to see Guns N' Roses, who at the time were the biggest band in the world. It was my first, and to date, only stadium rock experience. We took the subway, walked up Wembley Way hand in hand, and stood in the pitch's center circle, right in the middle of the enormous crowd. I was ridiculously overexcited. The Gunners were touring on the back of their pair of new double albums, *Use Your Illusion 1* and *Use Your Illusion 2*. However, because of a series of mysterious goings-on behind the scenes, the albums weren't actually out yet. This meant that we were all gathered in the stadium to watch them play a whole load of songs that nobody knew.

The Gunners came on two hours late—two hours of holding our bladders (or doing the old trick with the plastic bottle)—and as soon as they appeared, the crowd bounced us a good fifty yards from where Kathy and I had previously been standing together. They opened with a song nobody had ever heard before, but we didn't care; we were all G N' R disciples.

Ever since they'd burst out of the traps in 1986, Guns N' Roses had been my (and everybody else's) favorite band. And their spectacular meteoric rise meant that when heavy metal was killed by Kurt Cobain just a year after this Wembley gig, it was the Gunners that had the furthest to fall out of everybody.

Guns, Roses, Brickbats

Why did we all fall for Guns N' Roses so completely? This delinquent fivesome from Los Angeles all lived in a single room together, never washed, and had a singer with a voice that sounded exactly like my alarm clock; was there really anything new going on here? The main reason was that, suddenly, here was a band that was dark. We realized this straightaway, and were fearful. In the late '80s, there wasn't much else around in the way of darkness. All of Guns N' Roses's contemporaries were (despite the PMRC's paranoia) about as fluffy and intimidating as Easter bunnies, regardless of some Herculean drug-taking (Mötley Crüe) and Satanism (thrash metal).

Guns N' Roses were palpably dangerous, despite an early flirtation with bangles, Aqua Net hairspray, and pouting. They were the only band whose next move was impossible to anticipate. Their general unpredictability was one of the things that kept us on the edges of our seats. They might hurt themselves, we worried, which of course they ended up doing in quite spectacular fashion.

After decades of depravity from the likes of the Stones, the Zep, and the real 'Smiths, nobody was seriously expecting anyone to rewrite the rulebook on how to sabotage your own extremely promising career. Hadn't all these tales already been told? Their first trip to the U.K. inspired the *Daily Star* headline: "A rock band even nastier than The Beastie Boys is heading for Britain!" They urged us not to attend, which is always the worst thing to say.

Guns N' Roses were cunning right from the start in that they all looked different from one another, so there was something for all of us before you even got to the music. They appealed to everybody in rock, and that hadn't been done since the days of the Zep.

On cheery drums was chronic heroin addict Steven Adler. Adler was the one to appeal to your old-fashioned heavy metal fan; he could've slotted perfectly well into,

L–R: McKagan, Rose, Slash, Adler, and Stradlin

say, Iron Maiden or anyone of that ilk—fluffy blond hair, tight blue jeans, usually a cymbal manufacturer's logo on his black cut-off T-shirt, an annoying permanent grin, and of course a gleaming pair of ankle-hugging white sneakers. For me, he was their weakest link (he even smiled while he was playing the drums). Adler was soon fired; he hadn't been able to keep it under control like the others, and he sued the rest of the group for "forcing him into addiction." He spent his days spiraling further into the depths of his own narcotic consumption, while his opportunistic lawyers chipped away for snippets of the band's rising fortune as they all struggled with burgeoning habits of their own.

On the bass was their punk, Duff "Rose" McKagan. You could tell he was a punk because he wore a padlock on a chain round his neck, a ripped Ramones T-shirt, and big bulky high-laced boots, and was from Seattle. He talked about bands like the Misfits and Black Flag, who to us were obscure and scary, and it was only his fluffy bleach-blond hairdo that gave him away as being a little more metal than he was willing to admit. But Duff was cool. He was lanky and wore his bass at his knees, which was the correct way of wearing it. And he'd played in a band called the Fartz. Respect.

Izzy Stradlin, on rhythm guitar, was the coolest one, because he looked like a whacked-out cross between Johnny Thunders and Keith Richards. You hardly ever saw his emaciated face as he always wore a peaked cap over his eyes, and sunglasses, and whips of black hair that swept in across his jawline. He played a big hollow-bodied semiacoustic guitar, which meant that he was more of a junkie beat-poet character than a guitarist in a heavy metal band. He always seemed to be facing away in the photos, like he really didn't care whether he was there or not, which was in actual fact exactly how he *did* feel, and he left the band a few years later, bored by their dysfunction and excess. He'd been driving to the gigs in his own bus with his dogs and girlfriend, trying to be normal, which wasn't really allowed in G N' R.

Slash was the boozy comedy-wasted rocker—leather pants, creaky leather jacket, huge black cowboy boots, a tumbling heap of tight black curls (nobody saw his face until 1990, when he fell blind drunk onto his back in front of a photographer), a top hat and a swirling bottle of Jack Daniels superglued to his right hand, with a Marlboro in the other. Oh, and a Les Paul superglued to his knees. Slash was an alcoholic drug addict, and the best, most honest guitarist to emerge since Jimmy Page. He didn't seem to have a single care in the world, just so long as he had his Jack, his Les Paul, and his Marlboros. Indeed, he said so much himself, all slurred, in interviews.

And finally, with the microphone, metal's most charismatic man ever, W. Axl Rose (which is an anagram of oral sex, if you ignore the W). Somedays Axl dressed all in leather with a peaked cap, aviator shades and a T-shirt complete with pink Thin Lizzy logo. Often he wore a red paisley bandanna with just a pair of leather strides. Later he began to favor a leather kilt. And then some fantastically tight white Lycra shorts, which left little, if anything, to the imagination. He was covered in provocative tattoos—bright artless clumps all down his forearms. Axl was a redhead—fiery, unpredictable, a loose cannon, and extremely attractive, said girls (and the boys, in private). Axl was also blatantly unhinged—you could tell just from the way he danced (he couldn't—he just spun, arms wild, on the spot, and swayed a lot), and so he got grudging respect from the thrashers as well.

In 1986 G N' R released a live EP, half of cover versions, on their own record label. Yeah, whatever. But next came their masterpiece, one of the greatest albums ever made: the ruthless, the driven *Appetite for Destruction*. And it was the lengthy hangover resulting from this record's enormous success that finally sent Axl to the place in which he sadly still resides: tragic self-delusion.

Appetite for Destruction swings. It really, truly swings. It doesn't mope along in 4/4 time, pausing occasionally for a cup of tea and a ballad; it's one swaying, swearing, chopping, hopping, fiddledy-dee monster. It bites meat out of your ass then gives it a sweet methadone tonguing on the follow-through. It's music to wave your sweater around to. It's music to drink clear spirits to. It's music made for fighting, but fighting like they used to do in the olden days—fighting involving flinging things.

Appetite came out on the same day as Aerosmith's this-really-is-our-comeback-this-time *Permanent Vacation*, in the summer of 1987. We all listened to *Permanent Vacation* and were impressed at how awesome it was, and didn't get round to playing this new hyped L.A. band's debut, with cover art featuring a giant psychedelic monster poised to rape a young girl who looks like she's actually already just been raped anyway (banned almost straight-away), for a couple of days. But then, when we did, it was boom! Sorry Mr. Tyler, Mr. Perry, we may be gone some time.

A year later, *Appetite* was number one in America, and Axl's hips were swaying in spandex and white leather in the faces of the nation, as their record label plundered the album's very soul, for single after single after single. Which we thought was great, actually; singles meant videos, which were requested enough to get them onto real, normal TV, so we could feast our lovelorn eyes upon them as much as we wanted. The first single to be sheared off *Appetite* was a brave choice—a rattling punk statement of arrival—"It's So Easy" (which proved to be a prophetic title). It wasn't pretty—it only had about two notes in it—and halfway through, Axl breaks off from the barely even melodic menace to tell us to stop thinking we're cool and "Fuck off!" How exciting!

Live they were killer. Straight after they released *Appetite* they flew over to the U.K. for an introductory tour, and despite pressing redial fifty times, the Hammersmith Odeon's box office stayed resolutely engaged. About six of us were trying, too.

Guns N' Roses are the only band I know of that played live without set lists. They just played whatever came into their heads on the night. This is amazing when you think about it (even eXposed had set lists). They were an electrifying prospect, and Axl most of all. He was a whirling dervish personified: a squawking ball of negative energy, tossing off discarded clothing song after song, then disappearing stage left for a quick bandanna and kilt change; and let's trust a quick slug of Jack Daniels, too.

As their fame soared, the band released a mini-album of acoustic songs called *G N' R Lies*. This is where it all started to go wrong. Although they handled the switch from all-out physical attack to whimsical introspection surprisingly well, some of Axl's lyrics this time around were a little light on the whimsy and a little too heavy on the racism and homophobia. In his song "One in a Million," Axl requests that "niggers" get out of his way (he doesn't want to buy any of their gold chains), and muses upon the usefulness of "immigrants and faggots" and their "fucking disease"-spreading antics. Oh dear.

Now what do we do? Do we do anything? Do we take it back to the shop? Do we plug our ears when those lines come along? Or do we try to see it from his angle? That's what a lot of the metal press suggested. While not condoning his specific words, there were more than a few correspondents who said yes, that's all very distasteful and unpolitically correct, but just picture the terrible time Axl had during his (allegedly abusive) childhood in Lafayette, Indiana. He obviously felt like that while growing up, so why try and censor his raw artistic essence? It's *real life*, man.

Most people, thankfully, just said no, sorry, you can take your homophobic racist crap and stick it up your ass, you nasty, ginger little man. You're arguably the most famous rock star on the planet, the world's youth is hanging on your every casual utterance, your fans are in the unfortunate position of believing everything you say, you are in a quite frankly holy position to inspire. What you ought to be doing, surely, is singing songs about how cool drugs are. We forgave him, though, because we were already in love, spineless sheep that we were. Slash, who was half-black himself, was wheeled out to do the back-peddling on Axl's behalf. As usual, he slurred his way through the interviews.

Then began the long wait for what turned out to be an unprecedented simultaneous release of two double albums' worth of new material, the *Use Your Illusion* albums. The group's bloatedness was starting to define them. Not least the fact that suddenly there seemed to be twice as many people in the band as before. That evening in 1990, as Kathy and I hungrily consumed their Wembley performance, on top of the original band members there were now a whole new bunch of members who were pay-rolled instead of percentaged (an ominous sign): a new drummer, a keyboard player called Dizzy (not to be mistaken for Izzy), a trio of horn players, a percussionist, four female backing singers, and a bongos player. Axl dedicated his new Elton John–like ballad "November Rain" to the day's conditions, and we cheered as Slash, cigarette in mouth, climbed up onto the grand piano for some protracted soloing. Throughout the evening, Axl continued to rant against "unbelievers" and "pussies" and "everyone out to get me—and I mean everyone." Did that include us? He wasn't being very friendly, so we couldn't help but wonder.

A few weeks later, the band finally released the new albums. Kathy and I lined up outside Tower Records on Piccadilly Circus at midnight, which opened especially for the occasion. I stood in the line feeling sick, only having the cash for one of the albums, and as we half-stepped at grinding pace toward the gleaming piles of *Illusions*, I still hadn't made up my mind which one I was going to choose. Historical consensus has since decreed that *2* was the better of the twins, but I disagreed, as *1* had "Dead Horse" on it, which I believed to be a masterpiece (time has proved me wrong on this one). It was also the one I'd finally chosen at Tower Records, so I remained loyal to it. *2* featured a song called "Get in the Ring," which showcased yet more of Axl's fury, this time a personal attack on a couple of magazine writers who'd somehow irritated him in their line of duty. Axl was starting to look a little silly now; these paranoid rants were clearly and rather worryingly less cool than his old fighting talk on "It's So Easy."

Bless him, though, we all still said, hoping for the best.

Despite the records' flaws, they were taken very seriously by the world's press. Anything else that was happening in popular music temporarily halted while everybody attempted to digest the *Use Your Illusions*. Even the *NME* and *Melody Maker*—for years metal's archly superior enemies—devoted whole pages' worth of fussy text to each volume. Axl's spell had somehow entranced everybody, even those whose mission in life was to destroy such towering monoliths to excess. They were, right at this moment, arguably the biggest band on the planet. They could do anything they wanted. So from here, almost inevitably, it was all downhill.

Full-scale riots kicked off at their shows, most notably in St. Louis in 1991 after Axl decided at the last minute that he wasn't in the mood to go onstage. And whenever they did turn up, they were invariably several hours later than advertised, due again to Axl's whims and tantrums. Their increasing presence in the news pages (and for all the wrong reasons) was turning people further against them. Freddie Mercury died, and a tribute show was hastily arranged at Wembley Stadium. Axl, a huge Queen fan all his life, demanded Guns N' Roses play, so they were shoehorned onto the bill. *Hold on!* screamed the gay community. *Are you aware of what this man thinks of us? What the hell is this loathsome character doing playing at an AIDS charity event in commemoration of a homosexual man?*

Oh shut up, we all said. *This is Guns N' Roses, don't you know?*

By now, Rose had sole artistic control of the band, musically, financially, and in the hiring and firing. But the band's prepotency had infected his increasingly paranoid mind to the point where he was unable to switch it off. Even Slash and Duff, the only two original members left at the end of the mammoth *Illusion* tours, except for Axl, were intimidated by his erratic behavior and had long stopped arguing against any of his stupid ideas, such as his concept and plots for the superbly bad promo videos for "November Rain" and "Estranged." They set a low watermark for the medium that's still in place today.

The band toured on, breaking attendance records, sales records, amount-of-people-all-onstage-at-the-same-time records, and time-spent-keeping-the-audience-waiting-for-your-throat-to-"warm-up" records. At the end of it, they recorded an ill-advised cover-versions album which they mysteriously called *The Spaghetti Incident?* It didn't do very well, and things in the Gunners camp soon became very quiet indeed—in fact they disappeared for almost ten years.

Over this decade, Axl made no further public appearances, except by mistake. He became one of rock's missing persons—a casualty of his own success and self-regard. Rumors abounded as the years ticked by. He'd been arrested at an airport for some unknown mis-demeanor; the mugshot showed some crazed-looking fat bearded redneck. Surely that wasn't our Axl? His new bunch of hired hands had rerecorded the entire *Appetite* album in facsimile, "just for fun." They were about to release it. They didn't release it. It never existed anyway. *What the hell's going on here?* All we knew for sure was that Axl was now, officially, a recluse. Occasionally rumors surfaced of his plans for a repeat performance of world domination. He told us his new Guns N' Roses had an album on the way, and it was going to surprise us, and he was going to call it *Cockroach Soup*. Nope, scrub that, it was going to be called *2000 Intentions*. Ah, no, changed my mind, *Chinese Democracy*. It's been going to be called *Chinese Democracy* now for about five years and counting.

Axl actually pulled it together to play a few shows recently, but after announcing a full American tour he played his faithful old trick of canceling dates at the eleventh hour, provoking, all over again, riots outside the venues. Then he canceled the rest of the tour and fired the remnants of his backing band. Even his remaining admirers are finding it hard to care so much anymore.

Is This Love?

Everything was looking fantastic. Cat Ballou were cooking, I had enough cash for my speed, Kathy and I were a cool rock couple, and I was keeping my devotion to Faye under control. It had just turned 1991 and London was under a blanket of snow.

"Only two months to go now until I'm deported!" said Kathy breezily over a late breakfast one afternoon. "I hope I can find someone to marry soon!"

I watched her. "Well if you really can't find anyone else then I suppose I could do it," I said quietly.

"Oh no, you couldn't."

"I really don't mind. It would be a laugh I reckon, probably."

"Oh no, I'd never ask you. That would be much too close to the bone. It wouldn't be healthy."

"I'm just saying that if you can't find anyone else, then I'm happy to marry you. That's all."

"It won't come to that, forget about it."

"But if it does."

"It won't."

A few weeks later she admitted it looked like she was going to have to marry me after all. She had a way with words like that. She phoned her family to tell them, and her father immediately insisted on paying for us both to fly out to Montreal to attend a big party for the Jewish side of the family. *Your grandmother will be so delighted!*

"You did tell him it wasn't for real though, right?" I asked her.

"Oh yes. They're just a little . . . excitable on that side of the family."

"But why are they throwing this big party?"

"Oh, any excuse for a celebration!"

I felt curiously dispassionate about marrying Kathy. As most of our world existed outside normal everyday society anyway, this felt like just one more surreal incident in my winding path to glory. To me, it was a big joke, a fine example of my high-art agenda and overriding irreverence in the face of "duty." And I got to go to Canada, which was cool. Also, Kathy (through her father) had promised me money—about a thousand pounds—as a discreet financial thank you.

I would have done anything in the world for a thousand pounds.

I phoned Small to tell her what I was about to do, and the silence was deafening. But what could she do? I was all grown-up now, she reminded me, grittily, after she'd recovered from the shock.

"I'm going to have to tell the rest of the family about this, you know," she told me.

"But why? It's not for real."

"Will you be inviting Uncle Geoff to the wedding? He'll be very angry if you don't."

"But it's just going to be in a register office. We're not inviting anyone except for our friends, for the photos, which we need to prove it's real to the Home Office."

"You're not even inviting your own mother to your wedding?"

"Small, it isn't real."

She went back to telling me how angry Uncle Geoff was going to be. And she was right, he was.

In Canada we stayed with the Catholic, French-speaking side of Kathy's family. None of them spoke any English, and her brother was a socially inept clairvoyant who sat at the dinner table staring me out.

Her father was rotund and spent money like water; he drove

around in a cream limousine and was excessively jovial. He took Kathy and me into downtown Montreal, handed me a wad of Canadian dollars, and told me to spend it on whatever I liked. I bought a worryingly expensive pair of cowboy boots which I then wore to that evening's wedding celebration party. It was in her father's luxury high-rise apartment with the Jewish side of the family. The place was hot and airless, there was too much food, and I became drunk very quickly. The family were all lovely—much nicer than the Catholics. Kathy's grandmother repeatedly slapped my ass.

We were married in a register office in Willesden, and then trudged up the road to a pub for the wake. Martin took the wedding photos in the beer garden. We all looked very smart—we fastened our top buttons and donned those string ties cowboys sometimes wear, with what look like brooches at the top.

Kathy and I then had to go to Croydon for our Home Office interview. We answered all the questions correctly and showed them Martin's photographs, and Kathy came away with her new working visa.

Despite the fact that our marriage wasn't entirely authentic, Kathy and I now felt increasingly odd in each other's company. The fawning treatment we'd received in Canada only added to a new, pressurized, synthetic closeness. We somehow felt an obligation to act as if we were genuinely married. Maybe this hadn't been such a hilarious practical joke after all. Even our friends— who all knew what had happened—now perceived us as husband and wife; probably because, I mused to myself one lucid evening, we actually were.

To reclaim my lost status as a metal stud, I immediately began an affair with a Hollywood actress who'd turned up at the Fratton office one day for a few days' work. *Just to pay my phone bill, OK?*

Her name was Christina, and she wore a curly black wig, and to everyone's amazement it turned out that she actually *was* almost a proper film star. She'd played bit parts in films with

Michael Douglas and Melanie Griffith, she informed us all, constantly.

"I don't want any of you scum talking to me, OK?" she said matter-of-factly, as we left the office after her morning's training.

"OK," I said, joining in with everyone else and mouthing *bitch* behind her red, Versace-clad back.

We arrived at our street corner and spread out to entice the working women. I watched Christina in action. She was terrible. Although she did manage to get lots of women to stop, contempt dripped from her lips as she addressed them. I went over to offer some advice.

"Try smiling!" I said, smiling.

"Fuck you," she told me. She went to stand at the top of the road and desisted from actually approaching anyone at all.

The rest of us watched her with amusement. Instead of touting the leaflets, she was talking loudly into a cellphone the size of a brick—one of the first we'd ever seen. When she finally finished her calls, she came over.

"I'm hungry," she said. "Where's lunch?"

"Wherever you like. Maybe get a sandwich or something."

"A *sandwich*? I thought you said lunch was included in the deal, asshole."

"No one said that."

"*You* fucking said that, hair-boy."

I stared at her. She was very attractive. I thought I saw something. And I was hungry too.

"If you'll buy me lunch," I said, "then I know a Chinese restaurant just round the corner where we can have sex in the toilet."

She stared at me for fifteen seconds. Then she lit a long, stupid cocktail cigarette.

"Alright," she said.

Romance blossomed. She lived on a barge on the Thames behind Paddington, which swiftly became our love boat nest.

Sometimes she even took the wig off. She dated rock stars, she told me, so I would have to stay secret, which was fine by me. We went at it like rabbits, wherever we could find—in restaurants, graveyards, parks and alleyways, but mostly pub toilets. She eventually became relatively civil toward the working women, and stayed a while longer than it took to pay her phone bill.

Cat Ballou, meanwhile, needed a record deal to pay for our drugs, so we booked a session at a Hornsey studio to record a three-song demo. We recorded "What You Gonna Do," our staple live opener, which came out sounding wired and punky, and "For All Your Sins," one of my songs. I thought I'd been clever writing this. It was full of counterpointing chords that ground together really nicely. However it hasn't stood the test of time; it's a funereal dirge and features the worst backing vocals I've ever heard (mostly me). The final selection, "I Can't Help You," was our attempt at dance music; or rather it was a ham-fisted nod to the Stone Roses's "Fool's Gold." It was funky and the drums rattled and the guitars dropped out on the verses where Pat growled about getting shot by a preacher man back in 1969, and things like that. It was our best song and sounds perfectly passable even today. It has, ahem, a particularly good wah-wah guitar solo. We were pleased with how the tape ended up. To our relief, we sounded like we hoped we'd sound: fast, aggressive, and a little like the Stooges. We did nothing with the finished cassettes, though, because everyone was busy taking drugs and we couldn't really be bothered. We still played occasional support slots around town, at the Wag Club, the Camden Underworld, the Borderline; we even played the Johnny Thunders tribute show at the Marquee. Having cheated death for years, Thunders, everybody's favorite heroic junkie loser, had finally fallen. We'd been waiting for him to die for years. It was the end of an era.

Then, one morning, red alert.

"Have you seen *Kerrang!?*"

"No, why?" Heart beating faster. "We're not . . . ?"

We are!

There was a review of our recent performance at the Camden Underworld. I phoned Owen immediately.

"Hello?"

"Owen, it's Seb. Have you seen this week's *Kerrang!*?"

"No, I don't really buy it anymore."

"Go to Smith's, *now.*"

"OK, I'm going, I'm going."

"How's the concept album going by the way?"

"Well it's funny you should ask me that, because—"

"Goodbye." *Slam.*

And then a profound sense of anticlimax descends. And after that one begins the tedious but inevitable process of trying to read between the lines of the review. What does he mean, *pleasant*? What does *capable* mean exactly? How come he's mentioned Pat but not me? And so on. The review was average and very short. It said we looked good, were low-down and dirty and sounded quite dangerous. *Tick.*

We recorded another demo tape. This time it sounded even better, and we did a photo shoot for the cover in Martin's front room. We hung dark-red velvet drapes behind us, stripped off and sprawled over the sofa wearing just hats and tight black strides, with cigarettes stuck to our lips. This time around, we were going to try and do something serious with the demo tape.

"Get it played on the *Friday Rock Show*!" exclaimed our random knobhead bassist. The *Friday Rock Show* was Radio One's sole concession to metal. It aired every Friday night at ten o'clock and was presented by the iconic and gravel-voiced DJ, Tommy Vance. He played Magnum and Iron Maiden and Helloween. It was shit.

"And get a record deal with Def Jam!"

"Atlantic Records."

"EMI."

"Parlophone."

"*Geffen.*"

Drugs, delusion, inertia, indolence.

My Fratton money was slowing down and I was having to rely increasingly on income support and borrowing from Kathy to get by. We never made any money out of the band—what rare money we did receive from gigging was ploughed directly back into the drugs pool, or used to get Martin's photographs developed. Occasionally I was handed five pounds, for which I was effusively thankful.

Martin wrote the credits for the inside of the new demo in spiky writing. He listed the three songs, and then, underneath, the band members. As usual, the order went Pat first, Martin second, me third, and the bassist and drummer below. We were all OK with that, until I saw how he'd credited us. He'd put:

Pat: Vocals

Martin: Red guitar

Seb: Gold guitar

Outrageous!

"Martin, I'm happy to be listed below you, man, but I don't think it's fair to deny me credit for what I play. If you feel upset about me being called lead guitar for whatever reason, then I'd rather go at the bottom of the list than not have 'lead' mentioned at all," I said pompously.

He wasn't having it. He actually tried to argue that it was just "cooler" written like that.

"Red guitar, gold guitar. It's democratic," he snarled.

"But I don't want to be red guitar, gold guitar! I just want to be on there as lead guitar, because that's what I play. I play all the solos, I play everything, and now it looks like you're playing more than me, which isn't fair."

Martin picked up the remote control and I could tell he was preparing to whack it.

"I'm not changing it," he said.

I complained to Pat, I complained to everyone, and Martin was forced to amend it, against his will, to:

Martin: Red rhythm

Seb: Gold lead

We were all getting on each other's nerves.

Chapter Fifteen

hysteria

Our latest drummer was a young, crazy dude named Scott. He had a black Mohican, and was charismatic, hyperactive, and hard to pin down. Scott was a brilliant drummer—organic and instinctive—and we gelled brilliantly. Cat Ballou now rattled.

Scott liked taking speed too; in fact he liked taking everything. His favorite thing of all was to take whatever he could get his hands on, all at once, like a drug-crazed Animal out of *The Muppets*. And he got away with murder. No matter how many times he fucked up, disappeared, mislaid all of his worldly possessions, caught sexually transmitted diseases, didn't show up for rehearsals, stole money, or drunkenly agreed to join everybody else's bands, he was always able to charm his way out of the situation. I was in awe of his powers.

One evening, I was sitting alone at home watching television when I got a call from Scott's girlfriend, a spiky-haired biker chick called Sam, who was also friends with Kathy.

"Sorry to bother you like this, but I'm a little bit worried about Scott," she said. "He hasn't been home for two days, and I was wondering whether you'd seen him around."

This wasn't an unusual occurrence. Scott went missing all the time.

"Nope, sorry. I'm sure he'll be back soon."

Good old Scott! I thought, hanging up, looking forward to hearing the gruesome details of his exploits at our next rehearsal. A few hours later, it struck me that Kathy hadn't come home from work. In fact, thinking about it, she hadn't come home the night before either. I'd just assumed that she'd slept over at a friend's place. I called Sam back.

"I've got the same problem with Kathy," I said. "I don't suppose she's over there with you, is she?"

"No, sorry, I haven't seen her for ages."

"Maybe they've run off together!" I joked.

"Ha!"

"Funny!"

We hung up and went back to waiting. Sam phoned again at three in the morning.

"I've found out what's happened," she said.

"Oh, OK," I replied blearily. "And you want to talk about this now?"

"I think you'll want to hear it."

They had run off together.

OK, Kathy and I were hardly Romeo and Juliet, but I thought I'd have seen something like this coming. We'd recently moved into a large, airy apartment just around the corner from our rehearsal studios in Hornsey, and things were going along perfectly averagely. Was this really happening? Sam drove around

London on her motorbike, looking for them, while I sat at home building up an indignant fountainhead of self-righteous steam.

Two nights later, Kathy returned to the flat. I'd just been sitting there in a glaze of denial, a strange twilight zone of emptiness, speaking to Sam on the telephone, trying to piece together exactly how this had happened. Kathy went straight through to the bedroom without saying a word, and started packing up her stuff. I followed her through, open-mouthed.

"What the fuck's going on?" I demanded.

She ignored me, flinging clothes into bags.

"Speak to me, for Christ's sake!"

She continued ignoring me and I became hysterical. I shouted and pushed her against the bed. She said she was sorry, but it had just happened, and that was that. She felt I was more like a brother to her than a boyfriend, and yes, she was off to go and live with Scott, our drummer. I threw books and record covers around and wept tragically—hypocritically, considering my antics with Christina.

"But what about the apartment?" I whinged through red eyes as we grappled at the front door. "You can't just *leave* like this!"

"You owe me for rent anyway." She clattered down the steps. "I don't give a shit." And she was gone, leaving behind almost all of her possessions. A couple of weeks later, Scott and Kathy went to live in San Francisco and I never saw her again.

Sam and I grieved together over a vodka bender that lasted almost two weeks. We became close, and sexually fumbled, but it was just a confused friendship thing, and a vodka thing, and she soon became a lesbian anyway (that's the effect I was starting to have). I couldn't afford to keep the apartment by myself and was booted out, leaving most of my things helplessly behind.

By this time, Cat Ballou were altogether too self-important to care about our audience. Martin had become deeply involved in the drug underworld, and boasted constantly about his gangland connections. Most of his time was spent issuing scary threats to everyone. Pat was also taking way too many drugs, all kinds, usually all at once, and it was becoming increasingly difficult to talk to him down at the Hellfire Club.

"Hey there Pat, man. How's it going?"

"Pfff. Gl. Kkkkkkkl . . . kl . . ."

"Is it the drugs, Pat?"

"Gggggggg."

"If it's the drugs, just nod."

Ever so slowly, his chin would slump, full of drizzle, onto his chest, and then rise tremulously up again.

"Is that a yes?"

And then he'd fall to the side, but because he was turning into a rock star, he'd land on a chair at a rakish angle, and in the next chair would be a foxy chick who'd find his blurred catatonia sexually provocative. She'd be Scandinavian, and would buy him drinks all night that he'd spill down himself. All this while he was DJing.

The Last Command

I think I know what signaled the end—certainly for me—and if it wasn't exactly a white flag, then it certainly came across as a final, desperate cry for help from the heavy metal community.

Penelope Spheeris's feature-length documentary film, *Decline of Western Civilization Part Two: The Metal Years*, was (with ten years' worth of hindsight) a portrait of a money train literally seconds away from smashing into the painful buffers of reality.

You could call it a suicide note.

The film features Ozzy, Kiss, Aerosmith, Poison, W.A.S.P., Motorhead, Megadeth, and a vicious selection of deluded young up-and-coming Los Angeles wannabes who literally line up in front of the camera to commit cinematic hara-kari for our visceral delectation. It's a masterful piece of give-'em-enough-rope film-making, but you can't help but think that all Spheeris needed to do was just aim, focus, and let these pathetic souls express their motivations, desires, and alarmingly giant egos under their own steam.

Kiss's fifty-something Gene Simmons is filmed fingering fabric at a lingerie store, boasting about his sexual conquests and commenting on the backsides of the passing customers, all of whom ignore him.

Ozzy Osbourne is attempting to cook himself breakfast in his kitchen, but can't because his hands are shaking so much.

Poison are smug and unlikable.

W.A.S.P.'s Chris Holmes rambles drunkenly from a pool raft in the dark in his swimming pool, surrounded by empty floating vodka bottles, while his elderly mother sits poolside watching in silence.

Motorhead's Lemmy stands outdoors in the wind with his hands in his pockets, and is dry and dismissively witty about it all, but his very participation marks him as guilty by association (sorry, Lemmy).

Kiss's Paul Stanley reclines in a cushion-strewn room, surrounded by spread-eagled bikini-clad lovelies, spouting cringe-worthy sexist drivel.

And a selection of young Hollywood hopefuls reply to questions asking what they'll do if they don't become rock 'n' roll stars.

"But I will be."

"But what if you're not?" asks the narrator softly.

"But I will, don't you see?"

"But say you *don't* become famous. What will you do then?"

"But don't you see? I *will* become famous. I just will, I know it."

That's how I would've replied as well, although I refused to admit it to myself. We watched through our fingers. Look at all those idiots, said we idiots, idiotically.

The film showed quite clearly that all the good things about metal—the passion, the punch, the positivity, the posturing, the *entertainment*—had disappeared, and been replaced by this drug-addled, alcohol-bloated, deluded swollen troupe of Californian refugees. All of our cocksure rebellion had turned to mush. There's nothing in this world more jaded or tragic than the characters on parade in this film. They were ripe for the picking, for a cull, for death—and that was exactly what happened next. We had nothing left to offer the kids. We assumed the kids would swallow even our most foul-scented effluence—they'd done it a million times before for God's sake! Why not now?

When we first saw Cobain, it wasn't at all clear that he was the assassin who'd come to slit our throats. He had long hair for a start, professed a love of Black Sabbath, and, with his grubby bandmates had made a snotty but hardly radical debut album called *Bleach*. That was OK; metal was assimilating this nascent Seattle-based movement, tentatively described as grunge, pretty well. There certainly weren't any lines in the sand—not yet, anyway. There was Mother Love Bone, Tad, Mudhoney, Soundgarden, and the dreadful Pearl Jam, all enthusiastically frothed over by the metal press. So where's the threat? They had long hair and played guitar solos, and the kids moshed, and the bands sang about alienation, which made a pleasant change from songs about shagging and booze. All good. We were glad to see this grunge; it made a refreshing change from the hairspray diet we'd been on for the last five years.

Until *Nevermind.*

Even though Cat Ballou were on the very edge of all that was cutting, and considered ourselves leagues above anything so coarse or vulgar as (whisper it) heavy metal, from the outside I suppose I can understand why people still perceived us as just that. This was a problem when it came to attempting to recruit the drummer we needed to replace Scott. His name was Vic, and he was "above" the sort of thing we were doing, or so he claimed. Vic had ginger dreadlocks, wore a Hawaiian shirt, and smoked hand-rolled cigarettes, and his face looked like it had been through serious bouts of industrial drug abuse. He told us he'd once given himself a malt liquor enema.

"What happened?"

"I passed out."

"Oh my God."

"Yeah, it was alright."

Vic played drums for a semifamous grebo band (grunge wasn't quite there yet, but in reality that's what he was, the superior bastard) called Milk, who were known for having no tunes and being dirty. Vic smiled ironically whenever he was in our company; he was laughing at us. Even Pat and Martin were scared of Vic, so you can imagine my response. I was mute; I stared at my shoes in his company. He played a few rehearsals with us, and wasn't that bloody good anyway, so what's all the fuss about, guys? Vic smirked indulgently at my guitar solos as he tapped at his high hat.

He gave us more credibility, though. He agreed to join the band part-time, just for a laugh, and to help us out, seeing as he was quite friendly with Martin. Vic said that he had a friend who worked in a record shop, who'd gotten his hands on the second album from Seattle-based threesome Nirvana, and to watch out for it, because in his opinion it was going to blow people's minds.

"I've heard it," said Vic. "And it's true."

Vic knew more about that kind of thing than us, so we trusted him and bought it on the day it came out. We stuck it on. Yep—it's powerful; crikey—it's *angry*. It was pretty fierce stuff, and it began to get spun a lot down at the Hellfire Club, especially the first track, "Smells Like Teen Spirit." This tune was suddenly the sound of the times. We fed off it and felt it was ours, even though it wasn't. It was laughing at us. Little did we know that it was delving through our music at a million miles an hour; a burrowing virus rooting down toward the very core of everything we knew and loved and cherished and were made of.

Kurt Cobain Kills Us

Kurt Cobain was born in Aberdeen, Washington, in 1967. He was lower middle class. His family splintered while he was still young and he received his first guitar on his fourteenth birthday, exactly the same as me. He left home at seventeen, exactly the same as me. There are lots of books about him, not so many about me. At nineteen, Kurt claimed to know all there was to know, or rather all he needed to know, about rock 'n' roll. He understood all that lay behind and before him, and could see a path he hoped he'd be able to follow through its shit-encrusted corridors.

In Kurt's mind, everything had already been done, so the only route left to him was a self-necessitating mix of trailer-park guitars, a nihilistic and carefree U.S. punk attitude, and his own specific opiate of pure pop melody with lilting melancholic side salad that came mostly from a small clip of minor Scottish indie bands. He topped all this off with a fierce sense of individual self-expression. These were his tools, and his agenda.

Until *Nevermind*'s release in 1991, the guy still in charge at the harder end of rock was W. Axl Rose. We knew his reign was starting to totter when word came of run-ins he was having with Kurt and his new (according to some, evil psycho) wife, Courtney Love, backstage at awards ceremonies. Axl was starting to make a fool of himself. Kurt and Courtney would attempt to taunt him, leaving innocuous messages, saying "hello" and "how are you?," all of which were guaranteed to send Axl into a gigantic frothing rage. He couldn't see what Kurt could see, which was the fundamental ridiculousness of the whole rock circus. Axl didn't understand irony. He responded with apoplectic barrages of insults and warnings for Kurt to *keep his fucking bitch out of his fucking face or else.*

So, the metal world pondered, *if Kurt's not scared of Axl, who is he scared of? Is there nobody in metal prepared to take him on? Look at him there in his eyeliner and his cardigan and his little blond bob. Come on boys, if we all charge him at once, then surely . . . ?*

But Kurt was intelligent and opinionated. He knew who he was and knew what needed to be done, unlike metal, which had finally run out of ideas. Metal could only stand feebly by and watch "Smells Like Teen Spirit" endlessly rotate on MTV, killing off our traditional legends one by sinking, stinking one. Revolution was in the air.

The metal bands, alarmed at these developments, didn't panic, not yet. They were all safely ensconced in their plush Beverly Hills studios, with Bob Rock or Ron Nevison or Robert "Mutt" Lange, airbrushing their latest albums to perfection. But when their records were finally released in all their sickly pomp, no one came out to buy them. When Tower Records opened at midnight to sell the new Crüe album to the hardcore fans, the fans were nowhere to be seen. And when they booked the standard enormodomes for another sordid trek across America's midwestern bosom, they found themselves playing to empty seats.

Kurt and his band, Nirvana, and the newly empowered bands that tumbled down the mountainside beside him, swept heavy metal away; away from the malls, from the televisions, from the clubs, from the rehearsal rooms, from the record shops, from the guitar shops, from the radio stations, from the cultural landscape it had so effortlessly straddled. The giant heavy metal inflatable had been popped; twenty-five years of the devil sign and the squealing guitar solo undone in a matter of minutes.

Really, I'm not exaggerating—it happened virtually overnight. Some metal bands struggled on postapocalypse. They grew goatees, donned flannel shirts, and moved to Seattle, where they attempted to blend in with the new crowd, unnoticed. They even ditched the glitzy axes and switched to minimalist models instead. They tried to sing a little gruffer, and wrote about how sad they were feeling inside. But they weren't used to acting like this, and were unable to express their sudden disenfranchisement sufficiently within their canon; they were missing the cocaine, the pneumatic breasts, the leather, and all the Jack Daniels and fun they'd been having before.

And nor did it pass. Kurt wasn't just a blip on the scene—he was the prime mover, the cipher. The new rock tore through the halls, ripping up the furniture and setting it ablaze. Sonic Youth, the Breeders, Superchunk, Sebadoh, the Jesus Lizard, Pavement, the Lemonheads, Dinosaur Jr., Buffalo Tom, Flaming Lips, Screaming Trees; you could hear the momentum just in their names.

And, as with every movement, the shit slides darkly in and sucks up the deaf and the impressionable at double speed. Pearl Jam, Stone Temple Pilots, Smashing Pumpkins; this tiresome grunge lite became the new staple for the kids previously hooked up to Poison and Bon Jovi, and the new currency of the charts for the '90s.

Kaboom, metal was dead.

Leave Them All Behind

I fell in love with Kurt Cobain straightaway. I got it all, saw it all, and knew that he was right—we had to die.

Cat Ballou (all now hating each other) recruited a coarse young bass player from Leeds named Gordon. Gordon got through chicks like I got through cigarettes. He was attractive, weather-beaten, thick as pig shit, and he swaggered like his heels were pendulums. He was also homeless, though he did have a bass, which he carried over his shoulder like Dick Whittington. And since I'd been kicked out of my old apartment, I was now homeless too.

Gordon had a shady friend named Dave who'd told him we could stay in a squat he sometimes slept at, just off the Old Kent Road in southeast London. Gordon and I were desperate, so we agreed to move in. We carried our plastic bags of possessions down to the address we'd been given, and found a tired old half-collapsed house on a street lined with burned-out cars. There wasn't a bell, so Gordon knocked on a dirt-streamed, cracked bay window, while I waited by the curb with our stuff. Eventually, an elderly black man inched open the front door holding a baseball bat and asked who the fuck we were.

"It's OK," said Gordon, arms raised. "We're friends of Dave."

"Who the fuck is Dave?" replied the black man, moving through the door enough to be able to strike Gordon a decent blow with the bat if he felt like it.

"Dave," repeated Gordon, not moving, impressively confident.

"I don't know no one called Dave." The black man pushed up his thick glasses and squinted down at me. I smiled hopefully and mouthed *Dave?*

The man raised the bat. Gordon flinched.

"I'm not giving you a fucking key for the bottom lock. You can have a key for the top lock." He handed Gordon a latch key, spat on his doorstep, and slammed the door shut, turning the bottom bolt behind him so we still couldn't get in. We stood in the warm descending dark, unsure what to do, but then the man appeared again from behind his net curtains and shouted that we could get in if we negotiated through the semidemolished basement flat, up the back steps, and in through the broken glass of the back door, where there was another key in the lock.

We followed his advice and got into the house, where our new landlord was boarded up in his front room. The rest of this huge house was empty, and we had no idea what the etiquette was, so we chose a large room on the ground floor and fell asleep, scared and squalid on a stinking mildewed double mattress, hoping for the best but expecting more of the worst.

I awoke in the morning beside sweaty Gordon, his alarmingly large pornography collection and a single bare bulb hanging from the ceiling. We decided to explore the rest of the squat. There was an oily kitchen at the end of the corridor, and upstairs a filthy bathroom with a power shower that could just about dribble you clean if you were really determined. There was a locked door on the top floor—Dave's room, presumably there for whenever he needed refuge from his daily diet of crime and punishment, whoever or wherever he was. I never met Dave.

"Dave's sound," said Gordon. "Dave's a top guy. Don't fuck with Dave."

"I'm not going to," I replied.

"He'll fuck you over harder if you try."

"Honestly, I've no plans to try and fuck Dave over whatsoever."

"Let's hope not, for your sake," said Gordon.

We discovered that the old black guy downstairs was named Chapman. Sometimes there'd be a knock on the front door and we'd watch him go through the routine with the baseball bat again; it always involved lots of shouting with whoever wanted to come in. Even though it was almost empty, the house throbbed with paranoia. Whenever I felt brave and made a cup of tea, I'd open the cupboard to reach for a chipped mug, but I'd slam the door too loudly. *Shit, man, I can hear Chapman coming out. That's his cup.* I'd run back to our room empty-handed.

On the third day in the squat, we arrived home to discover our room had been flooded. A pipe had burst and the room was underwater. It was dark, the light didn't work, and it stank. We could hear Chapman's television blaring in the next room, but he didn't come out and say anything. Gordon's porn had suffered the most, along with all our clothes, but they needed a wash anyway, we supposed. This was the final straw for Gordon. The very next morning, he fled back to his parents' house in Leeds; he even left his bass behind, which, two days later, I pawned on Denmark Street for thirty quid.

I waved Gordon off, lifted out my remaining soaked clothes, and climbed the stairs to a small and empty boxlike room that was flooded with sunlight and had a narrow but clean mattress in one corner. I furnished it with a small cassette player from downstairs, and my notebooks, and stared out onto the summer trees that swayed over the street.

I couldn't afford to eat. I sat there for days, in a trance, watching the turning, divining branches heave and lift. I survived on water and cigarette butts and lots of sleep.

Despite this pitiful squalor, I was actually fine. You see, I had discovered two things.

A week beforehand, I'd gone to a Screaming Lord Sutch gig at the George Robey pub in Finsbury Park. I went with Sam and Faye, who were friends, and for once there was no Martin or Pat, nor anyone else from the scene to have to act cool in front of. Standing next to Faye, halfway through the show I suddenly grabbed her hand and held onto it tightly. Her body tensed, but she didn't let go. After the gig, we walked back to Sam's flat and drank beer. Neither of us mentioned the incident; Faye didn't even look at me. But the alcohol was wracking up the tension. A few minutes after Faye had left the room to visit the toilet, I leapt to my feet and ran down the corridor after her. I pushed clumsily at the bathroom door but it was locked.

"Faye!" I yelled through. "Let me in!"

"Go away," she whispered hoarsely. "*Go away.*"

"But I love you!"

There was a stunned silence. I stared at the door.

"*It's true. I love you! I've been in love with you for ages. Open the door. We were meant to be together. Please. Open the door!*" I rattled at it, but Sam had heard all the noise and dragged me away saying I'd had too much to drink and to come and lie down. But she hadn't let go of my hand, see? She hadn't let go of my hand!

The second thing propping up my draining body in my little room was the music on my cassette player. It was an album Kathy had left behind called *Dolittle*, by a group that I knew was on our banned list, the Pixies. I played it over and over again and could actually feel the walls inching down inside my head as I let a new consciousness slide upward. I had another tape too. *Screamadelica* was the new album by a band called Primal Scream. It sounded to me like *aliens*. I wandered, stunned, around South London with these albums on my headphones, almost weeping with new understanding. Utterly emaciated, jammed with unrequited love, it didn't matter. I had discovered the Music of God. I hollered and whooped in the street at passing old women. I walked for miles and miles, through summer rainstorms with holes in my shoes, dizzied by the burning asphalt. I cut my hair off.

Bad idea.

"What the *fuck* do you think you're playing at?" asked Martin as I sat in band headquarters, the Intrepid Fox pub on Wardour Street in Soho, with my new black bob hanging shamefully over my eyes.

"Why the fuck have you done that?" he screamed. Worse than the hair, I was also not wearing a pair of tight black jeans, for the first time in approximately five years. I was wearing a pair of blue jeans, and they were baggy on purpose. Passing rockers in the Fox glanced at them with displeasure; they were like garlic to vampires in here.

"And will you take those fucking headphones off and listen to me? And stop all that fucking smiling. What the hell's the matter with you all of a sudden? You're ruining the vibe of the pub.

What's that shit you're listening to, anyway?" He grabbed at my personal stereo and yanked out the cassette.

"Ride." He sneered at it. "What in fuck's name is *Ride*?"

"I love them," I smiled back. "Would you like to have a listen?"

"No I would not."

We got another gig at the Marquee. Beforehand Pat and Martin sat me down in a corner and told me that we had several record companies sniffing around us at the moment, and that now was a crucial time for the band, and it was important that we perform at the very top of our game, OK? I was surprised by this, as nobody had shown any interest in the group for months now.

"So the point of the matter is that it's important to project the fact that we're one cohesive unit out there, right?"

There was always trouble around the corner when Martin started speaking like a bank manager.

"Right?"

"Right," I mumbled.

"Which means that it's probably best, for the sake of the band, if you don't wear those trousers onstage tonight."

"Pardon?"

"I think it'll be better if you wear your tight black trousers tonight," said Pat. "Like normal."

"But I've had enough of tight black trousers. I want to wear these."

"I don't care what you think you've had enough of. We're Cat Ballou, not some shitty indie band of wankers. Now, if you want to be a fucking dickhead and go around in public wearing that . . ." Martin eyed me with disgust. I was also wearing a cardigan. ". . . that *shit*, then that's your own stupid fault. But when you're here on band business, you'll wear what you're told."

"But I don—"

"Shut up. You wear the black trousers tonight, OK? Or else . . ."

"Else what?"

"You'll regret it."

They stalked away, their jewelry tinkling. I didn't dare tell them that I'd also traded in my glorious golden Les Paul for a shitty old mustard-colored Fender Telecaster—the most un-show-offy axe I could think of.

I came damn close to wearing the blue jeans onstage, honest I did, but at the last moment I decided that I could wear the tight black ones and still be subversive, just with my upper half instead. I wore a tight black T-shirt with half arms, and stood cooly at the back of the stage in my hanging bob, a thousand times more relaxed than normal, and able to play properly for once. I played guitar solos of just feedback, missed whole verses just for a laugh, and sang my backing vocals with passion rather than apology. I didn't care any more—there was no pressure—I was a star. Afterward all our rival bands came up and complimented me on my insouciant "punk rock" performance and casual new bearing.

"Seb, you were like . . ." It was hard for them to say it. ". . . actually really cool up there."

"Thank you very much," I replied, rather baffled.

I could feel things from Faye, too. I sensed she'd seen this thing we shared, she'd opened her eyes to it, was blocking her heart from it like crazy, but it was there. We were in love, together, I knew it.

"I'm going to make it work with Martin," she told me. "I owe it to him."

"OK," I said. But I could hardly get the syllables out.

A splinter gang had emerged from the Hellfire scene, all of whom went back to Martin and Faye's flat after it closed to see in the morning behind heavy drapes. They'd started taking acid; halves of tabs to offset all the speed. I sat on the floor with a bag of white powder, whirring my way through clenched hours, clutching a rolled-up banknote and trying to get Primal Scream or Ride or

Teenage Fanclub or someone else they all hated onto the stereo, while surreptitiously staring at Faye through my new fringe. Sometimes they let me have one song, but usually took it off halfway through to relieved cheers, and on went Alice in Chains or Metallica or a Cat Ballou demo. Faye and I in our own universe of denial, on drugs yet again. Feelings so huge they dwarfed the room, the house, the street. We just stared at each other as often and as much as we could, trying not to get caught.

With the help of the local housing benefit office, I moved into a sublet on Highbury Grove, above a dry cleaner's, and tuned into John Peel on the radio. I sat on my bed, marveling at the Fall, and Pavement, and dance music, and daydreaming of being free from this rancid, dying scene. Metal was atrophying before everyone's eyes, and I was the only one who appeared able to see what was happening.

I took a deep breath and decided to leave Cat Ballou. What the hell. Enough stalling. I told them I'd had enough. Or rather, I told someone to tell somebody else to tell Pat. Not Martin; Martin scared the living shit out of me.

Bad plan.

First of all they confiscated all of my equipment: my Marshall stack, my Telecaster, all my effects pedals, and my entire record collection, which had been stored round at Martin's flat. And then all my friends dried up. Doors were suddenly shut in my face. I didn't mind this at all; all I wanted was to be out of it, and to be with Faye, but I was still surprised by the blanket hostility. After considerable begging, I got my guitar back, but nothing else. The rest of my things stayed in the basement of the Intrepid Fox, and I never saw them again.

Meanwhile, Faye had discovered that Martin had been cheating on her, and left him. He'd been treating her like shit for years, and her perspective had arrived at last. I knew she needed space right now, so I tried not to get in her way. I was having enough trouble over in Highbury. I appeared to be back at square one, yet again.

One late summer day, I'd just stepped out of the communal shower with a towel around my waist—still soaking wet—when I saw there were two people standing outside my bedroom door. It was Martin and his friend Glover.

"Hello Martin. Hello Glover." I knew something was terribly wrong. Martin sneered, and Glover, usually a sweet, placid guy, stood thuglike behind him, his backup in a floral print shirt.

"We're here to talk about Faye," said Martin.

"What about her?" I fumbled with the knob and they followed me into my room. I sat dripping on the edge of my bed, trying to smile.

"What have you been doing with her?" asked Martin, standing over me, jaw jutted out.

"Nothing." Shit. Who told him?

"I've heard you've been seeing her, Hunter. Is that fucking true?" He kicked at my stereo and the top clattered off.

"No, we're just friends, man, I promise."

Martin wiped everything off my small kitchen surface with his forearm, and it all fell noisily to the floor. "You don't fucking see her, alright?"

He lurched down and punched my wet chest.

"Alright," I said. "I'm not seeing her anyway, man. We're just friends, man. Calm down."

"You'd better fucking not be." And he started to kick my naked wet legs with his combat boots. I raised them up onto the bed, so he started punching my slippery torso instead. With all these blows, the towel shook loose around my waist, so there he was slapping a naked wet guy who wasn't defending himself, and I think he started to feel a bit self-conscious, so he stopped.

"If I hear one more word about this, then I'm going to come back here and kill you. Do you understand?"

"Yeah, I understand."

Martin stalked out with Glover close behind.

"See you, Glover," I said, but Martin had slammed the door shut. He'd picked up my keys as he left. I peered out of my window and watched him throw them over a fence as they strutted away down the alley.

I went out, but when I got back later I found that Martin and Glover had visited my flat again, and this time they'd really smashed the place up. All my books were torn up, my stereo was smashed, and there was paper everywhere. Records were snapped, clothes ripped, and my red lightbulb swayed forlornly. I couldn't have missed them by much. I found out later they'd had a second wind and come back to hurt me properly.

Love Knuckle

That was the last contact I ever had with Martin. He did break into my flat once more a few weeks later, but again, fortunately, I wasn't around. He just ripped stuff up and smashed a window.

Faye and I got together soon after. We were fantastic.

This is nearly the end, except I decided to have one last go at the band thing. I'd learned a lot. I knew how not to do it. My head was swilling around with all this wonderful new music I'd discovered.

Bring it on—I want my own fuckin' band!

It happened fast and from out of nowhere, like all the best things. It started as a jam session. Me and two girls.

Sam: Scott's old girlfriend; drummer; still half-affiliated with the Hellfire/Pat/Martin scene, but independent-minded enough to contemplate playing a little music with me on the side, so long as they didn't find out.

Jo: I didn't know Jo, but she was nice—long blonde hair; dyke;

a damn good bass player; up for playing some good music without agendas.

Me: Guitarist; singer; songwriter; focal point; leader. No agendas either (except those).

The music we made was the best I'd ever been involved with. At our first rehearsal together we locked into a wonderful hypnotic groove and the buzz was thick in the air along with the deep bassoonlike feedback. Even our feedback had vibes. We blissed out and lost track of time. None of our songs had names; we improvised wildly and built things into crescendos and trails and stutters and yawns and back up to white-noise howling. I put my guitar through the hoops and it was magnificent. We were great. We chopped these sonic squalls into song shapes and sizes and gave them nicknames and talked about getting a singer; I didn't have enough confidence yet to do it all myself. We auditioned a few and they were terrible, so I sang more until I got better, and then quite good, and then (this is my book so I'll write what I like) *stupendous*. I ripped off Kurt Cobain badly. The quiet bit followed by the blasting sandpaper bit.

I played a tape of my vocals to Owen and asked him to guess the singer.

"No idea," he said.

"It's me!"

"*No.*"

"It's really me!"

"It sounds like Kurt Cobain!"

"I know! But hang on—not that much like him. I'm my own man first and foremost."

"Are you sure this is you?"

I was proud. All three of us were; we were genuine quality; we were organic; we sounded like the ocean.

But the other two walked all over me. I don't know why but they did. When it came to naming the band, they wanted to call us Love Knuckle.

"That's the worst band name I've ever heard," I said evenly, prepared for discussion. We discussed it briefly, and then it was back to Love Knuckle again.

"I can't be in a band called Love Knuckle," I protested. "It sounds disgusting! It sounds like pornography!"

"We don't care," they replied.

"Hang on, this isn't fair! I have to have a say as to what we're fucking well called, surely? I'm the fucking singer and stuff! I hate the name Love Knuckle. Please guys, can't we change it to something else?"

"No, we like it. Too bad. Just deal with it."

Love Knuckle we were, then.

We booked a gig in Islington and were good, if nervous. I wasn't really one for writing lyrics (I barely had words for the choruses), so I improvised 90 percent of the lyrics up there onstage. I don't know if anyone noticed.

We recorded a demo, coincidentally at Vonn's studios off the Holloway Road—the very same place the Trash Can Junkies had recorded five years before. Things were souring though, the girls on one side and me on the other. All my ideas were "shit," my ace avant-garde guitar solos were vetoed, and my vocals were recorded with no kind words of encouragement, which, because I was new to this, were needed. The whole situation became increasingly hostile. It was the worst fun I'd ever had in a studio. But the demo sounded good. My vocals were low enough in the mix so that you could hardly hear them, and that kept the girls happy at least. We made up a load of tapes, did nothing with them, and bickered. Hooray for rock and fucking roll.

I asked Faye the other day how Love Knuckle ended, as I couldn't actually remember. I seem to have erased the final act from my memory.

"Sam kicked you out, didn't she?"

"What!"

"Sam booted you out of the band. I'm sure that's what happened. Because of all the bullshit that was still going on with Martin, she kicked you out."

"Of my own band? Are you sure?"

"Pretty sure, yeah."

All this put me off playing in bands, and I haven't been in another one since.

I moved in with Faye, we slotted together perfectly, and the big hole in my middle that had required rock fame and fortune suddenly disappeared; it had been filled. I locked the Telecaster away in a closet and tried to forget about it.

"So what are you going to do now?" Faye asked.

"I don't know," I replied. "Maybe I'll write a concept album about everything that's happened."

fa

Fa died in March 2001. For the last seven or so years of his life, he'd gradually withdrawn into hermithood, living in a single room that we were never allowed to see until he was physically unable to keep us out, in a dusty old house with a retired colonel who Fa told us used to be a spy. His drinking was now just a steady trickle, slowly visible out of the corner of our eyes: sips of red wine from a sick-stained toothmug. Despite the kind attentions of a carer, he stopped eating, stopped doing anything except being laboriously sarcastic, escorting the colonel and his giant Alsatian to the pub less and less, and dipping at the red wine like bobbing for apples. It was when he drank vodka that he got sick, and kept nearly dying, and we'd have to drive him up to the hospital, where the drips and luke-warm meals would show us glimpses of normal, lovely Fa. But the

nurses knew and they were unsympathetic toward this endless pro-
cession of alcoholics, in here for some R&R before their next
seven-day bender. We thought these brusque nurses were horrid,
but they weren't really, they were just saving their care for the properly sick. He just needs to stop drinking, we were told a million
times—heard every single day by families of alcoholics all around
the world every single day. Stop drinking, Fa, or you'll die. But if
the drink went, so did his life. The drink was all he'd been for the
last twenty years. Who could ever possibly want the sudden clarity
of what one had become after a lifetime of waste and abuse?
Waking up sober in a tiny crap-filled room, having to take stock of
who you've actually been all this time, and who the hell to start
being now. Starting over somehow. Jesus, out of hospital I wanted
to pour him his first toothmug of red wine myself.

Jake, the colonel's Alsatian, died, and soon after the colonel died
too. Fa had a mad, surreal day in Winchester Crown Court when
the colonel's son tried to have him evicted from the house. Fa's
lawyer acquitted himself relatively well throughout the proceedings, but inevitably duly evicted, the council put him in a big
apartment that his behavior had hardly merited. It was brilliant,
and featured not just the one, but a whole selection of light-
streaming rectangular rooms. Wow!

We fixed up his bedroom, lined up rows of pot plants in his bay
windows, put up shelves, got the books out of their dusty boxes,
and oxidized his concomitant knickknacks. He began to eat again.
His mates rediscovered him. They came round and fixed the place
up even better. Fa would sit contented in the bar across the road,
holding his half pint of Old Dog Fucker in his personalized jug,
grinning lazily at his fellow daytime patrons. He was happy. He
developed a taste for eccentricity. He began to collect hats.

"Hats?"

"I've always collected hats!"

"No you haven't!"

"Yes I bloody well have. Bugger off, the lot of you." He proudly pulled today's hat down over his eyes. He wore a different one each day. Mel and I bet he took them off when we weren't looking.

I was fond and tolerant. Cynical because I knew him too well. Fa and I both knew this, and it was fine. Indeed it meant we could often just sit in complete silence, raising eyebrows at one another, him with a bloody fireman's helmet on his head. Mel, though, right up until the end, kept hold of him in her mind as an all-functioning, proper father figure. She'd still go to him for advice, which fantastically he still doled out, and she took most of it with thanks and appreciation. Those two still needed each other—I was an outsider. That was OK. Too much time with him and I got upset and disoriented anyway; too much reality seepage.

Fa developed cancer of the tongue, and he took the news like the curmudgeonly old pro he'd effortlessly morphed into. In recent years he'd become a death's door–quipping stylist. Self-deprecating black wit tumbled from his swollen mouth as we drove him around the specialists, organizing to get him fixed up. The specialists were miracle workers, and, best of all, never judged him. They were amazing. They cut out the cancer with a laser and we piled down to his recovery ward in Southampton, wondering what to expect. Would he be conscious? Still under? Bleeding?

He was sat up in bed in a silk dressing gown, wearing a fisherman's hat and watching the telly with the *Sunday Times* spread over his knees. He grinned proudly, trying really hard not to, trying to look ill like he was supposed to be. Best of all was his new comedy lisp now half his tongue had been lopped off. We tricked him into saying words that made it sound funniest, like *saucy*, which was now *thorthy*.

Local TV transmitted a morning show from the hospital, and they interviewed Fa. He was fantastic: arms crossed, hat on, silk gown, lisp. He pontificated about how he used to be in a band with David Steel, when he'd been a big cheese in the Liberal

Party back in the '70s. About how he and Paddy Ashdown were mortal enemies, and that if he ever saw him again he'd punch his lights out (they cut that bit). He was boastfully modest about the way he'd dealt with his disease.

He was soon back home again, but a month later they found more cancer and this time treated it with chemotherapy. Then he needed some more, and then an intensive residential course of it. He became depressed. I drove down to see him on a Sunday and he lay in his room in the dark, in and out of sleep, unwell, down. There was a Grand Prix on his little portable TV that he wasn't even watching. I lay on the floor beside his bed and read the paper as he dozed. He woke up and asked to borrow some money, so I drove around looking for an ATM and came back with the twenty quid he'd asked me for but he was asleep again. He woke up and asked for it, then I helped him down to the smoking room where we had a few ciggies. I took him back up to his room and he said that he wanted some proper sleep now. We had a frail hug, and I never saw him conscious again.

A few days later Fa had a massive internal blood hemorrhage. In intensive care they flushed through fifty pints of blood and kept him alive on machines. After two days of vigil and fingernails, having counted nine separate pieces of equipment hooked up to his organs, my mother, my sister, and I knew that it was time for him to go, and switched them all off. We held on to him and watched his low green lines gradually flatten, and away he went. He was fifty-six, and a beautiful creation, and the more time goes by, the more I miss him, which I don't know why, but I wasn't expecting.

THANK YOU!

Neil Taylor, Nick Davies, Martin Fletcher, Andrew Dunn, Owen Oakeshott, Faye Brewster, Small and Mel and Pete—my family, Aimee Roche, Peter Newsom, Rachel Skerry, Rachel Connolly, my pals on the eleventh floor, Knut Ellingsen, Bill Massey, Malcolm Dome and Jerry Ewing, Pat Begent, Sir Rodney of Troubridge, Emma and Paul at Idols, Joe Rudzinski in Texas and his band Surveillance, Kevin Lightner, and everybody else who has given me support and encouragement. Special thanks to Brian Wilson. XO Elliott.

No thanks to:

Glenn Collins

WHERE ARE THEY NOW?

Owen is an actor. He's done lots for the Royal Shakespeare Company and appeared in *The Bill* and *Birds of a Feather*, but likes doing theater the best, except for the shitty money. He's still the same and I love him.

Trapper works at Abbey Road Studios in London, doing remastering and stuff, mostly with classical music.

Johnny works for Hampshire County Council and gives drum lessons in his spare time. He's the only one of us who still plays in bands.

Pat is the landlord of the Intrepid Fox pub in Wardour Street, Soho. He'll give you a discount on a pint if you go in with a copy of this book. Maybe.

Martin lives on a sheep farm in New Zealand.

Faye is the sales director for a major U.K. publishing house.

Sam works in catering in London. She also paints pottery.

Paul Bavister I've no idea. His post on Friends Reunited sounds rather glum.

Dominic is a chef in Winchester.

Mark works for IBM in Winchester.

Bob I'd heard was dead until someone told me he was actually considering becoming a fireman.

Rinse is now a bodybuilder.

Kathy I don't know.

Scott Ditto.

Danny I bumped into in Ealing a year or so ago and he had a mad look in his eyes. He studied the bass and now gives bass lessons privately. He suggested we have a "jam" and kept phoning me up about it, but eventually stopped.

An addendum from Owen, explaining his lyrics to "Striptease Louise": "It should be noted that this song represents an ironic exposé of the libidinous society that we inhabit, as well as a damning indictment of the exploitation of women in contemporary urban culture. Taking as its point of view the frenzied imaginings of a pubescent male teenager, it explores the interplay between lurid oversexed fantasy and the concurrent brutal reality of the male disavowal of any natural human warmth and tenderness. As such, it is a piece of observational satire, and by no means itself exploitative. Honest."

My Top 5 Metal Albums Ever
Rocks Aerosmith
Highway to Hell AC/DC
Physical Graffiti Led Zeppelin
Appetite for Destruction Guns N' Roses
Reign in Blood Slayer

Owen's Top 5 Metal Albums Ever
Back in Black AC/DC
Overkill Motorhead
Rocks Aerosmith
The Real Thing Faith No More
Creatures of the Night Kiss

Faye's Top 5 Members of Hanoi Rocks
Nasty Suicide
Mike Monroe
Andy McCoy
Razzle
Sam Yaffa

Owen's Top 5 Iron Maiden Albums
Number of the Beast
Killers
Piece of Mind
Powerslave
Live After Death

Malcolm Dome's Top 5 Metal Albums Ever
Physical Graffiti Led Zeppelin
"Apart from *Physical Graffiti*, I just can't do it, sorry." —Malcolm

My Boss Pierre's Top 5 Prog Rock Albums
Meddle Pink Floyd
Nursery Cryme Genesis
Close to the Edge Yes
Aqualung Jethro Tull
In the Court of the Crimson King King Crimson

Seb Hunter: Discography (Original Material)
Solo artist
"Go!" / "Wake Up!" / "Keep on Rocking" / "Off the Leash" / "Teenage
Rebel" / "I'm at Your Mercy" / "Vomit on Your Head" (w. Melissa Hunter)
Armageddon's Ring
"Armageddon's Ring" (org.) / "Armageddon's Ring" (w. guitar solo) / "The
Demons of Ozgarth"
Excalibur
"City Boy" (7" mix) / "City Boy" (alt. version) / "City Boy" (extended mix) /
"City Boy" (the ultimate extended mix)
eXposed
"She's Frigid" / "Ernie Is a Cunt" / "Empty Vodka Bottle Blues" / "Miss
Piggy's Gotta" / "Red Hot & Heavy" / "Pissed in the Daytime Blues" /
"Under the Table" / "You're So Missed" / "Do You Feel Strange?" / "Fuck the
Parrot"
Rag 'n' Bones / Trash Can Junkies
"Magazine" / "Lickin' the Ashtray" / "Manhunt" / "Just Because" /
"Steamroller You" / "Gangbang" / "Under the Table" / "Gravity 1086" /
"(Trash Can Junkie) Suicide" / "Minor Blues" / "Black Shrine" / "Striptease
Louise" / "Rio" / "Roulette" / "Where Have All the Angels Gone?" / "The
Apology Song" / "Rain Coming Down" / "Loving You" / "Blue-eyed Jo" /
"On Parade"
Cool Hand Luke / Cat Ballou
"What You Gonna Do" / "For All Your Sins" / "I Can't Help You" /
"Disconnected" / "Halfway Home" / "Is This All?" / "Mystery Girl" / "Lay
Me Down" / "Waste of Time" / "Rocket" / "Under the Table" / "End of the
Century" / "Siamese Crawl" / "Original Sin" / "Something Sweet" / "(I
Don't Want) Another Lover"
Love Knuckle
"Revolver" / "Rising Son" / "Better Man" / "Out and Start Again" / "The
Last Thin Aerial Twigs of Noise"

Seb Hunter plays Fender guitars, Ernie Ball strings, and plectrums he finds in the
street, exclusively. He doesn't currently own an amplifier.

PHOTO CREDITS

All professional images courtesy Ross Halfin, Pete Cronin, Tony Wooliscroft, Ola Bergman, Mike Prior, Mark Weiss, Mick Hutson, Michael Johansson, Fryderyk Gabowicz/Idols Licensing, and Publicity Limited.

For the synths, many thanks to Kevin Lightner www.synthfool.com

For Rick Nielsen's guitars, thanks to Steve Pitkin and Rick Nielsen.

All Great Kat photos © 2003 The Great Kat http://www.greatkat.com

Iron Maiden is available on EMI
Reign in Blood is available on American
Fistful of Metal is available on Megaforce